THE AMERICAN
PULP AND PAPER
INDUSTRY, 1900–1940

The American Pulp and Paper Industry, 1900–1940

Mill Survival, Firm Structure, and Industry Relocation

Nancy Kane Ohanian

Contributions in Economics and Economic History, Number 140

GREENWOOD PRESS

Westport, Connecticut • London

Library of Congress Cataloging-in-Publication Data

Ohanian, Nancy Kane.
    The American pulp and paper industry, 1900–1940 : mill survival,
firm structure, and industry relocation / Nancy Kane Ohanian.
        p. cm.—(Contributions in economics and economic history,
ISSN 0084–9235 ; no. 140)
    Includes bibliographical references and index.
    ISBN 0–313–27366–9 (alk. paper)
    1. Paper industry—United States—History—20th century. 2. Wood-
pulp industry—United States—History—20th century. I. Title.
II. Series.
HD9825.037   1993
338.4'7676'09730904—dc20   92–18362

British Library Cataloguing in Publication Data is available.

Library of Congress Catalog Card Number: 92–18362
ISBN: 0–313–27366–9
ISSN: 0084–9235

First published in 1993

Greenwood Press, 88 Post Road West, Westport, CT 06881
An imprint of Greenwood Publishing Group, Inc.

Printed in the United States of America

The paper used in this book complies with the
Permanent Paper Standard issued by the National
Information Standards Organization (Z39.48–1984).

10 9 8 7 6 5 4 3 2 1

To Lee

Contents

Tables

Acknowledgments

I am especially grateful to Lee E. Ohanian for his review of the manuscript and numerous suggestions. I also appreciate the comments and suggestions on portions of this work from Professors Stanley Engerman, Shirley Svorny, and Nancy Virts. I would like to thank Professor Joe Brown at the Rochester Institute of Technology for lessons on handmade papermaking and Mr. Bill Shafer, president of the Flower City Tissue Mills in Rochester, New York, for a tour of his tissue mill. Responsibility for any errors or omissions remains my own.

THE AMERICAN
PULP AND PAPER
INDUSTRY, 1900–1940

1

Introduction

This book examines the U.S. pulp and paper industry between 1900 and 1940, the period of relocation of U.S. pulp and paper production from the North to the South and the West. In addition to the critical role of this relocation in the development of the paper industry, this was among the most influential shifts of industrial production of the twentieth century. In fact, the extent of outmigration of the pulp and paper industry from the Northeast ranks second only to the widely studied exit of the cotton textile industry that occurred in approximately the same period (Fuchs 1962, 22; Kane 1988). Industry relocation is of interest not only to economic historians and industrial economists, but also to students of economic geography, development economics, and regional economics.

Production from mills in the South and in the West grew from insignificant levels at the turn of the century to represent the majority of U.S. pulp and paper production after World War II. The reasons for this remarkable shift in production and the impact on the organization of the industry are the focus of this research. This study is an empirical investigation of pulp and paper firm behavior during the process of relocation, with an emphasis on the interrelationships among firm location, industrial structure, vertical integration, and firm survival and growth.

The primary data source is the annual *Lockwood's Directory of the Paper and Allied Trades*, which provides information about each pulp and paper mill operating in North America in this period. The directory data supply a complete geographic and size distribution of firms in the industry. By identifying individual mills, research based on the directories can address questions about entry and exit, takeover of plants, plant scale, vertical integration, survival, and other firm-lifecycle issues. This collection of data provides a better basis for evaluating the behavior of firms in this specific industry and in general studies of firm behavior compared to previous studies that typically have been based on less complete samples.

A second but smaller data set was created from the detailed financial reports found in annual issues of *Moody's Manual of Investments* published in the 1930s. Company histories and other descriptive details about leading paper firms that were listed in Moody's are used to supplement the information available from the directories.

Data from the *Census of Manufactures* and other secondary sources are used to provide background detail about aggregate production, imports and exports, and other industry trends. Although these data could not be used for firm-level analysis, the government sources reported the information in sufficient detail to disaggregate the data to regional and product-grade categories and provided valuable information that was not available in the directories or the Moody's reports.

PLAN OF STUDY

This introductory chapter provides a summary of the economic background of the pulp and paper industry in the period 1900–1940. This summary is culled from several general histories of the industry, most written during the period. Familiarity with the basic features of the development of the industry during this period is assumed for the discussions that follow in the remaining chapters of the book. This chapter concludes with a description of the primary data source used in the original research in this study, *Lockwood's Directory of the Paper Allied Trades*. This source provides the basis for the results discussed in Chapters 3 through 7.

Chapter 2 continues with a more detailed description of the economic trends in U.S. pulp and paper production between 1900 and 1940. Original statistics based on data from the *Census of Manufactures* and other government sources are presented to document the growth of the industry and the changing composition of production in this period. Other developments, including industry cycles, imports and exports, and new technology are reviewed. An overview of the data collected from the directories is presented. The directory data are shown to be consistent with the census figures when aggregated to the industry level and are therefore a reliable source of information about the industry in this period.

The relocation of pulp and paper production to the South and the Pacific Coast is analyzed in Chapter 3. Census data and the directory data are presented to measure the regional distribution of production in the four major regions and to document the changes in the location of production in this period. Reasons for the relocation, particularly lower production costs in the new regions, are evaluated. The process of relocation is investigated by identifying the firms that entered each region during the 1920s and 1930s. The directories also make it possible to distinguish whether entrants built new mills or acquired existing plants. The relocation is shown to have been marked by the addition of new capacity in the growing regions, in contrast to the turnover of existing plants in the older regions. These differences in the method of entry contributed to faster growth of capacity in the new regions compared to the North and Lake regions. The role of branching by northern firms into the South during this period is also highlighted.

Chapter 4 deals with the structure of the pulp and paper industry in light of modern industrial organization theory and challenges the traditional oligopoly view of the industry. This chapter presents a number of measures of industry structure and firm organization that are calculated from the directory data, including market concentration ratios and statistics about multiplant operations, forms of ownership, and the distribution of plant sizes. Evidence of entry and exit of mills provides a measure of barriers to entry into the pulp and paper industry in this period. A study of economies of scale is conducted, following Stigler's well-known survivorship technique. Firm conduct and a brief history of antitrust actions in the industry are reviewed.

The vertical integration of pulp and paper production is the special topic of Chapter 5 and 6. The directory data base is ideal for the measure of both the incidence and the extent of vertical integration in this period. Moreover, because regional patterns of integration varied widely, this period offers an opportunity to explore intraindustry determinants of vertical integration, an area of much current research. In Chapter 5, the directory data are used to document vertical integration by region and by product markets over the period. In addition, changes in integration over the life cycle of the mill and among entrants in each decade are analyzed. In Chapter 6, a transaction-cost model of the determinants of integration is estimated by regression methods. Vertical integration is found to be associated with local pulp and paper concentration ratios, mill size, and the grades produced.

Mill survival and mill growth are analyzed in Chapter 7. This research draws on the rapidly emerging industrial organization literature on firm survival and offers a case study that yields insights into an area not yet well understood by economists. Statistics drawn from the directory data that measure mill survival, entry and exit, mill location, and mill age provide the basis for regression analysis of mill survival and growth. A comparison of the summary statistics for surviving and nonsurviving mills each year suggests some factors that may explain mill performance in this period. A summary of regional patterns of entry and exit highlights the role of mill location in the process of mill survival and in the relocation of the industry in this period. Groups of entrants are followed across time to compare the experiences of age-cohorts in each decade and to investigate the role of age in mill performance. Finally, the role of several mill characteristics, such as mill age, mill size, location, and grades produced, in the process of mill survival and mill growth is analyzed by regression methods.

Chapter 8 offers a review of the major findings of this historical study and some general implications for the study of industrial organization. Lessons learned from the directory sources about how an industry relocation occurs, what effect the relocation has on industrial structure, and clues about the process of firm survival are summarized to conclude the study.

Three appendices present details for the interested reader. Appendix A reviews the process of papermaking and includes a brief history of the major discoveries that led to modern pulp and papermaking techniques. Appendix B reports the methodology of data collection from the pulp and paper directories and other data sources. Special problems that were encountered in using the directories are also addressed. Detailed statistics of regional market concentration by grade of paper and pulp products are summarized in Appendix C, which extends the discussion of market structure from Chapter 4.

ECONOMIC BACKGROUND[1]

The first U.S. paper mill, the Rittenhouse paper mill, was built in 1690 in Germantown, Pennsylvania (near Philadelphia). By 1800, there were 100 small paper mills in the United States, concentrated in Pennsylvania and New England. The early paper mills were located near waterways, because water was an important source of power until the adoption of the steam engine in the midnineteenth century allowed mills to build independent of a stream flow. Clean water was also critical to the pulp and papermaking process, and mills typically were built in rural areas to avoid contaminated urban water supplies. In fact, the quality of the local water supply in large part determined the types of papers produced by the mills;

fine grades of paper required clear water that was free of impurities. In addition to water considerations, mill location was dependent on local supplies of capital, skilled labor, and raw materials, such as rags, waste paper, and later when wood was utilized for pulp, pulpwood timber stands. Paper mills tended to locate in the outskirts of population centers, where demand for paper was highest and rags and waste papers were available.

Papermaking was concentrated in the Northeast and Lake states in the eighteenth and nineteenth centuries but shifted westward and to the South with the outmigration of the U.S. population from the East. As the demand for newspapers and other published materials grew in these developing regions, pulp and paper mills were established near these new markets to save the costs of transporting the finished product to the market and to assure a reliable supply of paper for the publishers (newspapers, in particular). Census reports showed evidence of the beginning of this relocation as early as 1860, when 53 mills were reported in the West and 24 in the South (although the industry did not become significant in these regions until the 1920s). In addition to market forces, the relocation in later years was driven by the availability of raw materials, especially pulpwood, in the South and the Pacific regions.

Several technological developments led to key turning points in U.S. pulp and paper production. The Fourdrinier and the cyclinder paper machines, introduced in the early nineteenth century, made large-scale production of paper feasible by producing a continuous sheet of paper. Mechanized production had almost completely replaced handmade methods by the middle of the century (the last handmade paper mill in the United States closed down in 1906). The introduction of chemical and groundwood pulping revolutionized the industry by substituting wood for scarce rags in the pulping process. The important pulp discoveries, which are described in greater detail in Appendix A, were the soda process in the 1850s, mechanized groundwood production in the 1860s, the sulphite process in the 1880s, and the development of sulphate (kraft) pulp, first produced commercially in the United States in 1910.[2] The replacement of rag with pulpwood and other materials containing cellulose fibers (straw, in particular) lifted the constraint that the scarcity of rags had placed on pulp production and significantly reduced production costs. The use of wood also contributed to the relocation of the industry because the eventual depletion of pulpwood timber in the Northeast and Lake states prompted the shift of pulp production to locations near new sources of timber in the early twentieth century.

Differences in the species of pulpwood available in each region led to regional specialization in pulping technologies and types of paper produced. The earliest chemical process utilized straw, which readily replaced rags in the production of lower-grade papers and permitted the spread of pulping to regions outside the Northeast. Straw pulp was concentrated in the wrapping paper and strawboard mills located in the midwestern farming states and New York, but these mills turned to waste paper for their pulp stock by the 1920s. Before sulphite pulp was available, high-grade book and writing papers were made from soda pulp (in addition, rags were used for high-quality, fine papers). The soda process initially used the poplar and aspen pulpwoods of the Northeast and Lake region, and these regions specialized in high-grade papers. By the end of the century, the soda process was replaced by sulphite pulp, which utilized spruce found in the Northeast and Lake regions and western hemlock in the Pacific Northwest. Sulphite pulp produced a wide variety of papers, including book, writing, and wrapping papers. Groundwood pulp, which produced a relatively weak paper suitable for newsprint and catalogues, utilized the spruce and balsam softwoods found in the North (especially Maine and New York) and the Pacific Northwest, and in a relatively small proportion of timber in the Lake region.

The discovery of the sulphate pulping process in the early twentieth century was responsible for the growth of production in the southern states. Sulphate pulping was well adapted to the southern pine, an abundant, fast-growing, and relatively less expensive softwood that was too resinous for use in the soda or sulphite processes. However, an early drawback of the sulphate process was the difficulty in bleaching the resins from the pulp, and the colored pulp was not suitable for fine grades of paper. As a result, southern paper production during this period was specialized in kraft wrapping and board papers (until the bleached sulphate process was developed). The introduction of sulphate pulping also benefitted the pulping industry in the Pacific Coast region by permitting use of the predominant Douglas fir, which had not been suitable for sulphite pulping.

Imported wood pulp supplied a significant part of U.S. pulp requirements in this period. After 1900, about 20 percent of U.S. consumption was comprised of foreign pulps; the share rose to near 30 percent following the Underwood–Simmons Act of 1913, which allowed wood pulp to be admitted duty-free.[3] In this period, the United States imported about half of its unbleached sulphite requirements (primarily from Sweden) and one-third of its bleached sulphite needs (primarily from Canada). With the exception of newsprint, paper imports played a small role in U.S. paper markets because most papers were dutiable and were uneconomical to ship great distances (particularly the lower grades). However, newsprint imports soared after the Underwood-Simmons Act of 1913 made newsprint duty-free. Canadian newsprint exports to the United States grew from negligible amounts before 1913 to supply more than half of U.S. newsprint consumption after 1925.

LOCKWOOD'S DIRECTORY

Howard Lockwood began publication of *Lockwood's Directory of the Paper and Stationery Trades* in 1873, one year following the first issue of his successful periodical, *The Paper Trade Journal.* The directory was published biannually (annually in some years) before 1900 and became available annually in the twentieth century.[4] The directory provides a comprehensive list of North American firms operating in the pulp and paper industry and a wealth of information about those firms. Although this information was not used in this study, the directory also lists firms in a wide range of related activities, including general paper merchants, paper box and paper bag manufacturers, rag and paper stock dealers, and wholesale and retail stationers, and includes a section on watermarks and brands, and trade associations. In addition to the complete edition, the directory was issued in an abbreviated traveler's edition that listed only the pulp and paper mills. In the preface to the 1931 edition of the directory, the editors note that the traveler's edition was "designed to be as compact and convenient as possible to meet the special needs of traveling men."

The research for this book was based largely on the directory listings of pulp and paper mills operating in the United States.[5] The U.S. mills were arranged by state, and each entry included: the name of the mill and proprietors or managers; town or city and population where each mill was located; description of the type of pulp and paper produced; pulp and paper capacities, measured in pounds per 24 hours; the number and description of pulp and paper machines (not utilized in this study); type of power (water, steam, and electricity); and remarks indicating whether the mill was idle, for sale, or in bankruptcy. The Lockwood Company gathered the information from questionnaires mailed to the firms and reported a high response rate (Stevenson 1940, 110). Indeed, the number of mills reported in the directories was consistently higher than the count based on *Census of Manufactures* reports in any given year, in part because the census excludes small firms (see Chapter 2).

The directories were selected for this study at ten-year intervals, from the 1900–1901 edition to the 1941 edition. Since the directories were based on reports collected in the preceding year, this provides data for 1900, 1910, 1920, 1930, and 1940. Data was collected for all mainland U.S. pulp and paper mills listed in the directory, including idle and bankrupt mills.

Each year, between 700 and 800 paper mills and between 200 and 250 pulp mills were included in the data. The data for mills producing both pulp and paper were combined as one observation, which brought the total number of cases to under 900 in each sample year.[6] For the most part, the mill entries based on combined pulp and paper operations correspond to descriptions of the firm, since the majority of firms operated just one mill. However, some of the largest firms, such as International Paper, operated more than one mill. For issues where the distinction between mills and firms is important, the analysis accounts for multiplant operations. Multiplant ownership is studied in detail in Chapter 4.

Table 1–1 summarizes some features of the directory data base. The total number of mills included in the data base each year is indicated; these mills are classified as pulp, paper, or integrated mills. About one-fifth of the paper mills were integrated, and a relatively small (and declining) share of mills were specialized pulp mills. The average mill size and total capacities of pulp and paper producers are indicated; both series grew dramatically over the period. The rural nature of the industry is indicated by the distribution of the populations of mill towns, also shown in Table 1–1. By 1940, 90 percent of mills were located in towns with populations of less than 100,000; 57 percent of mills were located in towns with populations of less than 10,000; and almost one-third of mills were in towns with populations of less than 2,500.[7] Similarly, most paper mill towns had just one mill; 77 percent of U.S. towns listed in the 1941 edition of Lockwood's directory were "one-mill" towns (404 of the total 528 towns).[8]

Although thousands of paper products were manufactured in this period, classification of products has been made manageable in this study by using six broad paper categories and five pulp categories. The paper groups are as follows (details provided in Appendix B):

1. newsprint: sold primarily to newspaper publishers; a mix of groundwood pulp (80 percent) and sulphite pulp (20 percent); a relatively weak paper with poor aging qualities.

2. book and writing papers: made from chemical pulp (soda or sulphite) or rag pulp; fine papers.

3. wrap and paperboards: used to protect goods in transit because of strength and toughness; includes wrapping tissue.

4. kraft papers: strong brown paper made from sulphate (kraft) pulp; a special category of wrap and paperboard.

5. sanitary papers: includes toilet issue, facial tissue, paper towels, and paper napkins.

6. industrial papers: includes building papers, absorbent papers, and insulation paper.

The pulp categories are generally the same as the pulps reported in the directories, except no distinction is made between bleached and unbleached pulps: (1) groundwood, (2) soda, (3) sulphite, (4) sulphate (kraft), and (5) semichemical (a combination of groundwood and chemical pulps that was introduced in the 1920s).

Four regions have been defined as follows: the North includes Connecticut, Delaware, Maine, Maryland, Massachusetts, New Hampshire, New Jersey, New York, Pennsylvania, Rhode Island, and Vermont; the Lake and Central region includes Illinois, Indiana, Iowa, Kansas, Michigan, Minnesota, Missouri, Ohio, and Wisconsin; the South includes Alabama, Arkansas, Florida, Georgia, Louisiana, Mississippi, North Carolina, South Carolina, Tennessee, Texas, Virginia, and West Virginia; the Pacific includes California, Oregon, and Washington.

The directories permit the quantification of a number of important issues in the pulp and paper industry between 1900 and 1940, including industry relocation, industry structure, and mill survival and growth. The regional distribution of pulp and paper capacity and types of products manufactured are easily established by sorting the mills into regional categories. The remarkable shift of production to the South and the Pacific Coast can be documented by tracing the changes in the regional distribution over the period (see Chapter 3). The observations of mill size allow the study of the optimal scale of pulp and paper production, as well as measures of the number and size of mills in various markets (see Chapter 4). The directory data are ideal for the study of vertical integration because the identification of paper mills that are affiliated with pulp mills and reports of the relative size of pulp and paper capacities allow unambiguous measures of integration of these two stages of production (see Chapter 5).

The time-series nature of the data permit the observation of each mill's life cycle during this 40-year period. The decade of entry and exit, and approximate mill age (in decades) are estimated by the history of each mill's appearances in the selected directories between 1900 and 1940. This information is exploited in a variety of approaches. First, the entry and exit of mills during each decade between 1900 and 1940 provide important evidence for evaluating whether barriers to entry exist in this industry (see Chapter 4). Second, mill exits each decade are compared to the surviving mills to analyze the factors associated with mill survival and failure, particularly mill age, mill size, location, and types of grades produced (see Chapter 7). Third, among surviving mills, mill growth is measured by the growth of paper capacity during each decade, and growth is evaluated as a function of the same factors that are considered in the analysis of mill survival (see Chapter 7).

NOTES

1. This section is based on several well-known historical studies of the pulp and paper industry: Weeks (1916), Stevenson (1940), Lockwood Trade Journal Co. (1940), Guthrie (1950), Sutermeister (1954), and Smith (1971). Specific references have been omitted.

2. The early sulphate process created a pulp that produced a tough brown wrapping paper. Both the pulp and the paper were known as "kraft," the German word for strong. Today, sulphate is the major pulp type. Unbleached sulphate continues to be used for brown wrapping paper and paperboards; bleached sulphate is used in finer grades.

3. Reliance on foreign pulp is lower today; about 8 percent of U.S. pulp consumption is met by imported wood pulp.

4. In 1987, Lockwood merged with *Post's Pulp and Paper Directory*, established in 1884, to form *Lockwood-Post's Directory of the Pulp, Paper and Allied Trades*.

5. Alaska and Hawaii were excluded. The Canadian listings were not utilized in this study.

6. The total number of mills ranged from 789 to 879 mills in the sample years. See Table 2–8.

7. Before 1950, the census definition of urban was incorporated places of 2,500 or more inhabitants (Perloff 1963, 16).

8. The share of "one-mill" towns in 1940 varied by region as follows: 72 percent in the Pacific region, 75 percent in the North, 78 percent in the Lake region, and 81 percent in the South. The total number of mill towns in each region was as follows: 282 in the North, 152 in the Lake region, 62 in the South, and 32 in the Pacific region.

Table 1-1
U.S. Pulp and Paper Mills: 1900–1940

	1900	1910	1920	1930	1940
Number of mills	879	874	877	874	789
Integrated	148	175	184	182	16
Paper only	624	627	626	636	579
Pulp only	107	72	67	56	46
Ave. paper mill capacity (thou. lbs/day)	28.7	52.9	79.1	123.5	168.3
Ave. pulp mill capacity (thou. lbs/day)	55.6	103.3	128.8	195.3	310.9
Total paper capacity (thou. lbs/day)	21,875.0	40,996.5	61,560.8	98,551.1	118,970.8
Total pulp capacity (thou. lbs/day)	13,801.5	24,584.0	31,299.0	46,089.0	63,422.0
% Mills in towns < 2,500 population	48.6	43.5	36.6	34.7	31.8
% Mills in towns < 10,000 population	78.0	71.5	66.9	61.1	57.4
% Mills in towns < 100,000 population	96.4	95.6	94.3	91.4	89.7

Source: Compiled by the author from Lockwood's Directory of the Paper and Allied Trades.

2

Trends in Pulp and Paper Production

This chapter reviews the development of the U.S. pulp and paper industry between 1900 and 1940. I present original statistics on industry trends that are based on data available from government publications. The focus is on aggregate trends in national production and other industry-wide issues; regional trends are discussed in Chapter 3. Most of the statistics are drawn from *Census of Manufactures* reports, which measure the growth in national production of pulp and paper products and reveal the changes in the composition of pulp and paper output over this period. Census reports also document the extent of vertical integration of pulp and paper production, capacity utilization, and pulp and paper imports and exports. A 1938 U.S. Tariff Commission report on the wood pulp and pulpwood industry is used to supplement the census data.

In the final section of this chapter, the census data are compared to data from *Lockwood's Directory of the Paper and Allied Trades* to confirm the reliability of the directory data, which will form the basis for the analysis of the remaining chapters. Aggregate measures of number of firms, daily capacity, composition of output, and extent of vertical integration that have been derived from the directories are checked against the corresponding census figures.

GROWTH IN PULP AND PAPER PRODUCTION

Production figures from the *Census of Manufactures* show remarkable growth in pulp and paper output between 1899 and 1939 (see Table 2–1).

Pulp and paper production each increased about sixfold in this period; the average annual compound rate of growth was about 5 percent for both pulp and paper production over the entire period. Growth was highest during the first decade, however, when output doubled in each sector (see Table 2–2). In the following decades, pulp production rose at a steady pace, while the production of paper exhibited a cyclical pattern of faster growth during the 1920s and a slowdown during the Great Depression decade.

Growth in production was accompanied by significant gains in labor productivity during this period. Output per man-hour in the industry between 1919 and 1929 increased at an average annual rate of 5.5 percent, followed by an increase of 2.6 percent between 1929 and 1939 (Riche 1962, 1115). Productivity was especially high in the 1920s, a period of mechanization and modernization of pulp and paper mills, and slowed in the 1930s during the depression years.[1] By comparison, the average rate of growth of output per man-hour in the pulp and paper industry in the period 1948–1979 was 2.8 percent (Kendrick 1982, 12).

Annual variations in pulp and paper output and prices have tended to follow the business cycle. Two periods of declining annual production in the pulp and paper industry occurred following World War I and during the Great Depression. Biennial *Census of Manufactures* reports show that between 1919 and 1921, the value added by the pulp and paper industry declined 31 percent, close to the decline in total U.S. manufacturing value-added of 28 percent. Production exceeded 1919 levels by 1923, however. The industry suffered a longer period of decline between 1929 and 1933, when pulp and paper value-added declined 37 percent, compared to the 53 percent drop in value-added by all manufacturing industries. Recovery had begun by 1935, and by 1937, pulp and paper production was above the level reported in 1929. Monthly production data from the Federal Reserve Board show more clearly that paper production generally corresponded to the cyclical movements of the board's Index of Industrial Production between 1919 and 1930 (Stevenson 1940, 160). The cycles of paper products dependent on advertising, such as newsprint and book paper, tended to follow the business cycle with a lag, however, due to the delay in adjusting advertising plans following changes in economic conditions (Fraser and Doriot 1932, 339).[2]

Pulp and paper prices tended to follow the same pattern as general price indices. The Labor Department's index of paper and pulp prices between 1913 and 1938 generally corresponded to an index of all commodities. Both series rose sharply during World War I and then reached a peak in 1920, and both indices showed a substantial decline during the Great

Depression period (Stevenson 1940, 152). Paper prices also followed the movement of the Commerce Department's price index of manufactured products in this period. Among the different paper products, prices showed similar general trends. However, newsprint and book papers, which were sold primarily under contract, were less variable than other grades, especially paperboard (Guthrie 1950, 118–20).

PULP PRODUCTS

The composition of pulp production was altered sharply between 1899 and 1939 (see Table 2–3). The declining role of groundwood pulp and the emergence of sulphate pulp are the most notable changes in the pulp sector in this period. The slow growth and shrinking product share of groundwood pulp corresponds closely to a similar pattern in domestic newsprint production, the primary market for groundwood pulp.

The first commercial use of sulphate pulp was reported in 1910, and by 1939 it had become the leading category of pulp. Sulphate production increased from 50 thousand tons in 1914 (when it was first reported in the *Census of Manufactures*) to over a million tons by 1931. During the 1930s, sulphate and sulphite production were nearly matched, until sulphate took the lead in 1939.

PAPER PRODUCTS

The shift away from domestic newsprint production to more profitable paper markets is evident in the production shares of major paper products between 1899 and 1939 (see Table 2–4). Once the leading category of paper production, newsprint gradually drifted to a distant fourth-place ranking by 1939. The combined shares of the book and writing paper segments remained fairly steady, fluctuating from a 19 percent to a 23 percent share of annual production in this period. Although wrapping paper production grew at an average annual rate of almost 4 percent over this period, its share of production slipped from 25 percent down to 18 percent of paper production by 1939. The share of paperboard products increased steadily in this period, due to growth in the demand for containers and boxes for shipping goods. Sanitary paper (toilet tissue, towels, napkins) was the fastest growing segment at an average annual rate of almost 9 percent between 1899 and 1939. Industrial products (primarily building papers) remained a steady 7 percent to 8 percent of total production (with the exception of 1919, probably reflecting the wartime slowdown in construction).

VERTICAL INTEGRATION

The census reports provide both direct and indirect measures of vertical integration of pulp and paper production in the period between 1899 and 1939 (see Table 2–5). Since the paper and wood pulp firms were combined for the census reports of 1909 through 1925, statistics are available that report both the number of firms and the value of pulp and paper output that was produced by integrated firms. During this period, from 20 percent to 25 percent of pulp and paper firms produced both products. However, the output of these firms represented about double that share in terms of the value of pulp and paper production, from 44 percent to 53 percent. Although vertical integration will be analyzed in greater depth in Chapter 5, these preliminary census data suggest that the vertically integrated pulp and paper firms were relatively large-scale operations, compared to specialized mills.

The incidence of vertical integration can be approximated over the entire period by observing the proportion of pulp that was produced for the pulp firm's own consumption, which was reported in each *Census of Manufactures* between 1899 and 1939 (see Table 2–5). That share reveals an upward trend in vertical integration over this 40-year period, from 45 percent of total pulp to over 80 percent by 1939. The major part of domestic pulp was used on site, from almost the beginning of the period. This nonmarket pulp represents production at vertically integrated pulp mills that by definition produce at least part of the pulp required for their paper operations. Although vertically integrated firms may either purchase some pulp requirements or sell pulp that exceeds their requirements, this measure of the share of pulp for own use should be directly related to the actual proportion of pulp from integrated mills.

CAPACITY UTILIZATION

Pulp and paper capacity data measure the normal output of a plant that operates on a continuous, 24-hour, six-days-a-week basis with existing equipment. Table 2–6 reports the annual capacity of pulp production and paper production in thousands of tons, at decade intervals. Annual capacity was reported in all the *Census of Manufactures* for both pulp and paper in this period; daily paper capacity data was first reported for 1904, but daily pulp capacity was not reported until 1929. Beginning with the 1927 census, annual capacity was based on a 310-day year, allowing for normal shutdowns for repairs and other factors that would cause a temporary suspension of operations (U.S. Tariff Commission

1938, 85). Although prior reports did not specify the number of days that was regarded as normal for the year, that number can be inferred by dividing annual capacity by daily capacity. This approach indicates, for example, a 315-day year in 1909 and a 306-day year in 1919, which was roughly the same standard operating year that was assumed in the later reports.

The *Census of Manufactures* reports of paper and pulp capacity reveal fairly stable rates of capacity utilization in both sectors (see Table 2–6).[3] Utilization rates were lowest in the pulp industry in the first two decades (73 percent in 1899 and 1904), largely due to excess capacity in the dominant groundwood pulp segment. As the composition of pulp production changed over time, however, pulp capacity utilization rates reflected those found among the sulphite-producing firms. A slowdown in the growth of groundwood pulp capacity also helped raise the overall utilization rates in the later decades.

In the paper industry, capacity utilization varied between 78 percent and 82 percent in the years shown in Table 2–6. Utilization rates varied across the paper segments, but were more homogeneous than in the pulp industry. The most notable development of the 1930s was the striking decline in newsprint capacity and the corresponding (but less severe) drop in groundwood pulp capacity, which are both further indicators of the competitive conditions that marked the newsprint segment in this period.

IMPORTS AND EXPORTS

The United States consistently imported more pulp and paper products than were exported in this period. Trade data from various *Census of Manufactures* and from a 1938 report by the U.S. Tariff Commission are shown in Table 2–7. Wood pulp imports comprised a significant share of the total wood pulp used in the United States, varying from 14 percent to 28 percent of total U.S. consumption over the period. The bulk of pulp imports were sulphite and sulphate pulps; groundwood imports were relatively unimportant because the final product, newsprint, was imported instead (U.S. Tariff Commission 1938, 9). The decline in domestic newsprint production led to a shift from unbleached to bleached sulphite imports in the latter part of this period; sulphate pulp imports were primarily unbleached. Sweden was the largest supplier of imported pulp, particularly unbleached sulphite and unbleached sulphate. Canada followed as an important source of bleached sulphite and the relatively small imports of groundwood and soda pulps (U.S. Tariff Commission 1938, 7). U.S. pulp exports in this period remained small compared to U.S. pulp imports. Pulp exports were mainly sulphite pulps, bleached and un-bleached, from the Pacific Coast mills.

U.S. reliance on imported paper products increased over the period; by the 1920s, more than 10 percent of paper consumption was met by imported paper. By that time, the value of paper imports and the net import balance (imports less exports) exceeded that of pulp. Newsprint was the single largest category of imported paper; Canada was the chief supplier. By the 1920s, newsprint comprised over 90 percent of total paper imports. Although U.S. paper exports remained a small percentage of imports, exports grew significantly over the period. Over time, the composition of exports shifted from primarily printing paper before 1920 to wrap and paperboards in the following decade.

AGGREGATED DIRECTORY DATA

The annual *Lockwood's Directory of the Paper and Allied Trades* lists all pulp and paper mills in operation in the United States each year. The directory entry includes the mill name, location, daily pulp and paper capacity (pounds per 24-hour period), type of pulp and paper produced, source of mill power, and a description of the equipment used. A summary of some of the information collected from the directories at ten-year intervals is presented in Table 2–8. Corresponding data from the *Census of Manufactures* (where available) are included in Table 2–8 to check the accuracy of the directory information.

The directory generally indicated a larger number of mills and a higher level of pulp and paper capacity than the *Census of Manufactures*. The discrepancy may be explained by the reporting conventions used in the census reports. First, the census consolidated the reports of multiple plants owned by the same firm if the mills were located in the same city.[4] For most of the period, only the "total number of establishments" was reported, and those figures are shown in Table 2–8. However, these census numbers would most likely be adjusted upward if the total number of plants or mills had been reported. For example, in the 1929 census, when both the number of establishments and number of mills were reported, 883 establishments operated 910 mills. Second, the census omitted establishments reporting paper or pulp production valued at less than $5,000 (beginning with the 1904 census). The number of reporting mills may be higher in the directories in large part because these small firms were not excluded.

Although the directory measures of capacity are higher than the census figures, both series grew at approximately the same rate over the period. For example, between 1910 and 1920, both measures of paper capacity increased 50 percent, and between 1930 and 1940, both increased 21 percent. The similarity in the patterns found in the two capacity series suggests that mills omitted from the census reports probably account for the differences in the two data sources.

The composition of paper production was measured as a percentage of total paper production from the census data for selected types of paper. However, since the directories do not provide measures of production or capacity by type of product, composition was estimated instead by the percentage of mills that reported the various categories of product. Still, the distribution of products according to the two sources is remarkably similar. Both sources show that wrap and board products were the leading category, whether measured by production or number of mills. Industrial products were relatively unimportant in both sources. Newsprint was a much stronger category if measured by production, but both data sources show the dramatic decline in this market. Also, it is not surprising that newsprint was underestimated by directory measures based on number of mills because the newsprint mills were operated on a relatively larger scale than other types of paper mills. Book and writing products, on the other hand, were a larger category if measured by proportion of mills than by the census production shares but remained a stable share of either production (from the census data) or total number of mills (from the directories) over the period.

SUMMARY

This chapter documents the rapid growth of U.S. pulp and paper production in the period 1900–1940, based on data drawn from the *Census of Manufactures*. The cyclical behavior of pulp and paper output and prices tends to follow average manufacturing indices, although the decline in pulp and paper production during the Great Depression was less severe than in other industries. Aggregate production figures also document the shift away from newsprint production and the gain in paperboard production during this period, as well as the redistribution of pulp production away from groundwood pulp and the dominance by sulphate pulp by the end of the period. The net importer status of the United States is explained by a reliance on imported sulphite and sulphate pulps and Canadian newsprint.

The census data generally verify the reliability of *Lockwood's Directory* as a source of data about the pulp and paper industry between 1900 and 1940. Similar patterns of capacity growth and changes in the composition of industry production were found in the two data sources. The directory information offers the advantage of a more comprehensive source of data than the census reports, however. More mills were included in the directory source, and mill reports were not consolidated, which will prove useful in the later analysis of industry structure and mill survival.

NOTES

1. Gains in labor productivity reflect a higher capital per labor ratio, cost-reducing technological progress, education and training of workers, and a number of other factors (see Kendrick 1982).

2. Physical output data reported by Fabricant (1940) also show a correspondence between paper production and total manufacturing cycles. Using an index of physical output equal to 100 in 1929, Fabricant's series show that paper output dropped 6 percent between 1921 and 1929, and declined 16 percent between 1929 and 1933, compared to declines of 11 percent and 37 percent in total manufacturing in the same periods (Fabricant 1940, 61).

3. The biennial data, not reported in Table 2–6, show that utilization rates were cyclical, however. Both paper and pulp capacity utilization rates dropped significantly in 1921 (to 63 percent and 61 percent, respectively) and again in 1931 (to 67 percent and 70 percent, respectively).

4. Beginning with the 1923 *Census of Manufactures*, reports of separate plants located in different cities of the same state were combined if each mill town had a population of less than 10,000. By the 1931 census, the different cities were required to be in the same county, but the population limit was not changed.

Table 2–1
U.S. Pulp and Paper Production: 1899–1939
(Thousands of tons)

	1899	1909	1919	1929	1939	Annual Growth[1]
Pulp[2]	1,180	2,496	3,518	4,937	7,153	4.61%
Paper[3]	2,168	4,217	6,099	11,140	13,510	4.68%

Source: Census of Manufactures.
[1] Annual compound growth rate between 1899 and 1939.
[2] Only wood pulp was reported prior to the 1927 Census of Manufactures.
[3] Paper and paperboard products.

Table 2–2
Pulp and Paper Production Growth by Decade: 1899–1939

Decades:	1899-1909	1909-1919	1919-1929	1929-1939
Pulp	7.88%	3.49%	3.44%	3.78%
Paper	6.88%	3.76%	6.21%	1.95%

Source: Census of Manufactures.
Note: Growth rates are average annual compound growth rates during each decade.

Table 2–3
Pulp Product Shares: 1899–1939
(Percent of Total Pulp Production)

	1899	1909	1919	1929	1939
Wood pulp:					
Groundwood	49.7%	47.3%	43.2%	33.2%	20.2%
Soda	15.0	12.0	11.7	10.5	6.2
Sulphite	35.3	40.8	40.4	34.1	27.2
Sulphate	–	–	3.4	18.6	41.4
Semichemical	–	–	–	0.8	2.1
Screenings	n.a.	n.a.	1.3	1.3	0.6
Other fibre[1]	n.a.	n.a.	n.a.	1.5	2.2
Total[2]	100.0%	100.0%	100.0%	100.0%	100.0%

Source: Census of Manufactures.
Note: "n.a." indicates data not available.
[1] Includes deinked pulp, cottonseed-hull shavings, cotton-linter pulp, and rag pulp.
[2] Columns may not add up to 100 percent due to rounding.

Table 2–4
Paper and Paperboard Product Shares: 1899–1939
(Percent of Total Paper Production)

	1899	1909	1919	1929	1939	Average Annual Growth[1]
News	26.3%	27.7%	21.7%	12.6%	7.1%	1.30%
Book&Writing	19.1	21.2	22.6	21.5	19.9	4.78
Wrap	25.3e	19.0e	15.6	15.9	17.8	3.76
Board	18.2	20.9	30.6	40.0	44.6	7.06
Sanitary	0.7e	0.9e	1.6	2.0	3.6	9.22
Industrial	7.2	7.8	4.5	7.6	6.7	4.48
Other	3.3	2.4	3.3	0.3	0.5	-0.29
Total[2]	100.0%	100.0%	100.0%	100.0%	100.0%	4.68%

Source: Census of Manufactures.
Note: "e" indicates figure is estimated by the author.
[1] Average annual compound growth rate.
[2] Columns may not add up to 100 percent due to rounding.

Table 2–5
Vertical Integration of Pulp and Paper Production: 1899–1939

	Pulp for Own Use[1] (% of Total Pulp)	Firms Producing Both Pulp and Paper[2]		
		# Firms	% of Total Firms	% of Total Value
1899	44.8%			
1904	59.4			
1909	63.5	158	20.3%	43.6%
1914	68.5	160	22.3	46.1
1919	68.7	171	23.5	47.9
1921	69.8	169	22.9	52.1
1923	71.9	172	23.1	53.1
1925	77.0	188	24.6	43.7
1927	86.6	165	21.6	n.a.
1929	84.4			
1931	85.4			
1933	84.9			
1935	81.8			
1937	79.4			
1939	80.5			

Source: Census of Manufactures.
Note: "n.a." indicates data not available.
[1] Pulp produced and consumed in the same plants or transferred to and consumed in other plants of the same company; total includes pulp produced for sale.
[2] Prior to the 1927 census, statistics were reported for the combined "Paper and Wood Pulp" industry, which permitted analysis of integrated firms. Thereafter, the paper and pulp statistics were reported separately and did not include a summary of the integrated firms.

Table 2-6
Capacity Utilization in Pulp and Paper Production: 1899–1939
(Total Annual Capacity in Thousands of Tons and % Total Capacity Utilized)

Pulp Industry

Year	All Pulp Cap	% Util	Groundwood Cap	%	Soda Cap	%	Sulphite Cap	%	Sulphate Cap	%	Semichem Cap	%
1899	1,536	73%										
1904	2,645	73	1,515	64%	245	81%	885	85%	–	–	–	–
1909	3,406	78	1,810	65	345	87	1,251	81	–	–	–	–
1919	4,349	80	1,975	77	464	89	1,656	86	253	48%	–	–
1929	5,951	82	2,351	70	631	83	1,971	85	849	108	59	68%
1939	9,000	79	2,123	68	562	79	2,525	77	3,368	87	157	98

Paper Industry

Year	All Paper Cap	% Util	News Cap	%	Book Cap	%	Writing Cap	%	Wrap Cap	%	Board Cap	%	Building Cap	%
1899	2,782	78%												
1904	3,858	81												
1909	5,293	80												
1919	7,671	80												
1929	13,704	80	1,695	81%	1,775	84%	670	95%	2,039	79%	5,697	78%	911	72%
1939	16,557	82	988	97	1,936	79	777	81	2,610	86	7,631	80	938	70

Source: <u>Census of Manufactures</u>.

[1] Capacity not reported by paper type prior to the 1927 <u>Census of Manufactures</u>.

Table 2–7
Pulp and Paper Imports and Exports: 1909–1935
(Quantities in Tons, Values in Thousands of Dollars)

Pulp	Imports	Exports	Net Imports	Ratio of Imports to Consumption[2]
1909[1]	306,504	10,325	296,179	20%
	$8,672	$449	$8,223	
1914[1]	572,304	13,481	558,823	29
	$17,125	$530	$16,596	
1919	636,016	40,057	595,959	15
	$37,048	$3,049	$34,000	
1921	697,100	28,483	668,617	20
	$39,396	$1,755	$37,642	
1923	1,234,465	20,596	1,213,869	25
	$74,702	$1,095	$73,607	
1925	1,491,988	33,924	1,458,064	28
	$81,864	$2,441	$79,423	
1927	1,679,468	32,006	1,647,462	28
	$86,086	$1,534	$84,553	
1929	1,886,000	n.a.	n.a.	n.a.
	$88,948	n.a.	n.a.	
1935	1,933,000	171,000	1,762,000	28
	$70,735	$8,633	$62,102	

Paper	Imports	Exports	Net Imports	Ratio of Imports to Consumption[2]
1909[1]	$ 5,314	$ 2,178	$ 3,136	4%
1914[1]	15,742	2,145	13,597	10
1919	47,801	40,319	7,482	7
1921	83,336	13,887	69,449	13
1923	106,781	13,299	93,482	12
1925	109,064	13,090	95,974	11
1927	136,021	15,516	120,505	14

Sources: Census of Manufactures for the years 1909-1927; U.S. Tariff Commission (1938) for 1929 and
1935 pulp data.
Note: "n.a." indicates data not available.
[1] As of end of June of that year.
[2] Quantity of imports divided by sum of total domestic production and net imports.

Table 2-8
Comparison of Directory and Census Data

Year[1]	Total Number of Mills[2]		Both Paper and Pulp (number of mills)		Paper Capacity (tons per 24 hrs)		Pulp Capacity (tons per 24 hrs)	
	Census	Directory	Census	Directory	Census	Directory	Census	Directory
1900	763	879	n.a.	148	n.a.	10,938	n.a.	6,901
1910	777	874	158	175	16,824	20,498	n.a.	12,292
1920	729	877	171	184	25,091	30,780	n.a.	15,650
1930	883	874	n.a.	182	44,208	49,276	19,198	23,045
1940	844	789	n.a.	164	53,411	59,485	29,032	31,711

Composition of Paper Production[3]

	Newsprint		Book & Writing		Wrap & Board		Industrial	
	Census	Directory	Census	Directory	Census	Directory	Census	Directory
1900	26%	12%	19%	28%	44%	71%	7%	11%
1910	28	10	21	27	40	67	8	15
1920	22	9	23	29	46	66	5	16
1930	13	7	22	30	56	68	8	22
1940	7	3	20	28	62	68	7	21

Sources: Compiled by the author from the Census of Manufactures and Lockwood Directory of the Paper and Allied Trades.
Note: "n.a." indicates data not available.
[1] Census of Manufactures data are for the preceding year.
[2] Census of Manufactures report the number of establishments, which may operate multiple mills. Census figures for 1929 and 1939 overestimate the number of mills because integrated firms were double-counted, as both paper and pulp mills.
[3] The census data report the percentage of total paper production; the directory data report the percentage of total paper mills producing that type of paper.

25

3

Industry Relocation

The period between 1900 and 1940 was marked by the steady relocation of pulp and paper production from the Northeast and Great Lakes regions to the South and Pacific regions. Rather than an actual migration of plant and equipment from the older regions, for the most part, the relocation was accomplished by faster growth of capacity in the new regions and a gradual decline in the older regions through failure to replace equipment and through liquidations.[1] The relocation was most pronounced from the Northeast to the South; the loss of pulp and paper jobs in the Northeast was nearly equal to the gain in the South in the period 1929–1954 (Fuchs 1962, 204). Moreover, the pulp and paper industry was among the most mobile of industries during this period. Interregional shifts in pulp and paper employment were ranked seventh among 20 manufacturing groups in the period 1929–1954; pulp and paper was the second most important source of job losses in the Northeast in this period (following cotton textiles) and was among the leading sources of employment gains in the South (Fuchs 1962, 22, 202–219, 240).

A number of factors contributed to the relocation.[2] Probably the most important impetus was the depletion of timber stands in the Northeast and later in the Great Lakes region, as the result of late nineteenth century lumbering practices (such as clear-cutting without reforestation) (Markusen 1985, 245). The location of the industry followed the timber sources to avoid the costs of shipping pulpwood. Because about half of the weight of the pulpwood was lost in the pulping process (depending on yield), mills avoided shipping pulpwood long distances (McLaughlin and Robock

1949, 53). Moreover, new pulping technologies, which were spurred by the scarcity of pulpwoods in the older regions, facilitated the shift to the South and Pacific by making feasible the use of local pulpwoods in these new regions. In particular, development of the sulphate (or kraft) pulping process that used the resinous southern pine was critical to the establishment of the industry in the South. In the Pacific Northwest, production was fostered by the suitability of western hemlock for sulphite pulping and, later, by the use of Douglas fir for sulphate pulping as well as by the extension of railroads into western forests (Cohn 1954, 64; U.S. Pulp Producers Association 1944, 31; U.S. Pulp Producers Association 1955, 9; Markusen 1985, 246). The relocation was also market driven, in part as demand for paper products and published materials grew in these new regions. Development of a transcontinental railroad network and other improvements in transportation contributed to the shift in the industry away from the Northeast.[3]

This chapter begins the analysis of the relocation of the pulp and paper industry by documenting the important trends in regional production and specialization in the period 1900 to 1940. The description of the regional industries is based primarily on *Census of Manufactures* data, which report the extent and type of pulp and paper production by state during this period. This study aggregates the census data to four regions: North, Lake (and Central), South, and Pacific. The states included in each region were listed in Chapter 1. A 1938 U.S. Tariff Commission report provides additional details of regional pulp production in the 1930s. Also, a regional summary of the data from *Lockwood's Directory of the Paper and Allied Trades* provides further evidence of regional patterns in the industry in this period.

The directory data are further analyzed to address the process of industry relocation. The firm-level data are utilized to study the entry (and exit) of mills into the four regions. By identifying the individual entrants, the directories offer the unique opportunity to ask whether entrants built new plants or acquired existing mills, whether entrants were related to established firms as branch mills, and how these features of entering mills varied across the four regions. Thus the disaggregated directory data allow insights into the process of relocation that are not available from traditional sources, such as census reports or other government documents, because the latter aggregate data to state or regional categories.

REGIONAL PRODUCTION DATA

Regional measures of paper production are available from the 1899 and 1904 *Census of Manufactures*, and from the *Biennial Census of Manufac-*

tures between the years 1925 and 1939. These issues provided total paper production figures by state, which were aggregated to find the regional production levels. The regional data are intermittent because the census reports between the years 1909 and 1923 provided state production in a different format. In these years, production data was arranged by product type and reported only the leading states that produced each type of paper. As a result, state and regional totals based on this incomplete data in this middle period would not be comparable to the data that is reported here.

Evidence of the striking pattern of relocation in paper production is shown in Table 3–1, which summarizes the regional shares of total U.S. paper production that were based on the census reports of state paper production (measured in tons of paper). Although the northern region dominated U.S. production of paper throughout this period, the northern share of production steadily declined from 67 percent in 1899 to just 38 percent by 1939. Production in the Lake and Central states peaked as a share of production at 39 percent in 1927 and then drifted down to a 32 percent share by 1939. Initially, production in the South and Pacific regions was a negligible share of U.S. production. By 1925, however, these regions had become significant producers. Growth in the importance of southern paper mills was especially remarkable. The southern share of U.S. production climbed to 21 percent by 1939 from only 4 percent in 1925. The Pacific region's share of paper production increased modestly from 5 percent in 1925 to about 9 percent in the 1930s. The last column of Table 3–1 represents production that was not identified by state in the census, to prevent disclosure of information about individual firms in the one-firm states or where state figures were relatively small.

Census reports of pulp production in each state were less complete than for paper production. As in the case of paper production, the census reports between 1909 and 1923 did not provide total pulp production by state and instead reported only the leading state producers of the various types of pulp. In addition, state pulp production was omitted from the 1929, 1933, and 1939 census reports; data for 1929 was available from the 1938 U.S. Tariff Commission report, however. Nevertheless, the data reveal a clear pattern of pulp relocation that is similar to the relocation of paper production (see Table 3–2). Northern pulp mills produced 81 percent of U.S. pulp in 1899, but that region's share was eroded to 32 percent by 1937. Lake and Central pulp production initially rose to a 25 percent share of production by 1927 and then declined to a 16 percent share in 1937. The shift in pulp production to the South and the Pacific regions was even more dramatic than in paper production. By 1937, southern pulp production had reached a 29 percent share and Pacific production, a 23 percent share, from small shares in the early period.

Regional specialization in pulp and paper was largely determined by the local varieties of timber found in each region (U.S. Tariff Commission 1938, 10–11). Although mills imported different pulps and pulpwood from other regions and from abroad, regions generally specialized in the paper products that required the kinds of pulp derived from native pulpwoods. In both the North and Lake regions, local spruce, balsam fir, and hemlock were used to produce groundwood and sulphite pulps. The Lake region also produced significant quantities of sulphate pulp from local Jack pine, beginning in the 1920s. These two regions concentrated paper production on newsprint and book and writing papers, which required groundwood and sulphite pulps. Once the sulphate pulping process made the resinous southern yellow pine a viable pulpwood source, the South specialized in that pulp and in kraft (sulphate) wrapping and board papers. Production in the Pacific pulp mills was concentrated in sulphite, groundwood, and sulphate pulps, and paper production was diverse.

The *Census of Manufactures* between 1909 and 1925 reported production of the leading states arranged by type of paper and pulp product. Although regional total production is underestimated by this source because production in the smaller states was omitted, the data provide an approximate description of differences in regional specialization and changes in specialization over the two decades. The census data are supplemented by regional pulp production figures found in the 1938 U.S. Tariff Commission report, which provides data for 1929 and 1935.

Regional paper production corresponded to the types of pulp that were produced locally. For example, newsprint requires groundwood pulp, and book and writing papers use sulphite and soda pulps. Regional specialization in paper products can be described first by the regional distribution of each paper type (see Table 3–3) and second, by the composition of regional paper production (see Table 3– 4). These calculations are based on *Census of Manufactures* reports that listed the output of leading states in each category of paper, which are available in the 1909 and 1914 census and in the biennial reports between 1919 and 1925. Because the leading paper states were located in either the North or Lake region in this period (low-producing states were omitted), regional totals and shares of total U.S. production were available only for these two regions. The category "other" in Table 3–3 represents the smaller paper-producing states in the North and Lake regions as well as all production in the South and Pacific regions.

Domestic production of most paper products became less centralized after 1909, with the exception of newsprint (see Table 3–3). Newsprint production remained concentrated in the North between 1909 and 1925. Northern mills provided between 59 percent and 69 percent of U.S.–based newsprint in this period. The remainder was divided equally between Lake mills and other regions. The North was also the primary source for book and writing papers in the early part of this period (1909 and 1914). However, by the 1920s northern mills contributed at most 36 percent of annual book and writing paper output, down from 55 percent in 1909. Production of this type of paper apparently shifted to the Pacific and South, shown by the increasing shares of unidentified "other" regions. Northern mills played a still smaller role in the production of wrap and board papers. Although the North was the largest source of these papers in 1909 (38 percent), the northern share had declined significantly to 21 percent by 1925, when other regions dominated this market. Interestingly, only the North experienced a loss of market share in these last two markets in the process of relocation, while the Lake region maintained a fairly stable share of each market. The Lake region maintained market shares in each category of about 20 percent of newsprint, 25 percent of book and writing, and 33 percent of wrap and board production (the sharp drops in market shares in the last two categories for the Lake region in 1919 may be explained by a less extensive listing of the leading states in that census, which would underestimate production in both the North and Lake regions that year).

Regional differences are highlighted further by examining the mix of papers produced in each region (see Table 3– 4). Newsprint was the largest category of paper production in the North, followed closely by wrap and board production. Newsprint comprised from 31 percent to 44 percent of northern paper production in this period, while wrap and board represented from 30 percent to 38 percent. Book and writing ranged from 20 percent to 26 percent of northern production. Production in the Lake region became dominated by wrap and board papers in this period, which reached 61 percent of Lake paper output by the 1920s. Lake production shifted away from newsprint as that share dropped to just 11 percent by 1925, from an earlier range of between 20 percent and 29 percent. Book and writing papers fluctuated from between 15 percent and 23 percent of Lake production, with no clear trend. Other paper, primarily building and sanitary papers, comprised a small share of output in both regions.

Regional shares of U.S. pulp production by type of pulp are shown in Table 3–5. These shares are calculated from census reports for the period 1909 to 1925, and from the U.S. Tariff Commission report for the years 1929 and 1935. The data series is incomplete because only the census reports in this middle period provided production data that was disaggregated by type of product and by state. The U.S. Pulp Producers Association was the source for the data reported by the Tariff Commission.[4]

The North dominated production of all pulp types except sulphate in this period, and northern groundwood and soda output remained as a high share of domestic production through the 1930s. However, the northern share of domestic sulphite production had declined sharply by 1935. Northern production of groundwood pulp varied between 61 percent and 70 percent of domestic production between 1909 and 1929, with no clear trend in the annual data, until the share dropped slightly to 59 percent in 1935. However, the North's share of sulphite pulp production declined from 58 percent in 1909 to 38 percent in 1935.

The Lake region became a larger participant in the sulphite and groundwood markets through the 1920s, which contributed to the increase in that region's share of pulp production, which was observed in Table 3–2. Lake pulp mills supplied 26 percent of sulphite pulp and 24 percent of groundwood pulp in the early 1920s. In addition, the Lake region was the source for a large part of the emerging sulphate market through the 1920s. By the 1930s, however, Lake production was displaced by sulphite and groundwood production in the Pacific region and by southern production of sulphate.

Census estimates of pulp production by type of pulp in the South and Pacific regions are available beginning in 1923, when production levels in those states had become large enough to report. In addition, the 1938 U.S. Tariff Commission report provides detailed statistics that include production in these two regions for 1929 and 1935. Although sulphate production was introduced in the Lake region as early as 1914, the South became an important source of sulphate in the early 1920s and dominated that segment by the late-1920s. The South also had a presence in the sulphite segment by the end of this period with a share of between 4 percent and 6 percent of domestic production. Pacific Coast pulp mills specialized in groundwood and sulphite pulp. By 1935, market shares in these pulps reached 35 percent and 20 percent, respectively. Sulphate production was also significant in the Pacific region, where production was 15 percent of domestic sulphate output in 1929 and 13 percent in 1935.

COMPARISON OF REGIONAL CAPACITY UTILIZATION RATES

The nature of pulp specialization in each region resulted in wide differences in capacity utilization across regions. Data reported by the U.S. Pulp Producers Association describes capacity and utilization rates by region and by type of pulp for 1934 and 1935 (U.S. Tariff Commission 1938, 89). In 1935, regional utilization rates in pulp mills were as follows: North, 59 percent; Lake, 68 percent; South, 85 percent; Pacific, 81 percent; U.S. average, 70 percent. Northern capacity utilization was considerably lower than other regions, in part because of that region's concentration of groundwood pulp capacity (61 percent of U.S. capacity in 1935). Although domestic capacity of groundwood pulp was shrinking with the decline in groundwood production in the 1930s, utilization rates remained lower than for other pulps (57 percent compared to 74 percent for sulphite and 83 percent for sulphate in 1935). The lower utilization rates in the North and Lake regions also reflected the disadvantages of these regions relative to the more competitive pulp and paper mills in the South and Pacific states, as well as competition from Canadian newsprint mills that were displacing domestic groundwood and newsprint production. The most likely reasons for the higher proportions of unused capacity in these regions in the 1930s were the smaller and less efficient pulp and paper machinery in the older mills of the North and Lake regions and higher production costs compared to the newer mills of the South and Pacific regions (U.S. Tariff Commission 1938, 90–91).

REGIONAL DIFFERENCES IN PRODUCTION COSTS

The fundamental reason for the relocation of any industry is higher profitability in the new region. In the case of pulp and paper, estimates of production costs in each region confirm that lower costs played a role in the shift of certain types of pulp and paper production to the South and Pacific regions. The most important advantages of the South and Pacific Coast mills were lower pulpwood and labor costs, the two largest components of pulp and paper operating costs.[5] The price of southern pine was consistently the lowest of all pulpwoods, followed by Pacific Coast pulpwood (Guthrie 1941, 149; Guthrie 1950, 144; Mouzon 1940, 182). The southern low-wage advantage has been well documented in comparisons of pulp and paper wage data (Guthrie 1950, 138). Pacific Coast wages, on the other hand, were generally higher than in the other three regions. However, Pacific labor costs were lower than in the North and Lake mills because greater labor productivity offset the higher wages. Pacific labor may have been relatively more productive due to a combination of greater labor efficiency, more efficient management, newer and more efficient equipment, or a higher ratio of machines per worker.[6]

Studies conducted in the 1930s found that the costs of producing groundwood and sulphite pulps were lower in Pacific mills, excluding transportation costs to eastern markets.[7] Comparisons of groundwood manufacturing costs showed that Pacific mills had a significant advantage of lower wood costs compared to the other regions. The cost of wood per ton of groundwood was about one-third lower in the Pacific because of significantly lower pulpwood prices in the West, reflecting the relative abundance of pulpwood in that region (Guthrie 1950, 144). Total manufacturing costs in the Pacific groundwood mills were 15 percent to 20 percent lower than in the Lake mills (in part because of the small scale of operations of the Lake mills, which produced limited amounts of groundwood for use in specialty papers). However, higher conversion costs than in the northern mills left little difference in total manufacturing costs between those two regions (U.S. Tariff Commission 1938, 243–244).

The cost advantage of Pacific mills in the production of sulphite pulp was more striking; sulphite manufacturing costs were 30 percent lower in the Pacific region compared to the North and Lake regions (U.S. Tariff Commission 1938, 209). The lower cost of pulpwood in the Pacific had a larger effect on sulphite costs because twice as much wood is used per ton of sulphite pulp compared to groundwood production (Guthrie 1950, 147). However, the advantage of Pacific sulphite in direct competition with Lake and Northern pulp was reduced by the costs of drying and shipping the pulp to eastern markets.

Comparisons among sulphate producing mills in the South, Lake, and Pacific regions showed that costs were significantly lower in the South, which explains that region's dominance of domestic sulphate production. Southern sulphate costs were 13 percent lower than in the Pacific region and 38 percent lower than in the Lake region (the North was not a major producer of sulphate). Most of the southern cost advantage stemmed from lower pulpwood prices, lower wages, and lower power costs compared to the other regions (U.S. Tariff Commission 1938, 229–230). Adding the costs of delivering sulphate pulp to New York, the southern cost advantage widened in comparison to the Pacific and Lake mills. Another advantage of southern mills was proximity to deep water harbors that permitted southern products to be shipped by water, which was less expensive than by rail (Mouzon 1940, 201).

The regional cost advantages in pulp production typically led to advantages in paper production as well. A 1928 study of newsprint production costs in Canadian, Pacific, northern, and Lake mills found that total costs, including transportation, were lowest in the Pacific mills. The Pacific cost advantage stemmed primarily from lower pulpwood costs, but among the U.S. mills, the Pacific mills also reported the lowest labor, power, fuel, and materials expenses (Guthrie 1950, 201). As in the case of pulp production, labor costs were lowest in the Pacific mills despite high wages because of higher labor productivity than in the other regions. A later study of manufacturing costs in 1940 showed that Pacific mills had maintained the cost advantage in competition with northern newsprint mills, again due to lower pulp and labor costs (Guthrie 1950, 152). Some limited comparisons of paper costs in the early 1940s suggest that Pacific mills were the lowest-cost producers of wrapping paper, tissue, ground-wood paper (tablet paper), and paperboard, stemming primarily from lower pulp costs (Guthrie 1950, 156–63).

REGIONAL DESCRIPTIONS FROM DIRECTORY DATA

Lockwood's Directory of the Paper and Allied Trades documents a number of features of U.S. pulp and paper mills, including paper and pulp capacity, type of product, whether vertically integrated, and other aspects of operations. Directories were selected at ten-year intervals between 1900 and 1940, and data was collected for all mills listed in the United States. Table 3–6 summarizes the statistics of all mills operating in each of the four regions.

The regional distribution of paper and pulp daily-capacity closely corresponds to the census-based measures of the regional distribution of paper and pulp production that were discussed earlier in this chapter. Although the level of northern paper capacity grew each decade, industry concentration in the North steadily weakened with much faster growth in new regions. The North's share of U.S. paper capacity fell from 64 percent in 1900 to only 39 percent by 1940. Lake capacity increased from 32 percent of U.S. capacity in 1900 to 38 percent in 1930, and then declined to 33 percent by 1940.

The striking growth in paper capacity in the South and Pacific regions is further evidence of relocation of the industry to these regions. Paper capacity increased tenfold in the South over the period, and the region's share of paper capacity jumped from 4 percent in 1900 to 21 percent by 1940. In the Pacific region, the share of paper capacity increased from 2 percent in 1900 to 7 percent by the end of the period, as paper capacity more than tripled.

Capacity data from the directories indicate that the relocation of pulp production to the South and Pacific regions was even more dramatic than the relocation of paper. Over the four decades, northern pulp capacity dropped from 73 percent to 27 percent of total U.S. capacity, and the level of northern capacity declined between 1930 and 1940. Pulp capacity also fell in the Lake region in the last decade, and that region's share of pulp capacity declined from 20 percent in 1900 to 15 percent in 1940. Rapid growth in southern pulp capacity, particularly between 1930 and 1940, raised the southern share of pulp capacity from 4 percent in 1900 to 38 percent in 1940, when the South became the leading pulp region (measured by capacity). The Pacific region had 19 percent of U.S. pulp capacity by 1940, up from 3 percent in 1900.

The directories provide information about several aspects of regional production that are not available from the *Census of Manufactures*. The average size of mills in each region was quite diverse. Mills in the established northern paper industry generally operated on a smaller scale compared to other regions in this period. Northern paper mills ranked third in average size between 1900 and 1920 (somewhat larger than southern mills in that period), but in 1930 and 1940, the northern average lagged far behind the three other regions. Pacific mills generally were larger than in other regions through 1930. However, by 1940 southern paper mills reported the largest average size following the entry of several relatively large integrated mills in the 1930s.

In pulp production, Pacific mills were larger on average than in other regions every year beginning in 1910. The average size of northern pulp mills initially ranked highest among the regions in 1900, and then fell to a distant second behind the Pacific region in 1910 and 1920. By the period 1930 to 1940, the average sizes of northern and Lake pulp mills were virtually equal, and both were significantly lower than in the South and Pacific regions.

The vertical integration of pulp and paper production was far more prevalent in the new regions of the South and Pacific compared to the North and Lake regions. In the older regions, only about 20 percent of paper mills were integrated with pulp mills each year. However, in the South and the Pacific, almost half of paper mills also produced pulp. The high proportion of vertically integrated mills is consistent with the higher average size of mills in these two regions compared to the North and Lake regions, for reasons that are discussed in Chapters 5 and 6.

Finally, the summary of the number of mills producing various products in each region indicates differences in specialization among the regions.[8] In all regions, wrap and board production accounted for the largest number of mills. In the North and Lake regions, book and writing was the second-largest category of mills, followed by industrial products and then newsprint mills. This ranking generally corresponds to the importance of each product in total U.S. paper production, with the exception of newsprint (see Table 3–4). Because newsprint was produced in larger scale mills compared to other types of paper, the ranking based on the number of mills will understate the relative size of actual production of newsprint.

Although southern and Pacific mills also were concentrated in wrap and board production, the distribution of other paper products diverged from the older regions. Kraft paper, a special category of wrapping paper, was the fastest growing category of southern mills and a much higher share of total mills than in the other regions (although southern kraft mills did not outnumber kraft mills in any of the other regions until 1940). Pacific mills were characterized by a relatively high proportion of newsprint mills compared to other regions. In both the South and Pacific regions, book and writing paper was a smaller share of total mills than in the North and Lake regions. Instead, industrial-paper mills followed wrap and board (including kraft) as the next largest category of paper mills in the newer regions.

THE PROCESS OF RELOCATION

Regional production was transformed over the period by the entry and exit of mills during the four decades covered by this study. The directories are used to identify the mills that entered and disappeared in each of the regions during the 1920s and 1930s, based on the beginning of decade editions (1921, 1931, and 1941). These 20 years mark the significant period of entry to the new regions of the South and Pacific Coast and the most dynamic period of relocation of pulp and paper production (entry and exit during the earlier decades are discussed in less detail in Chapters 4 and 7, however). A mioll was identified as an entrant during the decade if it appears in the later edition but not the earlier edition of the directory, and was an exit if the reverse was true.

In addition to quantifying the number of entrants and exits in each region between 1920 and 1940, issues about the method of entry and exit are addressed. Because the directories list mills by location, I determined when a new mill entered with a new plant and when it acquired an existing plant by comparing pairs of directories, city by city. In about half of the cases of takeovers, the directory indicated that the new mill was a successor to a former company, a consolidation of firms, or was "formerly" another company (whether these were cases of name changes or actual takeovers was not certain; if the management was different, I treated it as a takeover). I also treated as takeovers the cases where a company became a subsidiary or a division of another firm between the two editions of the directory. The remaining takeovers were inferred by the descriptions of the mill, including equipment, type of product, and names of the management. Where a virtually identical plant was listed under different names between the two editions of the directory, I assumed that the entrant had acquired an existing plant. Entrants that could not be matched to previous descriptions of mills in the same city were assumed to have built new mills during the preceding decade.

The statistics of regional entry during the 1920s and 1930s are summarized in Table 3–7. The total number of entrants to each region is reported, followed by the number and percent of entrants that had taken over an existing mill (the remaining entrants, not reported separately, are assumed to have built new plants). Acquisition of plants was the dominant strategy of entrants in the 1920s only in the Lake states, and the share of entrants that acquired mills was much higher in the established regions than in the growing South and Pacific regions. Overall, about 43 percent of entrants took over an existing mill rather than build a new plant, but the share was less than 10 percent in the new regions during the 1920s. During the Depression years of the 1930s, however, entrants were much more likely to acquire than to build. The majority of entrants in all regions except the South represented cases of takeover. Although the share of entrants to the South that acquired mills also jumped in the 1930s, the share remained less than one-fourth, far below that found in the other regions.

The data on entry of new versus acquired mills suggests that the relocation of production was a matter of faster capacity expansion in the new regions, especially the South, compared to the established areas. Although entry to the North and Lake regions remained strong between 1920 and 1940, growth of the industry in these regions was dampened by the tendency for turnover, rather than expansion, of capacity and production. By contrast, entrants to the South (and the Pacific Coast in the 1920s) were more likely to create new capacity than to operate existing mills, which resulted in relatively faster growth than in the older regions and to a relocation of the industry.

Another feature of the process of relocation that was explored in this study was the formation of branch mills by established paper firms. I identified all firms that owned multiple mills, and from that set of firms I found 39 firms that introduced branch mills during the 1930s. The regional distribution of these branches is shown in Table 3–8. The South attracted the largest number of branches of the four regions, and branch mills represented a much larger share of entrants in the South than elsewhere. Over half of the new mills in the South during the 1930s were associated with established firms, compared to about 20 percent of Lake entrants, 10 percent of entrants to the North, and just one mill (8 percent of entrants) in the Pacific region.

McLaughlin and Robock note the importance of branch plants in their study of manufacturing growth in the South: "The expansion into the South is thus largely a matter of establishment of branch plants of northern companies" (McLaughlin and Robock 1949, 7). In addition, they cite 1939 statistics that show the larger role of branches in the South compared to the rest of the United States: 27 percent of southern manufacturing establishments in 1939 were branches (71 percent of the value of manufactured products) compared to 19 percent of establishments in the United States (65 percent of the value of products) (McLaughlin and Robock 1949, 13–14). Southern manufacturing branches typically were associated with northern firms (all but two of the southern paper branches were affiliated with northern paper firms) and represented the transfer of northern capital and management skills to the developing South.

In the paper industry, southern branches were more likely to be new plants compared to branches in the older regions (which was also true for all entering mills, as discussed above). Table 3–8 separates the entering branch mills into new plants and existing plants that had been taken over. Whereas over two-thirds of branches in the North and Lake regions represented takeovers of established mills, only one-third of southern branches were takeovers. This pattern is consistent with the general tendency to expand capacity in the growing southern industry as production shifted to this region.

CURRENT REGIONAL DISTRIBUTION OF PRODUCTION

This study ends at 1940 because the major changes in regional production of pulp and paper had occurred by that time; regional aspects of the industry in the modern period are quite similar to those found before 1940. In the decades following 1940, the regional distribution of paper production continued to shift away from the North and Lake regions, but at a much slower pace than before the war. Statistics from a recent edition of *Lockwood-Post's Directory of the Pulp, Paper, and Allied Trades* provide a description of the current regional distribution of production.

The largest number of paper mills continues to be located in the North, but southern mills dominate U.S. production of paper and paperboard products by weight (see Table 3–9). In 1990, 599 paper mills and 347 pulp mills were operating in the United States. The total number of establishments was 782, which implies that 164 establishments (21 percent) had vertically integrated pulp and paper production. By number of mills, the North represented 33 percent of U.S. paper mills in 1990, followed by 28 percent in the South, 27 percent in the Lake region, and 12 percent in the Pacific region. However, southern mills produced 53 percent of domestic paper and paperboard production in 1990, compared to 18 percent by Lake mills, 15 percent by Pacific mills, and 14 percent by northern mills.

The South dominates pulp production in both number of mills and amount of production. Southern pulp mills accounted for 45 percent of U.S. mills in 1990, followed by 20 percent located in the Lake region, 18 percent in the Pacific region, and 17 percent in the North. Southern mills produced 68 percent of domestic pulp production in 1990, while Pacific mills represented 16 percent, followed by 8 percent each from Lake and northern pulp mills.

Regional production has remained specialized, as indicated by the location of specific types of pulp production (see Table 3–10). U.S. groundwood and sulphate (kraft) pulp mills were concentrated in the South, whereas sulphite production mills were located primarily in the Lake and Pacific regions in 1990. Among groundwood mills, 35 percent were reported in the South, 23 percent in the North, 20 percent in the Lake region, and 22 percent in the Pacific region. The Lake and Pacific regions each reported 38 percent of U.S. sulphite mills; of the remaining mills, 18 percent were located in the North and just 6 percent (one mill) in the South (two more mills were located in Alaska). Sulphate (kraft) production was dominated by southern mills, where 65 percent of U.S. mills were located. Pacific mills represented 15 percent of sulphate mills, followed by 11 percent of mills in the North and 9 percent in the Lake region.

The composition of types of pulp mills continues to vary by region (see Table 3–11). Groundwood was the largest category of pulp mills in the North and Lake regions (representing 26 percent and 19 percent of regional mills, respectively). In contrast, pulp production was dominated by sulphate (kraft) mills in the South and Pacific regions. The majority of southern pulp mills (54 percent) and about a third of Pacific mills (30 percent) produced sulphate pulp in 1990. Although a large share of the mills in each region, from one-third to one-half, produced "other" grades of pulps (such as semichemical, other mechanical, and nonwood pulps), these grades represent a small share of total regional pulp production.

SUMMARY

The relocation of the pulp and paper industry can be documented from both census data that describe the amount of production in each region and directory data that provide the number, size, and type of products of mills operating in each region. Together, these data show that the shift of production, especially away from the North and to the South, was dramatic between 1900 and 1940. Production shares remained fairly stable in the Lake region; production in the Pacific region grew more slowly than in the South in this period. Interestingly, the regional pattern of production of pulp and paper in the postwar period has changed little since the major relocation of the industry prior to 1940, based on statistics drawn from a recent industry directory.

Regional production was specialized, measured by the types and amount of various grades of pulp and paper products. Northern mills dominated production of newsprint and groundwood and soda pulps. By 1940, the new regions challenged the North and Lake mills in the production of kraft pulp and papers in the South and sulphite pulp in the Pacific region. However, the North and Lake regions continued to outnumber and outproduce the new regions in the other pulp and paper grades in this period. The older regions adapted to relocation by shifting the composition of regional paper production away from newsprint in favor of wrap and board, sanitary, and industrial papers, and to some extent, kraft paper. The directory data also indicate a much lower percentage of vertically integrated mills in the older regions and a shift away from integration after 1920. Disintegration and a reduction in the number of specialized pulp mills in the North and Lake regions reflect the greater reliance on imported pulp by the paper mills in these regions during this period. Regional patterns in vertical integration are explored more carefully in Chapters 5 and 6.

Studies of regional production costs reveal that lower pulpwood and labor costs were the most important sources of the cost advantages in the South and the Pacific. In studies of specific products, southern mills were the lowest-cost producers of sulphate pulp, while Pacific mills had an advantage in sulphite pulp and newsprint production. Although most products were shipped to local markets, the consideration of long-distance transportation costs to eastern markets enhanced the southern cost advantage but weakened the cost advantage of Pacific Coast mills. In Chapter 7, indirect measures of mill profitability, based on mill survival and growth, provide further evidence of the role of regional cost advantages in the process of regional relocation.

The directory data were used to identify entrants to each region in the 1920s and 1930s to learn more about the process of relocation of the industry to the new regions. Entrants to the South were far more likely to build new plants and to be affiliated as branches of northern paper firms than entrants to the other regions. The tendency for entrants to the North and Lake regions to take over existing mills explains the relatively slow growth of capacity in those regions compared to the expanding South in this period. The directory data suggest that the process of relocation in the paper industry was marked by turnover of capacity in the older regions and expansion of capacity in the South. The use of directory data to study entry (and exit) is one of the most powerful contributions of this data source and these issues are discussed further in Chapter 4 in relation to barriers to entry and industry structure and in Chapter 7 in the study of mill survival.

NOTES

1. Fuchs emphasizes that relocation is measured by relative growth rates among regions (Fuchs 1962, 8, 32–3, 105). However, some migration of equipment did occur in the relocation of the paper industry. For example, when International Paper Co. closed most of its original northern mills, some of the equipment was transferred to its mills in other regions and the rest was sold (International Paper Co. 1948, 19).

2. This is based on neoclassical explanations of industry relocation (e.g., Fuchs 1962, Perloff 1963).

3. Markusen argues that the shift of lumber milling to the Great Lakes preceded the relocation to the South because of the destruction of the southern railroads during the Civil War (Markusen 1985, 245). However, in the case of pulping, transportation developments would seem to be irrelevant until the sulphate pulping technique permitted the use of southern wood.

4. To check the consistency of this alternative source, total production figures from both the Census of Manufactures and the U.S. Pulp Producers Association were compared and only minor discrepancies existed for 1929 and 1935.

5. For example, in 1931, wood costs as a percentage of total pulp costs ranged from 33 percent for sulphate pulp to 69 percent for sulphite pulp (Mouzon 1940, 181). A 1928 study of newsprint manufacturing showed that wood costs were about 40 percent and labor costs 10 percent of total costs, excluding transportation (Guthrie 1941, 201). In the manufacture of kraft paper in the 1930s, wood comprised 20 percent of total costs and labor (and management) represented 30 percent of total costs (Mouzon 1940, 180).

6. The Tariff Commission conducted a survey of payroll data for May 1935 in 30 U.S. pulp mills. Average hourly wages were highest in the Pacific region, followed by the North, Lake, and South. Higher wages in the Pacific region were attributed in part to a higher proportion of skilled workers in the sample as well as higher wages for both skilled and semiskilled workers compared to the other regions. Southern wages for semiskilled and unskilled workers were the lowest among the regions, and the lowest wages for skilled workers were found in the Lake region (U.S. Tariff Commission 1938, 16, 109). For earlier data, see Guthrie (1950, 146), which represents data from a study by the Department of Commerce of regional pulp manufacturing costs in June, 1931.

7. Southern mills were not major producers of groundwood or sulphite pulps and so were excluded from the comparison.

8. The sum of mills across all products exceeds the total number of mills because some mills produced more than one product.

Table 3-1
Regional Distribution of Paper Production: 1899-1939
(Percent of Total U.S. Production)

Year	North	Lake	South	Pacific	Not Classified
1899	67%	29%	1%	1%	1%
1904	68	29	1	1	1
1925	50	38	4	5	3
1927	48	39	5	6	2
1929	46	37	8	8	1
1931	44	36	8	8	4
1933	41	35	14	8	2
1935	41	35	14	9	1
1937	40	34	16	9	1
1939	38	32	21	8	0

Source: Census of Manufactures.
Notes: See text for states included in each region. State production data was incomplete in the census reports between 1909 and 1923 (available for leading producers only; reported by type of paper produced).

Table 3-2
Regional Distribution of Pulp Production: 1899-1939
(Percent of Total U.S. Production)

Year	North	Lake	South	Pacific	Not Classified
1899	81%	17%	2%	0%	1%
1904	76	18	4	2	1
1925	56	24	6	8	7
1927	49	25	8	11	7
1929	45	24	16	16	0
1931	36	20	11	19	15
1935	35	18	26	21	0
1937	32	16	29	23	0

Sources: Census of Manufactures; data for 1929 from U.S. Tariff Commission (1938).
Notes: See text for states included in each region. State production data was incomplete in the census reports between 1909 and 1923 (available for leading producers only; reported by type of pulp produced). State pulp production not available in the census reports of 1929, 1933, and 1939.

Table 3–3
Regional Distribution of Paper Production by Type of Paper: 1909–1925
(Percent of Total U.S. Production of Paper Type)

Year	Newsprint			Book & Writing			Wrap & Board		
	North	Lake	Other	North	Lake	Other	North	Lake	Other
1909	60%	18%	22%	55%	25%	20%	38%	32%	30%
1914	65	19	16	52	26	22	34	33	33
1919	69	18	13	30	12	58	23	14	63
1921	59	20	21	35	18	47	25	30	45
1923	60	19	21	36	26	38	28	35	37
1925	61	17	22	34	24	42	21	32	47

Source: Census of Manufactures.
Notes: See text for states included in each region. Regional totals incomplete because only the leading states were included in the census reports of production by type of paper in this period. "Other" includes production of smaller producers in the North and Lake regions as well as production in other regions.

Table 3–4
Composition of Regional Paper Production: 1909–1925
(Percent of Total Regional Production)

North Region				
Year	Newsprint	Book & Writing	Wrap & Board	Other
1909	36	25	31	8
1914	36	26	31	7
1919	44	20	30	6
1921	39	20	35	6
1923	31	20	38	11
1925	34	23	34	9

Lake Region				
Year	Newsprint	Book & Writing	Wrap & Board	Other
1909	21	21	50	8
1914	19	23	53	5
1919	29	21	48	2
1921	20	15	62	3
1923	13	19	61	7
1925	11	20	61	8

Source: Census of Manufactures.
Notes: See text for states included in each region. Based on incomplete measures of total regional production because only the leading states were included in the census reports of production by type of paper in this period.

Table 3-5
Regional Distribution of Pulp Production by Type of Pulp: 1909–1925
(Percent of Total U.S. Production of Pulp Type)

Year	Groundwood North	Lake	Other	Soda North	Other	Sulphite North	Lake	South	Pacific	Other	Sulphate Lake	South	Other
1909	66%	14%	20%	67%	33%	58%	15%	n.a.	n.a.	27%	n.a.	n.a.	n.a.
1914	70	15	15	70	30	54	16	n.a.	n.a.	30	47%	n.a.	53%
1919	70	15	15	n.a.	n.a.	41	16	n.a.	n.a.	43	37	n.a.	63
1921	65	24	11	n.a.	n.a.	54	26	n.a.	n.a.	20	36	n.a.	64
1923	63	22	10	54	46	53	26	4%	9%	17	24	32%	44
1925	66	17	12	61	39	39	26	n.a.	20	26	36	35	29
1929	61	23	16	69	31	46	27	6	35	0	27	58	15
1935	59	21	20	63	37	38	23	4		0	15	72	13

Source: Census of Manufactures; data for 1929 and 1935 from U.S. Tariff Commission (1938).
Notes: See text for states included in each region. Regional totals incomplete because only the leading states were included in the census reports of production by type of pulp in this period. "Other" includes production of smaller producers in the North and Lake regions as well as production in other regions. "n.a." indicates data not available.

Table 3–6
Directory Data on Regional Distribution of U.S. Pulp and Paper Industry:
1900–1940

1900	North	Lake	South	Pacific
No. mills	608	223	27	21
Integrated	90	43	8	7
Paper only	444	161	10	9
Pulp only	74	19	9	5
Total paper cap. (thou. lbs/day)	14,123.8	6,912.2	335.0	504.0
Percent of U.S. total cap.	64%	32%	4%	2%
Total pulp cap. (thou. lbs/day)	10,042.0	2,708.0	575.0	476.5
Percent of U.S. total cap.	73%	20%	4%	3%
Ave. paper mill cap. (thou. lbs/day)	26.9	34.4	18.6	31.5
Ave. pulp mill cap. (thou. lbs/day)	62.8	44.4	33.8	43.3
Number of paper mills producing:				
Newsprint	48	34	3	5
Book & writing	155	50	6	4
Wrap & board	363	157	14	14
Kraft	0	0	0	0
Sanitary	7	1	0	0
Industrial	56	20	6	2

1910	North	Lake	South	Pacific
No. mills	590	238	33	13
Integrated	109	47	11	8
Paper only	431	176	15	5
Pulp only	50	15	7	0
Total paper cap. (thou. lbs/day)	24,406.5	14,476.0	1,074.0	1,040.0
Percent of U.S. total cap.	60%	21%	3%	3%
Total pulp cap. (thou. lbs/day)	16,389.0	5,229.0	1,704.0	1,262.0
Percent of U.S. total cap.	67%	21%	7%	5%
Ave. paper cap. (thou. lbs/day)	46.6	67.3	44.8	86.7
Ave. pulp cap. (thou. lbs/day)	107.8	87.2	94.7	157.8
Number of mills producing:				
Newsprint	47	24	1	5
Book & writing	151	59	4	1
Wrap & board	341	150	19	9
Kraft	9	4	3	0
Sanitary	21	2	0	0
Industrial	79	33	5	5

Table 3–6 (continued)

1920	North	Lake	South	Pacific
No. mills	556	252	48	21
Integrated	111	48	15	10
Paper only	407	187	22	10
Pulp only	38	17	11	1
Total paper cap. (thou. lbs/day)	34,202.8	22,613.0	2,263.0	2,482.0
Percent of U.S. total cap.	55%	37%	4%	4%
Total pulp cap. (thou. lbs/day)	19,224.0	7,161.0	2,559.0	2,355.0
Percent of U.S. total cap.	61%	23%	8%	8%
Ave. paper cap. (thou. lbs/day)	69.0	98.7	62.9	146.0
Ave. pulp cap. (thou. lbs/day)	132.6	117.4	98.4	214.1
Number of mills producing:				
Newsprint	47	17	0	5
Book & writing	154	72	2	4
Wrap & board	292	152	22	12
Kraft	20	15	7	1
Sanitary	27	9	1	1
Industrial	83	33	9	4

1930	North	Lake	South	Pacific
No. mills	498	257	69	50
Integrated	90	46	28	18
Paper only	385	200	32	19
Pulp only	23	11	9	13
Total paper cap. (thou. lbs/day)	44,916.1	37,312.0	9,695.0	6,628.0
Percent of U.S. total cap.	46%	38%	10%	7%
Total pulp cap. (thou. lbs/day)	19,895.0	10,230.0	7,820.0	8,144.0
Percent of U.S. total cap.	43%	22%	17%	18%
Ave. paper cap. (thou. lbs/day)	97.0	154.8	167.2	184.1
Ave. pulp cap. (thou. lbs/day)	174.1	179.5	217.2	271.5
Number of mills producing:				
Newsprint	31	16	1	6
Book & writing	156	74	7	4
Wrap & board	259	153	35	22
Kraft	36	22	21	5
Sanitary	47	6	1	5
Industrial	110	49	15	8

Table 3–6 (continued)

1940	North	Lake	South	Pacific
No. mills	425	235	81	48
Integrated	68	41	38	17
Paper only	340	187	35	18
Pulp only	17	7	8	13
Total paper cap. (thou. lbs/day)	46,229.0	38,688.8	25,400.0	8,653.0
Percent of U.S. total cap.	39%	33%	21%	7%
Total pulp cap. (thou. lbs/day)	17,219.0	9,974.0	24,141.0	12,088.0
Percent of U.S. total cap.	27%	15%	38%	19%
Ave. paper cap. (thou. lbs/day)	118.8	178.3	379.1	254.5
Ave. pulp cap. (thou. lbs/day)	207.5	207.8	561.4	402.9
Number of mills producing:				
Newsprint	14	4	1	6
Book & writing	112	74	9	6
Wrap & board	230	138	37	19
Kraft	25	20	26	5
Sanitary	56	14	1	4
Industrial	94	40	12	10

Source: Compiled by the author from Lockwood's Directory of the Paper and Allied Trades.

Table 3–7
Regional Patterns of Entry: 1920–1940 (Number of Paper Mills)

Mills	Total Entrants 1921-1930 % Entrants	Takeovers 1921-1930 No. Mills		Total Entrants 1931-1940 % Entrants	Takeovers 1931-1940	No.
North	153	74	48%	107	65	61%
Lake	93	53	57%	59	41	69%
South	35	2	6%	31	7	23%
Pacific	25	2	8%	13	10	77%
Total U.S.	306	131	43%	210	123	59%

Source: Compiled by the author from Lockwood's Directory of the Paper and Allied Trades.

Table 3–8
Entry Via Branching by Existing Firms: 1931–1940 (Number of Paper Mills)

	Total Entrants 1931-1940	Branches of Established Firms		
		Total Branches	New Plants	Takeover of Existing Plants
North	107	11	4	7
Lake	59	11	3	8
South	31	16	11	5
Pacific	13	1	1	0
Total U.S.	210	39	19	20

Source: Compiled by the author from Lockwood's Directory of the Paper and Allied Trades.

Table 3–9
Regional Distribution of U.S. Pulp and Paper Production: 1990

Region	No. Paper Mills	Percent of Total	No. Pulp Mills	Percent of Total
North	197	32.9%	57	16.5%
Lake	159	26.6	70	20.3
South	168	28.1	155	44.9
Pacific	74	12.4	63	18.3

Region	Percent of U.S. Production in 1987	
	Paper & Paperboard	Woodpulp
North	13.9%	7.8%
Lake	17.8	7.5
South	53.4	68.4
Pacific	15.0	16.3

Source: Lockwood-Post's Directory of the Pulp, Paper and Allied Trades, 1989 and 1991.

Table 3–10
Regional Distribution of U.S. Pulp Mills: 1990
(Percent of Grade Mills in Each Region)

	Groundwood	Sulphite	Sulphate
North	23.1%	18.8%	11.0%
Lake	20.0	37.5	8.7
South	35.4	6.3	65.4
Pacific	21.5	37.5	15.0
Total	100.0	100.0	100.0

Source: Lockwood-Post's Directory of the Pulp, Paper and Allied Trades, 1991.

Table 3–11
Composition of Regional Pulp Mills: 1990
(Percent of Regional Mills by Grade)

	North	Lake	South	Pacific
Groundwood	26.3%	18.6%	14.8%	22.2%
Sulphite	5.3	8.6	0.6	9.5
Sulphate	24.6	15.7	53.5	30.2
Other	43.8	57.1	31.1	38.1
Total	100.0	100.0	100.0	100.0

Source: Lockwood-Post's Directory of the Pulp, Paper and Allied Trades, 1991.

4

Industry Structure

Traditionally the paper industry has been viewed as an oligopoly structure that is dominated by a few large firms, such as International Paper. Many economists have argued that economies of scale led to an industry characterized by a few large mills that produced a high volume of standardized product (Cohen 1984; Guthrie 1940; Stevenson 1940). The benefits to large scale are explained by the high fixed costs of constructing a plant and purchasing the expensive paper machinery, which represent a barrier to entry that limits the number of firms in the industry. In this view, several analysts suggest that the absolute decline in the number of paper mills operating over the period (from 879 pulp and paper mills in 1900 to 789 in 1940) is evidence of barriers to entry and increased concentration of the industry.[1]

A detailed analysis of the paper mills operating in the period 1900–1940 contradicts this traditional view, however. This chapter presents evidence of a competitive industry structure with low barriers to entry, based on the descriptions of pulp and paper mills listed in the annual *Lockwood's Directory of the Paper and Allied Trades*. The data permit the measure of market concentration, the distribution of mills by size, and the number of mills entering and exiting the industry each decade. Although a number of relatively large firms were operating in this period, the large total number of firms results in fairly low market concentration measures (with the exception of the newsprint industry and certain narrowly defined regional markets). The survivorship technique suggests that economies of scale were achieved at a mill size that represented a relatively small share of total industry capacity. Moreover, the high rate of entry and exit during this period is direct evidence that barriers to entry were not substantial, despite the net decline in the number of firms.

The remainder of the chapter is devoted to a discussion of the conduct of paper firms, including pricing methods and the earnings of paper firms. Although often suspected of collusion, especially in the more concentrated newsprint industry, antitrust findings reveal that the pricing practices and earnings of paper firms were consistent with a competitive industry environment.

CONCENTRATION RATIOS

One widely used indicator of industrial structure is the concentration ratio. Typically the concentration ratio is measured by the combined market sales of the top four or top eight firms expressed as a share of total market sales. Concentration ratios range from 0 to 100 percent. Other measures of size, including value-added or number of employees, produce concentration ratios that are consistent with those based on market sales. In this study, concentration ratios utilize production capacity to measure market shares because individual mill or firm sales data are not available for most of the firms operating in this period. Two series of concentration ratios are measured, one based on individual mill capacities and another based on the total capacity of paper firms. Because many of the largest paper firms owned more than one mill, the firm-based concentration ratios are often higher than the mill-based ratios.

For concentration measures of total paper or pulp production, total mill capacity was used to rank mill size. However, for the individual product markets, mill capacity was adjusted to account for mills that produced more than one product. Mill capacity devoted to each category of paper or pulp product was assumed to be proportional to the total mill capacity because the directories did not list capacity separately by product. For example, a mill that produced both newsprint and wrapping papers is assumed to have used half of total capacity for each type of product.[2]

The concentration ratios for the paper industry that are based on mill capacities are generally low. For the paper industry as a whole, concentration ranged from 5 percent to 7 percent in the period 1900–1940 (see Table 4–1). These national concentration ratios are consistent with Stigler's judgement that the pulp, paper, and allied products industry was classified as unconcentrated, based on four-firm concentration ratios of 18 percent and 19 percent in 1935 and 1947, respectively. His criteria for unconcentrated industries was a national concentration ratio below 50 percent (Stigler 1963, 211–12).

In regional markets, concentration was high in the developing regions of the South and the Pacific Coast in the early twentieth century, but the total production from these areas was relatively small at that time.[3] Among the separate product markets, the national concentration ratios were high in kraft production when it was first introduced in 1910 and in the minor category of sanitary grades. The concentration ratios for the regional makets for each of the paper grade categories are shown in the tables provided in Appendix C.

When the capacities of paper firms, which in many cases operated more than one mill, are used to calculate concentration ratios, the values rise but remain moderate in most markets (see Table 4–2). Concentration ranged from 12 percent (in 1920) to 25 percent (in 1900) for the industry as a whole, which is higher than the mill-based ratios but still relatively low. Most of the increase in concentration is explained by International Paper, which owned many of the largest mills in this period. Among the separate product markets, the use of firm-level data makes the most difference in newsprint, where the concentration ratios were 64 percent in 1900, 47 percent in 1920, and 57 percent in 1940, all relatively high values. The ratios jump with the switch from mill-based to firm-based concentration ratios in this market because the largest newsprint producers, International Paper, Great Northern, and Crown Willamette, operated multiple, large newsprint mills.[4] The concentration in the newsprint market attracted antitrust investigations, as discussed below. The regional firm-based concentration ratios remained high in the South and Pacific regions because of the large concentration of capacity held by the Southern Kraft Corporation (a subsidiary of International Paper) after 1930 in the South and by Crown Willamette in the Pacific region throughout the period.

The measures of concentration in pulp production are restricted to the capacity of pulp produced for the market rather than for the mill's own use. Market pulp is assumed to equal the pulp capacity of the specialized pulp mills or the amount of pulp capacity in excess of paper capacity of the vertically integrated mills.[5] The total market-pulp capacity is consistent with the annual production of pulp "made to sell" that is reported in the *Census of Manufactures*, after adjusting for differences between annual and daily production (assuming a 310-day production year, as reported in the census reports beginning in 1927) and allowing for less than full capacity use.

The concentration ratios based on mill capacities are reported in Table 4–3. At the national level, market pulp concentration was quite low;

concentration ranged from 17 percent to 20 percent during the period. When separated by the grade of pulp, concentration was high only in the relatively small soda and semichemical markets and among the early sulphate (kraft) producers when it was first introduced. Regional concentration in market pulp was quite high in the South and Pacific Coast markets before 1930 but dropped to the levels found in the North and Lake regions by the end of the period. The concentration ratios found in the production of each pulp grade by region are shown in Appendix C.

As in the case of paper concentration measures, the firm-based concentration in market-pulp production was generally higher than the mill-based ratios, primarily because of the multiplant operations of the largest market-pulp producers (see Table 4–4). The nationwide concentration ratios among market-pulp firms ranged from 31 percent in 1900 to 29 percent in 1940, which was about 15 percentage points higher than the mill-based ratios. In 1900 and 1920, most of the increase was due to International Paper, which represented 20 percent of capacity in 1900 and 13 percent in 1920. In 1940, International Paper's share dropped to 6 percent, and the Pacific Coast firms Rayonier and Crown Williamette represented 13 percent and 6 percent of the national market, respectively. Among the separate pulp grades, firm-based concentration was higher than mill-based ratios only in the groundwood and sulphite markets. The most significant increase in concentration occurred in the sulphite market in 1940. Concentration increased to 57 percent that year, due primarily to the five-mill pulp-capacity owned by Rayonier, the single largest market-pulp producer that year.[6] However, groundwood concentration remained at relatively low levels throughout the period after accounting for the multiplant capacity of the largest firms. The soda, sulphate, and semichemical markets were led by relatively small, single-mill firms, and the concentration ratios were unchanged by the firm-based approach.

Regional concentration in the North and Pacific regions was most affected by using firm-based measures of market-pulp capacity. After accounting for the capacity of International Paper's market-pulp capacity, northern concentration increased about 20 percent points in 1900 and 1920, and increased 10 percent points in 1940 to a relatively high level of 52 percent. The Lake and South concentration ratios were either unchanged or rose slightly because the largest mills generally were operated by single-mill firms in these regions (the exception was the southern concentration ratio in 1900, which jumped to 73 percent due to the two-mill capacity of West Virginia Pulp and Paper that year). Firm-based concentration remained very high in the Pacific region throughout the period, though, because of the multiplant operations of Rayonier and

Crown Willamette. In the next chapter, the role of concentration among the market-pulp producers in the South and Pacific is shown to be a major factor in the high degree of vertical integration among paper mills in these regions.

A number of limitations in the use of concentration ratios should be noted. The most important theoretical criticism is that high concentration does not necessarily imply monopoly power. The threat of potential competition or foreign competition, which are not measured by the concentration ratio, may result in a competitive market even if only one firm operates in that market. Moreover, modern research on industrial concentration and firm conduct has found little support for the interpretation of high concentration as an indicator of monopoly power (Shughart 1990, 91–96).

Even if concentration ratios could identify monopoly structures, there are several practical problems. The measurement of the concentration ratio is sensitive to the definition of the market. The more broadly defined the market, both in terms of the product and the geographic boundaries of the market, the lower the concentration ratio. The economically meaningful market will include products and regions that compete directly, but the empirical measurement of the relevant market is difficult (Shughart 1990, 140–47). In this study, a series of concentration ratios based on different market definitions are reported, ranging from the entire paper (pulp) market combined to individual paper (pulp) products located in specific regional markets.

Another problem with the concentration ratio is the treatment of exports and imports. Exports are included in the measurements of firm size, whereas imports usually are excluded. The market shares of large firms that are exporters will be overestimated by this procedure, since the export sales should not be treated as part of the domestic market. On the other hand, the exclusion of imports in the measure of domestic consumption underestimates the relevant market. As a result, foreign competition is ignored and the market concentration of domestic firms is overestimated. Although pulp and paper exports were not significant in the period under study, the role of foreign competition should be taken into account in the analysis of concentration ratios in the import-sensitive paper and pulp markets (in particular, the newsprint and sulphite pulp markets).[7]

FORMS OF OWNERSHIP

The types of business organization found in the pulp and paper industry were documented by both census data and the directories. These sources reveal that the corporate form dominated the industry during this period. The census data also show that the proportion of incorporated firms was much higher in the pulp and paper industry compared to other manufacturing industries, presumably because that form of ownership facilitated the financing of larger investments in the capital-intensive pulp and paper industry.[8]

The *Census of Manufactures* for the years 1914 and 1919 report the character of ownership in leading manufacturing industries, including paper and wood pulp, for the years 1904, 1909, 1914, and 1919. Data for the years 1909 and 1919 are shown in Table 4–5. In 1909, 81 percent of pulp and paper firms were incorporated, compared to 9 percent operated by individuals and 9 percent by partnerships and other forms of ownership. By 1919, the share of firms that were corporations had increased to 89 percent of pulp and paper firms and 96 percent of the value of pulp and paper production. Only 5 percent of firms were owned by individuals, and another 7 percent of firms were operated by other forms of ownership.

By contrast, the ownership distribution across all industries was dominated by individual ownership in this period. In 1919 for example, 48 percent of all manufacturing firms were owned by individuals and 32 percent by corporations. However, firms owned by individuals produced just 6 percent of production, while corporations accounted for 88 percent of production in 1919. The pulp and paper industry as well as other capital-intensive industries (such as iron and steel) reported much higher shares of incorporated firms than labor-intensive industries (such as jewelry or bookbinding).

Another source of information about the forms of organization is the annual *Lockwood's Directory*. The directories were used as a supplement for the years not available in the census reports. The 1900 and 1940 editions of the directory were used to classify firms according to the directory listing, and the results are summarized in Table 4–5. If the company was listed with the names of the corporate officers it was classified as a corporation; if no officers were listed, or no information about ownerhsip was provided, the firm was classified as "other." Individually owned firms were listed with a single owner; multiple owners (partnerships) were classified as "other."[9]

The directory information documents the long-term shift toward use of the corporate form of ownership in the first half of the twentieth century. The share of corporations grew from 55 percent of firms in 1900 to 96 percent by 1940; as a share of paper capacity, corporations represented 99.5 percent of paper capacity in 1940. Interestingly, only 4 firms that were not corporations in 1900 survived through 1940 without becoming incorporated; another 41 noncorporations in 1900 survived that period, but were incorporated by 1940. The census data reveal that most of the shift to incorporation of the industry occurred between 1900 and 1910, when the share of incorporated paper firms jumped from 55 percent to 81 percent of firms. The popularity of the corporate ownership structure suggests that even if the high fixed costs in this industry formed a barrier to entry, firms were able to rely on the capital market for funds to finance entry and expansion by incorporating. As further evidence of the advantages to incorporation, the directory data reveal that the survival rate of incorporated mills was about double that of mills that were not incorporated in 1900; 31 percent of incorporated mills in 1900 survived to 1940, compared to just 16 percent of noncorporations.

MULTIPLANT OPERATIONS

Although the majority of paper firms operated one paper mill between 1900 and 1940, the proportion of firms that operated two or more mills gradually increased during the period. Table 4–6 reports the total number of paper firms and paper mills that operated during 1900, 1920, and 1940.[10] In 1900, one-mill firms represented 90 percent of paper firms, 74 percent of paper mills, and 62 percent of paper capacity. In 1920 and 1940, the number of one-mill firms gradually declined, despite a rise in the total number of mills in 1920. By 1940, one-mill firms accounted for 85 percent of paper firms, 62 percent of mills, and 48 percent of paper capacity.[11]

Most of the multiplant firms operated just two mills. The number of two-mill firms increased from 36 in 1900 (7 percent of paper capacity) to 44 in 1920 (12 percent of capacity) and then declined slightly to 39 in 1940 (11 percent of capacity). The number of firms that operated three mills almost doubled from 12 in 1900 to 21 in 1940 and represented 13 percent of paper capacity by 1940.

The number of mills operated by the remainder of multiplant firms ranged from 4 to 23 mills in 1900, from 4 to 22 mills in 1920, and from 4 to 20 mills in 1940. Although few firms operated four or more mills, the relatively large number of mills in this category represented a significant share of total paper capacity in this period (26 percent in 1900, 19 percent in 1930, and 29 percent in 1940).

A statistical comparison of the single-mill firms with the multimill firms is summarized in Table 4–7. The average paper capacity of the mills owned by multimill firms was significantly larger than that of the single mills. This suggests that multiple mills were not simply an alternative to expansion at a given site; otherwise, the single-mill plants would have been on average larger than the mills of the multimill firms (all else constant). The multimill firms apparently operated on a larger scale than the single-mill firms by building larger mills as well as multiple plants. The only other difference between the two types of firms that stands out in the data is that a larger proportion of the mills of the multimill firms were vertically integrated compared to the single-mill firms (but in 1940, the shares were almost equal). This result is consistent with the fact that larger mills were more likely to be vertically integrated, which is discussed in greater depth in Chapter 5.

Interestingly, the survival rates of the two types of mills were nearly identical in the years sampled. In 1900, 20 percent of the mills of single-mill firms survived to 1940, compared to 22 percent of the mills of multimill firms; the survival rates were 45 and 44 percent, respectively, in 1920. The similarity in the survival rates suggests that multiplant expansion was not necessarily a profitable strategy.[12] This is supported by the gradual decline in the average number of mills owned by the multimill firms over the period, from 8.4 mills per firm in 1900, to 6.1 mills per firm in 1920, and then to 5.4 mills per firm by 1940.

The multimill statistics reflect the failure of many early consolidations to maintain their original market shares over time. In her study of the merger movement in American manufacturing of 1895–1904, Lamoreaux argues that the paper industry was just one of many sectors where firms consolidated following this sequence of events: the rapid expansion of many capital-intensive industries in the early 1890s, the depression of 1893, price wars, and unsuccessful attempts to avoid the price competition of the 1890s through collusive arrangements (Lamoreaux 1985, 12, 45, 62). While the consolidations in some industries, including steel, were successful, "mergers in the paper industry had at best a marginal existence" (Lamoreaux 1985, 11). For example, two of the largest consolidations in the paper industry, the American Writing Paper Company and International Paper, operated 23 and 22 mills in 1900, respectively (see Table 4–8). However, by 1940, only 9 American Writing Paper mills and only 5 of the original International Paper mills were still operating. In the newsprint market, International Paper's share declined from 46 percent of total U.S. capacity in 1900 to just 7 percent of U.S. newsprint capacity in 1940 (from only 1 U.S. mill), as the company closed some mills and switched to other grades in the remaining mills. After International Paper acquired the Southern Kraft Corporation in 1930, the number of mills and market share of the firm were restored to near the earlier levels. As shown in Table 4–8, with the exception of International Paper, none of the multimill firms represented significant shares of U.S. paper capacity in this period.

Table 4–9 summarizes the number of multiplant firms that were located in more than one region. Although most firms remained concentrated in just one region, by 1940 about 30 percent of multiplant firms, or 5 percent of all paper firms, operated in two regions (and in four cases, more than two regions).[13]

In 1900, only 5 firms operated mills in more than one region. Three of these firms owned mills in both the North and Lake regions (American Writing operated 3 Lake region mills that did not survive to 1940), 1 firm operated a northern and a Pacific Coast mill, and West Virginia Pulp and Paper operated 2 northern mills and 1 southern mill (and continued to operate in these two regions through 1940). By 1920, the number of firms with interregional operations increased to 11. Seven of these firms operated in both the North and Lake regions. One (West Virginia Pulp and Paper) owned northern and southern mills; 1 owned northern and Pacific Coast mills, 1 operated mills in the South and Lake regions, and 1 firm operated in the North, Lake, and Pacific regions.

The number of firms with interregional operations jumped to 25 by 1940. Six firms had mills in both the North and Lake regions, 9 operated in both the North and South regions, 1 had mills in the North and Pacific regions, 4 operated in both the Lake and South regions, and 1 had mills in the Lake and Pacific regions. Three firms were operating in three regions: 1 firm had mills in the North, Lake, and South regions, and 2 firms had mills in the North, Lake, and Pacific regions. U.S. Gypsum operated mills in all four regions (5 mills in the North, 4 mills in the Lake region, and 1 mill each in the South and Pacific regions).

With the relocation of the industry to the South and Pacific regions well underway by 1940, a large proportion of these interregional firms, 10 out of the 25, were expanding their established North or Lake region operations to these new regions during the 1930s. (As noted in Chapter 3, branching by northern firms played a significant role in the growth of new pulp and paper capacity in the South.) Another group of 5 firms that operated in both the old and new regions in 1940 were new entrants during the 1930s. In addition, firms in the developing regions were establishing branches in the older regions to some extent: 3 established southern firms extended operations to the North or Lake regions during the 1930s, and 1 firm had operated mills in the North, Lake, and Pacific regions since the 1920s.

Few paper firms operated a separate pulp mill at a different location than the paper mill(s) during this period. In 1900, 8 firms listed a total of 14 pulp mills at locations separate from their paper mills (representing 8 percent of total domestic pulp capacity). In only one case, the firm's pulp mill was in a different region than the paper mill (southern pulp mill and northern paper mill); otherwise, the pulp mills were in the same county (3 mills) or in the same region (10 mills, including 7 owned by International Paper). In 1920, 20 firms operated 27 separate pulp mills (12 percent of pulp capacity); only 2 firms had interregional operations. In 1940, the number of firms with separate pulp mills dropped to 12 (14 pulp mills, 4 percent of pulp capacity). Almost all of these pulp mills were in the same region as the firm's paper mill(s); only 2 firms had interregional operations.

ECONOMIES OF SCALE

The relationship between production costs and firm size is an important determinant of industry structure. Given market demand, an industry is more likely to be concentrated if there are cost advantages associated with large-scale production. Economies of scale may be measured directly by estimating cost functions, which requires firm-level (or plant-level) cost data. The objective of the cost-study approach is to determine the nature of the costs as a function of firm output and to find the minimum efficient scale required to minimize average costs by fully realizing the economies of scale in that industry.

A report of labor costs and mill size conducted by the American Paper and Pulp Association in the 1930s revealed striking economies of scale in paper production (Hagenauer 1935). The results of a 1934 survey of labor costs and productivity among 389 paper manufacturers are replicated in Table 4–10. These survey results demonstrated that the labor cost per ton were generally much higher in the smaller mills than in the larger mills, and that labor productivity improved with the size of mill. The association report concludes that "The cost of production is considerably higher in the small mills than in the large mills. It is apparent that mills with the lowest production costs are those in the tonnage classes whose operating ratio tends to be higher . . . and operate at a higher rate of efficiency . . ." (Hagenauer 1935, 39).

Production costs and labor productivity varied by the grade of paper produced. The 1934 survey data were analyzed by type of product, and the results are shown in Table 4–11. Labor costs were lowest among the newsprint and kraft mills, which produced a standardized grade of paper. Higher grade papers produced by the book and writing mills required a more labor-intensive process, and labor costs were higher for these grades. Across all grades, however, economies of scale were evident. Another factor to consider, not shown in the data, is the quality of the paper produced at different-size mills. Particularly for writing mills, the smaller mills produced a very high quality of paper that was not comparable to the product of larger mills in the same grade class. So despite higher labor costs and lower labor productivity, the small writing mills remained competitive with larger mills because they served a market niche where higher prices compensated for the higher production costs (Hagenauer 1935, 36; Smith 1971, 619; Vogel 1959, 391).[14]

Alternatively, economies of scale and the optimal firm size may be estimated by the "survivor technique" developed by George Stigler. Rather than collect cost data, this method finds the efficient firm size by assuming that "competition of different sizes of firms sifts out the more efficient enterprises" (Stigler 1968b, 73). The survivor technique begins by classifying firms by size categories based on percentages of total industry production (or capacity). Then the market share of industry production (or share of capacity) originating from each category is observed over time. A rising market share is a measure of success that indicates that size-category of firms survived the competitive pressures of that industry. As a result, efficient firm size(s) will be revealed by a rising market share and inefficient size(s) by declining market shares over the period.[15]

Following Stigler, firm size in the paper industry for all paper grades combined has been estimated by capacity (because production was not reported at the firm level). Size categories are expressed as percentages of total paper industry capacity in each sample year to account for growth in industry and firm size over time. (As a result, the absolute size of the mills in a given category will rise in each period due to expansion of total industry capacity over time.) Table 4–12 reports the size distribution of paper firms in the period 1900–1940. The size categories are defined to delinate firm sizes among the small firms and are similar to those categories used by Stigler and others (e.g., Stigler 1968b, 76; Keeler 1989, 235).

Over half of all paper mills in each sample year reported capacities less than one-tenth of a percent of total paper capacity (see Table 4–12). However, the number of mills and share of industry capacity in the smallest size category declined over the period. Despite the fact that the majority of mills were small throughout the period, the survivor test emphasizes the trend away from small plants.[16] The next two categories, capacities ranging from 1/10 to less than 3/10 of a percent of total capacity, represented smaller shares of industry capacity in 1940 than in 1900 (but the shares had increased in some sample years during the period). The middle categories, from 3/10 of a percent to less than 1 percent of total capacity, grew over the period in terms of both number of mills and share of industry capacity. The largest mills, those sizes above 1 percent of total capacity, declined from 12.5 percent of industry capacity in 1900 to 7.8 percent of capacity in 1940, as the number of mills in these categories dropped from 9 in 1900 to 6 in 1940.

The evidence from Table 4–12 suggests that the surviving sizes ranged from 3/10 of a percent to less than 1 percent of total industry capacity, because these were the only mill sizes that gained shares of industry capacity over the period. The gradual disappearance of the smallest mills may be explained by the relative inefficiency of mill sizes smaller than 3/10 of 1 percent of industry capacity. Based on these results, it appears that the minimum optimal size of a paper mill is equal to 3/10 of 1 percent of industry capacity each year. The survivorship test indicates that economies of scale were exhausted with a mill capacity of more than 1 percent of industry capacity, because the shares of total capacity represented by mills that were larger than 1 percent of capacity declined over the period. These results confirm Louis Stevenson's assertion that the maximum paper mill size in the 1930s was between 500 to 750 tons per day (Stevenson 1940, 110). This capacity range is equivalent to the size category of 1 percent to 1-1/2 percent of total industry capacity in 1930 and 1940, which marks the start of decreasing returns to scale according to the survivor tests.

Additional analysis of the distribution of paper mills each year supports the conclusions of the survivorship test. Each year, mills were classified as survivors if they were listed in the 1941 issue of the directory and nonsurvivors if not. The proportion of mills surviving to 1940 by size category are listed in Table 4–13 for each sample year. Mills that were smaller than 2/10 of 1 percent of annual capacity consistently had lower survival rates than larger mills each sample year. The poor survival statistics for the smallest mills confirm that the minimum efficient plant size was likely to have been an intermediate size mill. Although the survival rate generally was highest among the largest mills (greater than 1 percent of annual capacity), the survivors generally drifted to lower-size categories in subsequent years. In 1900, five of the largest nine mills survived to 1940, but only one of these mills was larger than 1 percent of annual capacity in any subsequent year (and only in 1910 for that one mill).[17] Of the six largest mills in 1910, four survived to 1940 but only one remained larger than 1 percent of annual capacity (and was the only mill to report a large capacity in 1920). In 1930, five of the six largest mills survived to 1940, and two remained larger than 1 percent of annual capacity in 1940. In addition to these two mills, four new large mills were introduced in the South during the 1930s, and these six mills represented the only mills that were larger than 1 percent of capacity in 1940.

While industry-wide economies of scale is of interest for a discussion of paper production in general and for a comparison of the paper industry with other manufacturing sectors, a more careful analysis must control for the type of paper grade produced. Because newsprint mills generally were the largest of all paper mills, this grade of paper has been selected for a separate investigation of economies of scale. The survivorship technique has been applied to all mills that produced newsprint in any of the sample years. Newsprint capacity had to be estimated in the mills that produced other grades of paper in addition to newsprint, because mills rarely reported capacity separately for each grade. In these cases, the total mill capacity was divided by the number of grades produced (based on the six grade categories used in this study). Total newsprint capacity each year was measured by the sum of the estimated newsprint capacity at each newsprint mill.[18]

Table 4–14 presents the distribution of newsprint mills between 1900 and 1940. The size categories are percentages of total newsprint capacity each year. One clear trend that occurred over the period was the shift to relatively larger mill sizes, measured both by number of mills and capacity shares, as the total number of newsprint mills steadily declined. The largest three categories, ranging from 2.5 percent to 15 percent of total newsprint capacity, increased from a combined 47.9 percent of newsprint capacity in 1900 to 90.7 percent of newsprint capacity in 1940. The number of mills in these three categories increased from 9 to 16 mills over the same period. At the other extreme, the four smallest size categories were gradually eliminated over the period, as the distribution shifted to relatively larger sizes. The group of mills smaller than 4/10 of 1 percent of newsprint capacity declined from 5.5 percent of total capacity in 1900 to 2.1 percent in 1930 and then disappeared by 1940. Of the 34 mills in the first four size categories in 1900, only 7 survived to 1940 (a 19 percent survival rate compared to 28 percent for all newsprint mills); the survivors had grown to larger size categories in the meantime. As a group, the medium-size mills, those ranging from 4/10 of 1 percent of total newsprint capacity to less than 2.5 percent, also delcined over the period. These five categories declined from a combined 46.8 percent of total newsprint capacity in 1900 to only 9.4 percent of total newsprint capacity in 1940. The pattern of capacity shares for the intermediate sizes was erratic over the period, however.

The data presented in Table 4–14 suggest that the minimum optimal mill size in newsprint production was equal to 2.5 percent of total newsprint capacity, which was larger than for paper mills in general (less than 1 percent of industry capacity, as discussed above). The evidence that only the largest size categories of mills grew during the period, while the smaller size categories lost market share, supports the theory that newsprint mills shifted to larger-size mills (relative to total newsprint capacity) because larger mills were more efficient. The redistribution of the newsprint production to more efficient-sized mills is consistent with the difficult climate of this period, as domestic newsprint mills struggled to compete with imported newsprint from Canada.

These results are similar to the magnitude of economies of scale found in the late nineteenth century newsprint industry. Lamoreaux (1985) investigated the size distribution of eastern newsprint mills in 1892 and 1900, based on the 1892–1893 and 1900–1901 editions of *Lockwood's Directory* (the latter is the same issue used in the above analysis). Lamoreaux defined size categories by increments of 1 percent of total eastern newsprint capacity and applied the survivor technique to discover the pattern of changes in the distribution of newsprint mills during the competitive period of the 1890s. She finds "an expansion of mills with at least 2 percent of total capacity at the expense of their smaller competitors," which she concludes is the approximate minimum efficient size for a newsprint plant (Lamoreaux 1985, 42). This result is very close to the 2.5 percent figure that was found in the analysis of all U.S. newsprint mills in the later period between 1900 and 1940 and lends support to the conclusions that were drawn from Table 4–14.

BARRIERS TO ENTRY

Barriers to entry are factors that prevent or deter entry of new firms into an industry. Entry barriers may result in high concentration if the industry would otherwise support a larger number of smaller firms under free entry. It is interesting to note, however, that industry structure may not change when barriers are eliminated if entry results in the replacement of the encumbents by more efficient firms. In fact, the market could become even more concentrated if the encumbents are replaced by a smaller group of larger firms.

Barriers to entry have been defined in various ways. Traditionally entry barriers were described as conditions that block entry and allow existing firms to earn above-normal profits by setting price at higher than competitive levels. Supporters of this view list economies of scale, high capital requirements, ownership of a vital resource, and advertising as common barriers to entry. Others follow the more narrow definition suggested by Stigler, who described barriers "as a cost of producing (at some or every rate of output) which must be borne by a firm which seeks to enter an industry but is not borne by firms already in the industry" (Stigler 1968c, 67). Stigler's definition excludes factors such as economies of scale or high capital requirements, if the existing and entering firms face the same cost functions. Because the entrants have the same opportunities for achieving efficiency gains through large scale production and can establish firm reputations by advertising, many of the traditional entry barriers are seen to promote rather than obstruct allocative efficiency.

Both Cohen and Whitney report that the decline in the total number of mills listed in the directories before 1939 is indirect evidence that there were traditional barriers to entry in this industry (Cohen 1984, 791; Whitney 1958, 363). However, I argue that there is little evidence of barriers to entry (traditional or Stigler barriers), based on evidence drawn from the same directories that Cohen and Whitney examined. The focus on the total number of mills has misled some observers to conclude that entry to this industry was difficult.[19] It turns out that the period between 1900 and 1940 was marked by a tremendous amount of entry and exit of firms in the pulp and paper industry. Although the number of paper mills increased gradually from 772 in 1900 to 819 in 1930, and then declined to 743 by 1940, this relative stability in the total number of mills masks the underlying turnover that occurred throughout the period. In fact, a high rate of failure dramatically changed the composition of paper producers from one decade to the next.

The mills listed in the directories at ten-year intervals between 1900 and 1940 were used to document the number of mills entering and exiting during each decade of this period (see Table 4–15). The table summarizes the total number of mills and average size (measured in pounds of output per day) at the beginning of each decade, followed by the number and average size of mills that subsequently entered and exited during that decade. The total number of mills remained fairly steady over the period because the number of entering and exiting mills during each decade was almost balanced (until the 1930s, when exits exceeded entrants during the depression years). However, total pulp and paper capacity grew significantly, despite the constancy in the number of mills, because entrants on average were about double the size of mills that exited each decade (and also because surviving mills expanded each decade).

Entry occurred through either the takeover of existing mills or the establishment of new mills each decade (which was then mirrored by exit through the transfer of ownership of plants or the closing of plants). The relative importance of takeovers versus new plants varied by decade and by region, as was discussed in Chapter 3. Roughly half of entrants represented the turnover of existing plants, with a greater tendency for entrants in the older regions to acquire mills compared to entrants in the expanding regions of the South and the Pacific Coast (see Table 3–7).

Measures of the effect of entry and exit on industry structure are presented in Table 4–16. The entry and exit variables follow Dunne, Roberts, and Samuelson (1988, 502–3) and are defined as follows:

entry rate = number of entrants/the total number of mills at the end of the decade;

entrants' market share = entrants' capacity/total industry capacity at the end of the decade;

entrants' relative size = average entrant size/average encumbent size at the end of the decade;

exit rate = number of exiters/the total number of mills at the beginning of the decade;

exiters' market share = exiters' capacity/total industry capacity at the beginning of the decade;

exiters' relative size = average exiter size/average nonexiter size at the beginning of the decade.

The entry statistics reveal that entrants represented a significant but declining share of the paper industry in the first four decades of this century, from 46 percent of mills operating in 1910 to 28 percent in 1940. The market share of entrants was about equal to their entry rate because the average size of entrants was fairly close to the industry-wide average each decade (although much larger than the average size of exiters, as already noted). As a result, one can measure entry by the number of mills or by the amount of new capacity each decade, because each measure represents about the same impact on industry structure.

Mills that exited during each decade comprised a declining share of mills that were operating at the beginning of each decade, from 44 percent to 35 percent; however, the exit share declined more slowly than the entry share, resulting in an exit share greater than the entry share during the 1930s. Exits represented a smaller market share than was implied by the exit rate, because the average size of exiters was smaller than the industry average each decade. The exit rate tends to overstate the impact of mill failures on total industrial capacity. In terms of the impact on industry structure, exiters contributed to an increase in the average size of mills each year by the elimination of the relatively small mills. Entrants, on the other hand, had little impact on the average mill size because the average size of new mills was nearly equal to the industry average each decade.

In summary, the directories permit a more accurate means to measure the nature of entry barriers by identifying the individual entrants and exiters from one decade to the next. The striking rate of turnover in the firms that produced pulp and paper challenges the traditional view that entry barriers were high in this industry. This analysis also points to the fallacy in statistics based on the net number of mills each year, which do not distinguish the surviving mills from the new mills each period. This approach will be expanded in Chapter 7 to study the determinants of survival in the period 1900–1940.

FIRM CONDUCT

A number of factors contributed to competitive pricing and profits in the paper industry, even when concentration was high in the early twentieth century in some markets due to consolidations, such as International Paper. The homogeneous nature of most grades, especially standardized newsprint and kraft grades, weakens any one firm's market power because of the easy substitutability with other suppliers. Moreover, firms were able to switch the grade of paper produced on their paper machines by varying the pulp and the speed of the machine. Thus, as prices increased (decreased), firms could easily enter (exit) that market and stabilize prices. As noted in a *Fortune* article, "Flexibility (of paper machinery) is the great price leveler in all but the very fine papers. . . ." ("Economics of Paper" (1937, 184). In a similar view, Stevenson argues that "the paper industry is almost self-regulatory in regard to monopolistic attempts because of 'grade-shifting'. . ." (Stevenson 1940, 218). The reliance on foreign imports of pulp and certain paper grades, especially newsprint (tariff-free after 1913) also mitigated the market power of domestic mills.

The behavior of pulp and paper prices appears to be driven by market forces. For example, an index of paper and pulp prices between 1913 and 1938 moves in close correlation with a price index of all commodities; both rise sharply during World War I to a peak in 1920, decline gradually in the 1920s, and drop sharply during the Great Depression (although the paper price index fell relatively less than the general index) (Stevenson 1940, 152). The exception to market pricing occurred during the brief period of the National Recovery Administration (NRA), from 1933 to 1935, when price codes were established for the industry (Stevenson 1940, 177–79, 206; Guthrie 1940, 113).

Profits in the pulp and paper industry generally were regarded as competitive. A discussion of profits in this period is complicated by unreliable data and accounting methods because firms were unlikely to have accounted for depreciation prior to 1920 (Creamer et al. 1960). Profits apparently were lowest in the newsprint industry, where "the cost of new and modern newsprint mills . . . had made the profit margin much too narrow for all except the largest" (Smith 1971, 208). More reliable estimates of profits in the 1930s, 1940s, and 1950s, which account for depreciation, show that paper industry profits were comparable to average manufacturing profits. Using Stigler's calculations of rates of return (in 1947 prices) in the period 1938–1958, the average rate of return in the paper industry was 6 percent, compared to 5.28 percent for all manufacturing. However, the variance of paper returns was twice as high as for all manufacturing. According to modern financial theory, it is not surprising that the relatively more volatile paper industry exhibits higher profitability. The higher returns are consistent with competitive markets where risk averse investors must be compensated to hold riskier stocks.

Some branches of the paper industry have been suspected of periods of oligopolistic collusion or price leadership, but Guthrie holds that these attempts were ineffective "because of inherent characteristics of the industry which make difficult the successful restriction of price competition" (Guthrie 1940, 114). Lamoreaux (1985) argues that International Paper attempted a dominant-firm strategy in the early twentieth century newsprint market. However, the entry of competitors in this period, especially Great Northern, and the growing competition from Canadian newsprint rapidly diminished any power International Paper may have had to influence market prices. As evidence of the degree of price competition experienced at that time, *The Financial World*, reported during 1905 that International Paper lost a number of important newsprint customers to competitors and was "obliged to reduce its price" to other publishers to keep their business (*The Financial World*, March 1905, 10). Later that year, the paper was critical of International Paper's prospects because of

the increasing competition brought about solely by the arbitrary fixing of prices on newsprint by the company, and the loss during the past year of some of the company's principal and largest customers—big metropolitan newspapers which have organized their own paper manufacturing company, or have made contracts for the output of independent mills (*The Financial World* November 1905, 8).

In later years, International Paper diversified to other grades of paper and to power plants, which reduced its market share in newsprint to less than 15 percent by 1920 ("International Paper & Power" 1937, 135).

Evidence drawn from antitrust investigations of paper firms often failed to prove that paper producers were guilty of antitrust violations, with the exception of producer organizations that practiced episodes of price-fixing and quota plans.[20] As the most concentrated segment, antitrust attention often focused on the newsprint market in this period. Newsprint firms, primarily International Paper, were the target of investigations in 1900 and 1907, which were prompted by newspaper publishers' complaints of price-fixing in periods of rising newsprint prices. No evidence of collusion was found, notwithstanding the testimony of newspaper publishers. International Paper responded to the first investigation, which came just two years after the formation of the company, by testifying that the increase in newsprint prices at the turn of the century was to compensate for the costs of producing a higher quality of paper and to assure "a fair return" (to correct for low prices in the years before the consolidation when firms earned insufficient returns, according to the company) (U.S. Industrial Commission 1901, 435). In the investigation of higher newsprint prices in 1907, International Paper and other newsprint manufacturers testified that the increases were justified by the higher costs of pulp wood, wages, and other materials used in production. The Congressional committee conducting the investigation determined that

no combination in restraint of trade has been proven by the evidence to exist among the paper manufacturers . . . but that on the other hand the evidence does show that the upward tendency in the price of paper, which was so marked during the year 1907, reached its limit some months ago, probably as the result of economic conditions, and that at present the tendency of the newsprint market is downward (U.S. Congress 1908, 13).

These early findings did not deter continued surveillance of the industry, however. Between 1904 and 1951, there were 22 congressional investigations of newsprint manufacturers, probably to maintain "good relations with newspapers" (Whitney 1958, 351). At a later investigation, a committee reported that newsprint prices were set by collusion, but the conclusion probably refers to Canadian rather than U.S. producers. Whitney explains that the evidence against the newsprint firms was unconvincing for a number of reasons, including the use of buyer testimony (which is biased) and the legacy of cooperation fostered under the NRA.

A series of early twentieth century investigations of price fixing were directed against "pooling associations," which were formed to act as the common selling agent for a group of manufacturers. In 1900 a group of 26 wrapping paper and newsprint mills in Wisconsin, Michigan, and Minnesota created the General Paper Company (Ellis 1948, 29). General's alleged purpose was to operate as a western cartel, fixing prices and restricting output, to compete with International Paper's economic power in the East. The General Paper Company was dissolved under the Sherman Act in 1906, but Smith argues that the selling agency had become defunct before then because Kimberly-Clark had left the organization (Smith 1971, 207). Other pooling associations, including the Fibre and Manila Association, the American Paperboard Association, and the Eastern Boxboard Association, were dissolved by the antitrust authorities in the period 1905–1915 (Weeks 1916, 312).

In contrast to the pooling associations, trade associations were considered benign by antitrust authories (with the exception of the investigations discussed below). The general trade association was known as the American Paper and Pulp Association during this period (now the American Paper Institute).[21] The association had a number of affiliated service and divisional associations, including the Technical Association of the Pulp and Paper Industry (TAPPI), which was formed in 1915 to promote the exchange of information about the science of pulp- and papermaking, and groups representing various specialized manufacturers.[22] Although the association was originally formed in 1878 to attempt to stablize market prices (which had declined following the Panic of 1873), not all mills cooperated with plans to coordinate a reduction production in the late 1870s. This early failure to control the market led the association to take on functions that did not restrict competition, such as social meetings, public relations, dissemination of statistics, and the exchange of technical information among its members (Weeks 1916, 299; Smith 1971, 354; Whitney 1958, 367).

Investigations by the Federal Trade Commission in 1917 led to the dissolution of two trade associations formed by newsprint and book paper manufacturers, however. Although sharp increases in newsprint and book paper prices in 1915 and 1916 were probably explained by market conditions (higher wartime demand), the Commission took antitrust action against firms in these markets. In 1916, the Federal Trade Commission concluded that the recently formed News Print Manufacturers Association (NPMA) had indirectly attempted to control the newsprint market through allotment of customers, curtailment of production, and prevention of plant expansion.[23] After the commission presented its findings to the Department of Justice, the NPMA, seven leading newsprint executives, and 45 U.S. corporations were indicted for violation of the Sherman Act. In 1917, all but one party pleaded *nolo contendere* (the one that went to trial was later acquitted), and the manufacturers agreed to dissolve their association. Publishers were temporarily protected by maximum prices, administered by the Federal Trade Commission (other commodities were also subject to wartime price controls). That same year, the commission dissolved the Bureau of Statistics of the Book Paper Manufacturers Association.

Another wave of price-fixing cases were introduced in the late 1930s after the expiration of the NRA codes. In 1939, the Federal Trade Commission charged the Book Paper Manufacturers' Association (formed in 1933 under the NRA) with conspiracy to fix prices and other business policies. The group was issued a cease and desist order in 1945, but Guthrie argues that there was little evidence that competition was suppressed by the association (Guthrie 1940, 114). In 1940, the Kraft Paper Association was enjoined from using kraft paper quotas, following investigation by the Justice Department. A similar case was brought against the National Paperboard Association in the late 1930s, but the suit was dropped when the industry voluntarily withdrew the quota plan. Whitney notes that the paper industry has attracted more antitrust actions against trade associations than any other industry (Whitney 1958, 412).

SUMMARY

Descriptions of the individual pulp and paper mills listed in the directories clarify a number of issues concerning industry structure, including the number and size distribution of mills (and firms), multi-plant operations, and the rate of entry and exit of mills. The evidence challenges the traditional view of this industry as a highly concentrated oligopoly with high barriers to entry. Instead, the data suggest that in most markets concentration was fairly low (the exception was newsprint), economies of scale were achieved at a plant size representing a small percentage of market concentration, and that entry and exit of mills over each decade during the period 1900–1940 was extensive. Secondary sources confirm that the conduct of paper firms was competitive, and investigations into various branches of the industry (newsprint in particular) generally concluded that producers were innocent of antitrust violations in this period.

NOTES

1. The net rate of entry has been used as a measure of entry conditions in interindustry studies (Orr 1974; Duetsch 1975). However, Duetsch admits that it is an inadequate measure, particularly because it ignores firm turnover (Duetsch 1975, 450).

2. This approach will create errors to the extent mill capacity was not allocated in equal proportions across all products, or where the mill listed additional grades that were produced only in the event the mill chose to shift production to those grades when conditions in the primary market became unfavorable (U.S. Congress 1909, 148).

3. The markets for most paper and pulp products were not nationwide in this period. Most products were shipped within the regions as broadly defined in Chapter 3 (Guthrie 1950, 86–89).

4. These concentration ratios are consistent with those reported by Whitney, which are based on the production of the top five newsprint firms for the years 1913, 1920, and 1951 (Whitney 1958, 353).

5. This approach assumes that a pound of paper requires a pound of pulp and that integrated mills sell any excess pulp. However, the calculations will be inaccurate in the event an integrated mill sells all the pulp produced at the mill and buys all the mill's pulp requirements in the market, or if the mill stores rather than sells any excess pulp. I also assume that market pulp from a mill that is part of a multiplant firm is not transferred to another paper mill owned by that firm. This approach is supported by information found in the annual reports of International Paper in this period. Despite the fact that International Paper produced a net deficit of pulp across all mills owned by the company, the annual report of 1940 listed an annual production of market pulp that was consistent with the daily capacity of specialized pulp mills found in the directories that year. Moreover, later annual reports include a footnote that explains that only a small portion of the market pulp was shipped to other mills owned by International Paper.

6. Excluding Rayonier's capacity for specialized sulphite production (for use in rayon) in 1940, the market-pulp concentration ratios would be revised as follows: for the top four mills, all mills = .19, sulphite mills = .43, Pacific mills = .55; for the top four firms, all firms = .24, sulphite firms = .53, Pacific firms = .75. The notable changes are the increase in mill-based ratios for the sulphite mills and Pacific mills, primarily due to the relatively large drop in the denominator when Rayonier pulp is excluded.

7. For other criticisms of concentration measures see McGee (1988, 252–3); Scherer and Ross (1990, 76–79).

8. Modern economics textbooks explain that corporations are able to raise large sums of money because incorporation creates a legal entity that does not depend on the life of any one of the firm's owners and because the liability of the firm's owners is limited to their initial investment. Disadvantages of the corporate form include double taxation of dividends (taxed once as corporate profits and again as personal income) and the separation of ownership and control of the firm when owners do not manage the corporation. However, Hessen (1989) argues that this standard view of corporations is incorrect. He points out that the advantages attributed to incorporation are available to partnerships through optional clauses that can be included in the partnership agreement or in contracts arranged with creditors. Hessen believes that corporations became popular in the late eighteenth and early nineteenth century to obtain franchises (special privileges and exemptions) granted by state governments to promote economic development in an area. Nevertheless, the striking contrast in the share of corporations in high versus low capital-intensive industries suggests that financing advantages of incorporation at least played a role in the preference for the corporate form in the high-fixed-cost industries.

9. This approach follows Stevenson (1940), who investigated the trend toward incorporation based on the 1872 and 1934 issues of *Lockwood's Directory*. He defined the following four categories: "corporations" if the firm was listed as a company or corporation with the names of the corporate officers included in the directory entry; if no officers or owners were named, the organizational form was listed as "doubtful." "Partnerships" and "individuals" were listed as such in the directory. In 1872, the

corporate form represented just 13.8 percent of firms. The industry was dominated by partnerships (45.8 percent of firms) and individuals (35.8 percent of firms); 4.6 percent of firms were classified "doubtful." By 1934, however, corporations had jumped to 96 percent of firms, and individuals and partnerships each represented just one percent of total firms; another 2 percent were classified "doubtful."

10. Mills at the same location were treated as separate if the firm reported the directory information individually for each mill; if combined, the mills were treated as a single plant. These multiplant statistics do not include specialized pulp mills that were owned by a paper firm and located in a different town than the firm's paper mill(s); these cases are discussed below.

11. Similarly, Stevenson found that in 1939, 424 firms operated only one paper mill each, out of a total 536 paper firms and a total 736 paper mills operating in the United States that year (Stevenson 1940, 102).

12. Lacking data on operating costs, I do not analyze the profitability of multiplant operations in the paper industry. For a discussion of recent research on the economies of multiplant operation, see Scherer (1990, 120–40).

13. Stevenson concurs that most firms operated locally. He reports that only 27 corporations out of a total of 543 owned and operated paper mills in more than one state in 1934 (Stevenson 1940, 102).

14. A second study for the American Paper and Pulp Association confirmed the evidence of economies of scale in paper production. Stevenson analyzed labor productivity among paper mills in the period 1934–1946 and found consistently higher ratios of tons per man-hour among larger mills. Labor productivity also varied by paper grade; tons per man-hour were higher among the standardized grades (board, kraft, and newsprint) than book and writing papers (see OEEC 1951, 64).

15. However, this test does not imply how much higher than the optimal-size firm are the costs of the inefficient-size firms (Stigler 1968b, 77). For a discussion of the limitations of this method, see Shepherd (1967).

16. Shepherd is critical of the potential contradiction between the static distribution of plants and trends observed over the test period, where the survivor test may conclude that a size representing the majority of plants is nonoptimal (Shepherd 1967, 116). This result is probably not contradictory in this case study, however, because the evidence is clear that small mills were less likely to survive, as shown in Table 4–13.

17. In fact, the largest mill in 1900, the Great Northern Paper Company's mill at Madison, Maine, reported a capacity of 600,000 pounds in 1900 but capacities no larger than 200,000 in later years.

18. This method apparently underestimated actual newsprint capacity, based on a comparison with the available reports of newsprint capacity in the *Census of Manufactures*. In 1930, the estimated capacity was 81 percent of that reported in the census, and in 1940, the estimate was 92 percent of the census total. If the total capacity of each mill producing newsprint had been used instead, however, newsprint capacity would have been overestimated in 1930 and 1940 by 25 percent and 47 percent, respectively.

19. One exception is Lamoreaux, who emphasizes the degree of entry in the early twentieth century newsprint industry. She asserts that "there were no barriers to prevent the entry of new competition" (Lamoreaux 1985, 47, 128).

20. For a detailed discussion of antitrust proceedings in the paper industry, see Whitney 1958, Chapter 6.

21. Originally formed in 1878 as the American Paper Makers' Association, the name of the association was changed in 1883 to the American Paper Manufacturers' Association and in 1887 to the American Paper and Pulp Association, to admit pulp manufacturers (Ellis 1948, 173).

22. The American Paper and Pulp Association listed 4 affiliated service associations and 11 divisional associations in 1927, for example. The number of affiliations rose to 22 during the 1940s. For listings of the associations, see U.S. Department of Commerce, "Trade Association Activities" (1927, 199–200) and Judkins (1942 and 1949).

23. For details of the brief history of the NPMA, formed in 1915 and dissolved in 1917, see Ellis (1948, 92–108).

Table 4–1
Concentration of Top Four Paper Mills
(Four-Mill Paper Capacity as Share of Total Paper Capacity in Each Category)

| | FOUR-MILL CONCENTRATION RATIO | | | | |
	1900	1910	1920	1930	1940
All Paper	7%	5%	5%	5%	6%
By Grade:					
Newsprint	30%	25%	25%	26%	42%
Book & Writing	11	13	13	14	13
Wrap & Board	5	7	8	9	9
Kraft	--	45	28	24	26
Sanitary	80	56	47	46	39
Industrial	24	16	14	17	20
By Region:					
North	11%	8%	8%	9%	9%
Lake	10	10	10	11	11
South	42	41	34	31	26
Pacific	68	73	56	35	35

Source: Compiled by the author from Lockwood's Directory of the Paper and Allied Trades.

Table 4–2
Concentration of Top Four Paper Firms
(Four-Firm Paper Capacity as Share of Total Paper Capacity in Each Category)

| | FOUR-FIRM CONCENTRATION RATIO | | |
	1900	1920	1940
All Paper	25%	12%	16%
By Grade:			
Newsprint	64%	47%	57%
Book & Writing	24	25	19
Wrap & Board	20	11	20
Kraft	–	34	38
Sanitary	80	47	39
Industrial	27	18	22
By Region:			
North	32%	20%	17%
Lake	24	11	15
South	42	37	48
Pacific	68	85	52

Source: Compiled by the author from Lockwood's Directory of the Paper and Allied Trades.

Table 4–3
Concentration of Top Four Market-Pulp[a] Mills
(Four-Mill Pulp Capacity as Share of Total Pulp Capacity in Each Category)

	FOUR-MILL CONCENTRATION RATIO				
	1900	1910	1920	1930	1940
All Market Pulp	17%	20%	18%	18%	17%
By Grade:					
Groundwood	22%	19%	17%	24%	29%
Soda	59	55	62	63	87
Sulphite	34	42	21	35	34
Sulphate (kraft)	–	100	59	39	52
Semichemical	–	–	–	100	100
By Region:					
North	23%	24%	25%	32%	42%
Lake	41	33	32	45	41
South	59	69	57	46	46
Pacific	74	99	86	42	41

Source: Compiled by the author from Lockwood's Directory of the Paper and Allied Trades.
[a] Pulp produced for market; calculated as total pulp capacity of specialized pulp mills or pulp capacity in excess of paper capacity of integrated mills.

Table 4–4
Concentration of Top Four Market-Pulp[a] Firms
(Four-Firm Pulp Capacity as Share of Total Pulp Capacity in Each Category)

	FOUR-FIRM CONCENTRATION RATIO		
	1900	1920	1940
All Market Pulp	31%	29%	29%
By Grade:			
Groundwood	40%	37%	37%
Soda	59	62	87
Sulphite	38	21	57
Sulphate (kraft)	–	59	52
Semichemical	–	–	100
By Region:			
North	42%	43%	52%
Lake	41	35	44
South	73	57	46
Pacific	78	99	71

Source: Compiled by the author from Lockwood's Directory of the Paper and Allied Trades.
[a] Pulp produced for market; calculated as total pulp capacity of specialized pulp mills or pulp capacity in excess of paper capacity of integrated mills.

76

Table 4–5
Forms of Ownership: 1900–1940

	1900[a]	1909[b]	1919[b]	1940[a]
Number of Firms:				
Corporations	349	633	647	521
Individuals	137	71	33	6
All others[c]	144	73	49	14
Total	630	777	729	541
Share of Total Value of Products:				
Corporations	n.a.	92.8%	96.4%	n.a.
Individuals	n.a.	2.2	0.5	n.a.
All others	n.a.	4.9	3.1	n.a.

[a] Based on the 1901 and 1941 editions of Lockwood's Directory of the Paper and Allied Trades. Value of production not available from this source.

[b] Sources were the abstract of the Census of Manufactures: 1919, Tables 195,197, and the Census of Manufactures, 1914, Vol. II, Table 10.

[c] Includes partnerships, and for the directory data, cases where the type of ownership could not be determined.

Table 4-6
Multiplant Operations in Paper Production: 1900, 1920, and 1940

Mills Owned by Firm:	1900			1920			1940		
	Total Firms	Total Mills	Share of Capacity	Total Firms	Total Mills	Share of Capacity	Total Firms	Total Mills	Share of Capacity
One	569	569	61.8%	568	568	60.7%	459	459	47.8%
Two	36	72	7.4	44	88	11.8	39	78	10.8
Three	12	36	4.6	16	48	8.6	21	63	12.8
Four +	9	95	26.1	14	106	18.8	22	143	28.6
Total	630	772	100.0%	642	810	100.0%	541	743	100.0%

Source: Compiled by the author from Lockwood's Directory of the Paper and Allied Trades.

Table 4–7
Comparison of Mills of Single vs. Multiple Mill Firms: 1900, 1920, and 1940

	1900		1920		1940	
	Single-mill	Multimill	Single-mill	Multimill	Single-mill	Multimill
Number of mills	569	203	568	242	459	284
Ave. paper capacity (thou. pounds)	24	42	68	104	131	229
Ave. no. mills owned by firm	1	8.4	1	6.1	1	5.4
Percentage:						
Newsprint	.11	.13	.08	.11	.04	.03
Book & Writing	.25	.37	.26	.37	.29	.25
Wrap & Board	.76	.58	.64	.52	.60	.56
Kraft	.00	.00	.05	.06	.11	.10
Sanitary	.01	.00	.06	.02	.13	.05
Industrial	.11	.10	.16	.17	.19	.25
Survived to 1940	.20	.22	.45	.44	1.00	1.00
Vertically integrated	.18	.22	.21	.28	.22	.23

Source: Compiled by the author from Lockwood's Directory of the Paper and Allied Trades.

Table 4–8
Largest Multiplant Paper Firms: 1900, 1920, and 1940

		Number of Mills and Percent of Total Paper Capacity					
		1900		1920		1940	
Firm	Date Estab.	Mills	%	Mills	%	Mills	%
International Paper	1898	22	14.8%	15	5.7%	20	9.1%
incl: Southern Kraft Corp.	1930	–	–	–	--	15	7.1
American Writing	1899	23	2.7	22	1.6	9	0.4
American Straw Board	1889	15	4.6	6	0.9	–	–
Kimberly Clark	1872	7	1.6	8	1.3	8	1.1
Union Bag and Paper	1899	7	1.3	5	0.8	3	2.2
West Virginia Pulp & Paper	1899	3	1.1	6	1.8	7	2.4
Hinde-Dauch	1882	2	0.1	7	0.7	7	0.7
Great Northern	1899	1	2.7	3	2.5	3	1.9
United Paperboard	1912	–	–	11	1.7	3	0.5
Crown Willamette[a]	1914	–	–	4	1.7	3	1.5
U.S. Gypsum	1920	–	–	–	--	11	1.0
Consolidated Paper	1921	–	–	–	--	6	1.3
Container Corp. of Amer.	1926	–	–	–	--	9	2.6
Fibreboard Products	1927	–	–	–	--	6	1.3
Central Fibre Products	1931	–	–	–	--	6	0.9

Sources: Compiled by the author from Lockwood's Directory of the Paper and Allied Trades;
supplementary information on incorporation dates from Lockwood, 250 Years of Papermaking in America (1940, 80-135) and Moody's Manual of Investments.
[a] Became a division of Crown Zellerbach Corp. in 1928.

Table 4–9
Interregional Multiplant Operations: 1900, 1920, and 1940

Regions	Number of Multiplant Paper Firms		
	1900	1920	1940
Same region	52	63	57
North & Lake	3	7	6
North & South	1	1	8
North & Pacific	1	1	1
Lake & South	0	1	4
Lake & Pacific	0	0	1
South & Pacific	0	0	0
North, Lake & South	0	0	2
North, Lake & Pacific	0	1	2
All four regions	0	0	1
Total Multiplant Firms	57	74	82

Source: Compiled by the author from Lockwood's Directory of the Paper and Allied Trades.

Table 4–10
Labor Cost and Labor Productivity by Mill Size
(September 1934)

Capacity	Labor Cost per Ton of Paper Production		
(tons/day)	Northern Zone	Central Zone	Southern Zone
0-10	$36.09	$23.38	--
11-25	29.53	27.63	--
26-50	18.48	14.03	$5.82
51-100	12.49	21.66	--
101-200	11.86	11.45	9.08
201 and above	8.31	4.05	4.81

Capacity	Tons of Paper Production Per Man		
(tons/day)	Northern Zone	Central Zone	Southern Zone
0-10	1.18	4.11	--
11-25	2.13	1.53	--
26-50	3.87	4.14	9.82
51-100	5.92	3.09	--
101-200	6.82	5.76	4.87
201 and above	8.30	9.46	14.60

Source: Hagenauer (1935, 38), Tables XXV and XXVI.

Table 4–11
Labor Cost by Mill Size in Five Product Divisions
(September 1934)

Capacity	Labor Cost per Ton of Paper Production				
(tons/day)	Book	Writing	Newsprint	Tissue	Kraft
0-10	$44.26	$140.88	--	$21.00	--
11-25	34.98	60.38	--	18.00	$34.85
26-50	18.41	30.75	$12.74	15.99	13.50
51-100	22.92	24.96	10.80	20.62	8.88
101-200	18.18	16.07	7.79	13.69	15.32
201 and above	17.33	--	6.90	--	11.35

Source: Hagenauer (1935, 36), Table XVIII.

Table 4–12
Distribution of Paper Capacity: 1900–1940
by Relative Size of Mill Capacity

Mill Size (Percent of Industry Capacity)	Percent of Industry Capacity[a]					Number of Mills				
	1900	1910	1920	1930	1940	1900	1910	1920	1930	1940
Under 0.1	20.9	22.4	20.8	17.6	16.1	475	493	477	471	408
0.1 to 0.2	22.3	23.6	24.8	23.1	19.6	156	158	169	172	145
0.2 to 0.3	15.1	12.8	11.5	15.8	14.9	60	50	47	68	63
0.3 to 0.4	7.3	9.1	14.4	11.9	11.2	21	26	42	36	33
0.4 to 0.5	6.4	7.3	5.0	7.7	8.7	14	16	11	18	20
0.5 to 0.75	11.9	13.1	11.2	12.2	12.8	20	21	19	21	22
0.75 to 1.0	4.1	4.3	10.7	5.0	8.4	5	5	12	6	10
1.0 to 1.5	8.1	7.3	–	6.7	5.9	7	6	–	6	5
1.5 to 2.5	1.6	–	1.6	–	1.9	1	–	1	–	1
2.5 to 5.0	2.8	–	–	–	–	1	–	–	–	–
Capacity not reported						12	27	32	21	36
Total						772	802	810	819	743

Source: Compiled by the author from <u>Lockwood's Directory of the Paper and Allied Trades.</u>
[a] Columns may not add to one hundred due to rounding.

Table 4–13
Survival Rate by Size of Paper Mill: 1900–1940

Mill Size (Percent of Industry Capacity)	Percent of Mills Surviving to 1940			
	1900	1910	1920	1930
Under 0.1	.16	.26	.40	.60
0.1 to 0.2	.26	.33	.48	.67
0.2 to 0.3	.32	.40	.70	.77
0.3 to 0.4	.29	.42	.50	.86
0.4 to 0.5	.29	.44	.64	.83
0.5 to 0.75	.25	.62	.68	.81
0.75 to 1.0	.40	.40	.58	.83
1.0 to 1.5	.43	.67	–	.83
1.5 to 2.5	1.00	–	1.00	–
2.5 to 5.0	1.00	–	–	–

Source: Compiled by the author from Lockwood's Directory of the Paper and Allied Trades.

Table 4–14

Distribution of Newsprint Mills: 1900–1940
by Relative Size of Newsprint Capacity

Mill Size (Percent of Newsprint Capacity)	Number of Mills					Percent of Newsprint Capacity[a]				
	1900	1910	1920	1930	1940	1900	1910	1920	1930	1940
Under 0.1	11	3	1	0	0	.7	.2	.1	—	—
0.1 to 0.2	12	8	1	1	0	1.5	1.1	.1	.2	—
0.2 to 0.3	10	8	2	2	0	2.4	1.9	.5	.5	—
0.3 to 0.4	3	7	3	4	0	.9	2.5	1.1	1.4	—
0.4 to 0.5	11	4	9	0	2	4.6	1.8	3.9	—	.9
0.5 to 0.75	7	11	5	7	0	4.1	7.3	3.3	4.5	—
0.75 to 1.0	9	8	15	7	3	8.4	6.9	12.6	5.6	2.7
1.0 to 1.5	7	11	14	11	2	8.9	13.5	17.7	12.9	2.6
1.5 to 2.5	11	4	7	10	2	20.8	7.8	12.0	19.5	3.2
2.5 to 5.0	5	8	8	8	8	18.2	26.9	28.5	29.0	24.7
5.0 to 10.0	3	5	3	4	5	17.8	30.1	20.1	26.4	31.7
10.0 to 15.0	1	0	0	0	3	11.9	—	—	—	34.3
Capacity not reported	0	0	1	0	0					
Total	90	77	69	54	25					

Source: Compiled by the author from Lockwood's Directory of the Paper and Allied Trades.

[a] Columns may not add to one hundred due to rounding.

Table 4–15

Entry and Exit of Mills Between 1900 and 1940 (Number of Mills and Average Capacity, Lbs./Day)

Paper Mills

Decade	Beginning of Decade		Entering Mills		Exiting Mills	
	No. Mills	Ave. Capacity	No. Mills	Ave. Capacity	No. Mills	Ave. Capacity
1900–1910	772	28,783	369	56,336	339	22,035
1910–1920	802	52,899	329	74,834	321	38,796
1920–1930	810	79,127	307	120,427	299	62,945
1930–1940	818	123,498	212	176,089	287	88,791

Pulp Mills

Decade	Beginning of Decade		Entering Mills		Exiting Mills	
	No. Mills	Ave. Capacity	No. Mills	Ave. Capacity	No. Mills	Ave. Capacity
1900–1910	254	55,428	115	101,473	122	30,970
1910–1920	247	102,862	88	116,918	84	90,928
1920–1930	251	128,802	84	183,675	97	85,172
1930–1940	238	195,292	68	412,746	96	151,277

Table 4–16

Market Share and Relative Size of Entrants and Exiters for Paper Mills by Decade

	1900-1910	1910-1920	1920-1930	1930-1940
Entrants				
Entry Rate	.46	.41	.37	.28
Market Share	.48	.38	.36	.29
Relative Size	1.13	.91	.96	1.07
Exiters				
Exit Rate	.44	.40	.37	.35
Market Share	.34	.29	.29	.25
Relative Size	.65	.62	.71	.63

Source: Compiled by the author from Lockwood's Directory of the Paper and Allied Trades.

5

Vertical Integration in the Pulp and Paper Industry

Economists have long debated the merits of vertical integration as an alternative to purchasing required inputs from outside suppliers. While vertical integration is thought to bring the benefits of lower production costs and control over input supplies, not all firms in a given industry are integrated. A case study of the pulp and paper industry offers an opportunity to explore the determinants of vertical integration, because only about one-fifth of paper mills chose to integrate backwards to pulp production. Based on information from *Lockwood's Directory of the Paper and Allied Trades*, this chapter compares the integrated paper mills to mills that purchased their pulp requirements from outside suppliers. The directory entries report the amount of pulp and paper capacities and types of pulp and paper products for each paper mill, which permits a careful analysis of the decision to integrate at the mill level.

A summary of the data from the directories measuring integration is presented in a wide variety of formats to uncover the important features of the integrated mills in this industry. Modern theories of integration are summarized and the economies of vertical integration in the pulp and paper industry are considered. Other aspects of integration that are explored include integration among mills within cities, integration within multiplant operations of firms that owned multiple paper mills, the pattern of changes in integration in individual mills over time, the extent of integration among mills entering and exiting each decade, and the apparent link between integration and mill survival in this period.

Finally, the backward integration of paper firms into the ownership of timberland during the 1930s is explored. Information about timberland ownership by paper firms is drawn from issues of *Moody's Manual of Investments* that were published during this period. This sample, when combined with the data found in the directory listings for the same firms, provides a basis for analyzing the role of pulp production, paper capacity, paper grades, and mill location in the paper firm's decision to own timberland.

The next chapter extends the analysis of vertical integration with statistical tests of the determinants of the decision to vertically integrate and to alter the extent of integration among integrated mills over time, based on a transaction-cost model of integration. The descriptive details of the directory data that are described in this chapter form the basis for the tests and models that are developed in Chapter 6.

DEFINITION OF VERTICAL INTEGRATION

Vertical integration exists when two stages of production are performed within the same firm. Specifically, a firm is vertically integrated if production of the "upsteam" (earlier stage) process is dedicated to use in the "downstream" (later stage) process, or if all of the requirements of the downstream process are met by the upstream process. Partial integration occurs when part of the upstream output is sold outside the firm and part of the input for the downstream process is bought outside the firm (Perry 1989, 185). The key feature of vertical integration is the substitution of internal exchange within the firm instead of reliance on market exchange, known as the "make or buy" decision.

The type of vertical integration of interest here is the production of pulp (the upstream process) by a paper firm (the downstream process).[1] The incidence of vertical integration in the paper industry can be measured by data drawn from *Lockwood's Directory of the Paper and Allied Trades*. Because the directory combines the details about the pulp and paper operations for each mill into a single entry, vertical integration may be inferred by those listings that provide information about capacity, machines, or grades for both pulp and paper production.[2] Several situations may occur that satisfy the above definition of vertical integration: if all the firm's pulp is used within the firm as its only source of pulp supply, or if, in addition to its internal supply of pulp, the firm supplements its pulp requirements with pulp bought in the market, or if the firm sells its excess pulp production in the market. These cases are approximated by values of the ratio of pulp capacity to paper capacity equal to one, less than one, and greater than one, respectively.

One limitation of the directory data is that full and partial integration cannot be distinguished by this source. Partial integration occurs when part of the pulp output is sold outside the firm, and at the same time, some pulp required for paper production is bought from other suppliers. However, the directory listings do not provide information about market sales or purchases of pulp that would identify partial integration. For example, even though a match between pulp and paper capacity suggests that the firm produces all of its pulp requirements, it is possible that the pulp was sold rather than transferred within the firm. With this caveat in mind, pulp is assumed to be used internally by the firm, except when pulp capacity exceeds paper capacity and the difference is assumed to be sold to outside buyers. In other words, all integration is treated as full vertical integration in this study. This is probably a safe assumption, though, because firms usually produced types of pulp that were required for the types of paper manufactured (e.g., groundwood pulp and newsprint).

ARGUMENTS FOR VERTICAL INTEGRATION

The basic economic rationale for vertical integration is that the firm can produce the upstream input internally at a lower cost than if the firm negotiated a contract with an independent supplier or if the input was purchased in the spot market. The cost savings may be attributed to a variety of sources, which Perry has broadly classified as technological economies, transactional economies, and market imperfections (Perry 1989, 187–89). These potential economies must be weighed against any costs incurred by integration. Firms may sacrifice the advantages of specialization at one stage of production when they enter the new stage of production, particularly if increasing returns to scale exist at the original stage (Hyman 1988, 289). The costs of managing the integrated firm may also offset the advantages of integration, depending on the experience and skill of the managers. By committing the firm to integrated production methods, flexibility is reduced and adjustment to changes in the market at one stage of production is more difficult. Integration also raises capital requirements and investment expenditures when the firm expands operations (Buzzell 1983, 94).

Technological economies occur if fewer resources are used to produce the downstream output if the upstream process is vertically integrated. In the steel industry, for example, the integration of smelting with later stages of production saves the energy that would be required to reheat steel if it were purchased outside the firm. The extent of technological economies will vary by industry but are available to all firms within an industry. The fact that not all firms within a given industry are integrated, however, suggests that technological savings may not be sufficient to explain the decision to integrate (McGee 1988, 281).

Transactional economies refer to the reduction in transaction costs when integration replaces external exchange. The integrated firm avoids the costs associated with negotiating a supply contract, which includes assuring such features as the price, quantity, quality, and delivery of the goods. The incentives to integrate will be higher, the higher the cost to the firm of a shortage or interruption of input supplies. Transaction costs arise from problems monitoring a contract when there are informational asymmetries between the supplier and the "downstream" producer (Shugart 1990, 336). Another source of transaction costs occurs when assets involved in the production of the upstream product become specialized to that transaction. When assets become specific to a particular transaction, the firm is vulnerable to opportunistic behavior by the supplier. The potential loss is measured by the appropriable quasi-rent, or the difference between the value of the asset in its current use and its value in its next best use (Klein, Crawford, and Alchian 1978). The higher the "asset specificity" associated with the transaction, the higher the costs of market exchange and the greater the incentive to integrate (Williamson 1985, 90). The integrated firm can also reduce transportation and storage costs by producing the upstream and downstream products at the same site.

Market economies stem from substituting integration for exchanges in imperfect markets. Unlike the transaction-cost theories, this approach ignores the costs of exchange. Instead, these theories focus on the avoidance of costs attributed to monopoly or monopsony market power, price controls and rationing, and problems associated with uncertainty (Perry 1989, 190–212). Following Caves and Bradburd (1988), this class of models will not be evaluated in the following discussion. There is little empirical evidence that the pulp and paper markets are consistent with these market imperfections (see Chapter 4), and certain conditions of some of these models are difficult to observe in any case (Caves and Bradburd 1988, 268).

In addition to explanations based on these benefits of integration, other theories focus on intertemporal patterns of integration. Stigler incorporates market growth in a theory of integration that addresses the pattern of integration over the life cycle of an industry (or firm, presumably) (Stigler 1968a, 135–36).[3] Stigler argues that over the lifetime of an industry, firms will integrate when the industry is young, disintegrate as the industry matures, and then integrate when the industry reaches the final, declining phase. Initially, the new industry is integrated because firms require new materials and specialized equipment, so must make their own. As the market (final demand) grows, firms specialize in one process to take advantage of increasing returns to scale. The firm disintegrates and independent suppliers take over tasks that had been internalized by the original firm. Firms will return to vertical integration in the final stage of development as the market size declines and no longer supports specialization.[4]

ECONOMIES OF INTEGRATION OF PULP AND PAPER PRODUCTION

Pulp and paper production is subject to technological economies of integration, and observers of the industry before 1940 attributed these technological economies to the high rates of integration found in certain paper segments during this period. One significant advantage was the saving of the cost of drying the pulp. Integrated mills allowed pulp to be transferred in slush form to the paper plant, whereas specialized pulp mills had to dry the pulp before it was shipped (U.S. Tariff Commission 1938, 94–95). Integration also saved the water and energy costs of converting the dried pulp to slush form at the paper mill. The technological advantages of integration may have been offset by a number of disadvantages, however. One consideration was transportation costs at the other stages of production. Because pulp production usually was situated near sources of pulpwood, integration meant locating papermaking at the pulping site and shipping paper to the markets. In some cases, the transportation costs may have been minimized by separating the pulping and papermaking sites, particularly if materials other than pulp were used in papermaking, such as waste paper (U.S. Tariff Commission 1938, 95).

These technological economies appeared to be greater for some products than others. Standardized papers that were produced on a relatively large scale, such as newsprint and kraft, were more likely to be integrated with pulp production. Coordination between pulp and paper production may have been facilitated because these papers required large batches of only a few grades of pulp, which also took advantage of the economies of scale in pulp production. Finer grades of paper, such as writing papers, were often produced to order in small quantities and required a wide range of grades and types of pulp. As a result, a far greater proportion of groundwood and kraft pulps and newsprint and kraft papers were produced in integrated mills compared to sulphite pulp and other papers.

Some observers continue to attribute vertical integration in the industry primarily to the type of paper grade produced. In a recent study, the Organization for Economic Cooperation and Development (OECD) explained international differences in the extent of pulp and paper integration across OECD countries by the grades produced in each country, in addition to the size of mills and the rate of modernization of paper machinery. The OECD study found that more than 75 percent of paper produced in the United States and Scandinavian countries was integrated with pulp production, compared to between 11 percent and 55 percent in the United Kingdom and European countries. The OECD analysts concluded that the higher proportions of integration were explained by the production of standardized grades, such as newsprint and paperboards. Integration offers cost advantages in these bulk grades, where paper is produced in large-scale operations and it becomes economical for the firm to produce its own pulp requirements (OECD 1982, 7).

Modern studies also have explored the transactional economies involved in the integration of pulp and paper production. Livesay and Porter (1969) investigated trends in integration in U.S. manufacturing between 1899 and 1948, based on a sample of over 100 of the largest U.S. industrial firms in that period. In the subsample of firms included in the combined category of lumber and paper products, the percentage of those integrated with an "upstream" process increased from 50 percent in 1899 to 89 percent in 1948. (The authors indicate that all categories included at least four firms, but did not provide the actual sample size of the lumber and paper category.) More of the lumber and paper firms were integrated backward toward raw materials than forward into wholesaling or retailing, although there was a trend toward greater integration in both directions. Livesay and Porter argued that backward integration in the industries that were dependent on raw materials, including lumber and paper, may be viewed as a defensive strategy to control raw material supplies and avoid exploitation by independent suppliers.

Globerman and Schwindt (1986) take a transaction-cost approach to explain the observed pattern of integration in Canada's 30 largest forest products firms. They explain variations in integration in different activities, from forestry to packaging, by the degrees of asset specificity required at each stage. "Upstream" integration by Canadian firms into logging and ownership of timberlands is high, they argue, because the processing mills (pulp or sawmills) are specialized to specific timber stands and are therefore vulnerable to opportunistic behavior by owners of the timberlands. Similarly, the specialization of pulping assets to a particular paper machine, and the fact that the salvage value for a mill or componet asset is low, leads to integration at the level of papermaking (especially among newsprint manufacturers).

Modern theory also suggests that vertical integration is likely to be high in the paper industry because of the fixed-proportions and continuous-process nature of papermaking. The technology implies a greater potential loss from the interruption of input supply (a form of opportunistic behavior associated with asset specificity) compared to variable-proportions or batch-process industries (Hennart 1988, 283).

DIRECTORY EVIDENCE OF VERTICAL INTEGRATION, 1900–1940

Vertical integration was not the dominant strategy by firms in the paper industry between 1900 and 1940. Data from *Lockwood's Directory of the Paper and Allied Trades* in this period show that the proportion of vertically integrated paper mills each year varied between 19 percent to 23 percent in the sample years, with no clear trend over the period (see Table 5–1). However, a substantial part of domestic paper capacity was integrated in the period. Because the integrated mills were on average larger than nonintegrated mills, integrated capacity each year ranged from 38 percent to 47 percent of total capacity in the sample years.

Vertical integration was more predominant in the statistics based on the domestic pulp industry, where the majority of pulp mills were associated with paper mills. The proportion of integrated pulp mills steadily increased from 58 percent in 1900 to 78 percent by 1940. The percentage of pulp capacity that was integrated was higher than the share of integrated mills because the integrated pulp mills were on average larger than the nonintegrated mills. Integrated pulp capacity represented from 64 percent of total pulp capacity in 1900 to 83 percent in 1930 and 1940. The substantially higher proportion of integrated pulp capacity compared to the proportion of paper capacity is explained by pulp imports. Although integrated paper and pulp capacities were approximately equal in each sample year, total domestic pulp capacity was less than total domestic paper capacity by the amount of pulp imports each year (see Table 2–7). When the integrated pulp capacity is expressed as a share of domestic pulp capacity, the percentage is higher than in the same calculation for the paper capacities due to the smaller denominator for pulp capacity.

Integration was far more common among mills in the new regions of the South and Pacific compared to the established North and Lake regions (see Table 5–2). The share of integrated mills fluctuated between 41 percent and 52 percent of all paper mills in the South and between 44 percent and 62 percent in the Pacific, while the rates in the North and Lake regions ranged from 17 percent to 21 percent of paper mills. (Today, there remains a wide disparity in regional vertical integration. In 1990, the share of paper mills that were integrated with pulp production in each region is estimated to be approximately 65 percent in the South, 51 percent in the Pacific Coast region, 23 percent in the Lake region, and 7 percent in the North. These estimates are based on a comparison of the total number of establishments with the number of pulp and paper mills in each state, as reported in the 1991 edition of *Lockwood-Post's Directory*.)

Chapter 6 explores the relationship between the regional differences in vertical integration and the significantly higher concentration ratios among the pulp and paper mills in the South and Pacific regions compared to the North and Lake regions, which were shown in Chapter 4 (see Tables 4–1 through 4–4). Economic theory suggests that the higher integration that was found in the less developed regions may reflect higher transaction costs if market exchanges were among small numbers of suppliers and buyers in those regional markets. Because most market-pulp was sold by contract (rather than spot sales), paper mills would be more vulnerable to opportunistic behavior related to the negotiation and enforcement of contracts in the more concentrated markets (U.S. Tariff Commission 1938, 190). This theory is tested in the regression analysis in the next chapter.[5]

Another measure of vertical integration is the ratio of pulp to paper capacities in each mill. The distribution of the pulp ratio among integrated mills is summarized in Table 5–3. The pulp to paper ratio was symmetrically distributed about a sample mean of 1.0. A significant share of mills, between 10 percent and 20 percent, reported equal pulp and paper capacities during this period. However, the standard deviation of the ratio was relatively large and indicates a wide dispersion of the ratio among integrated mills each year. The range reported in Table 5–3, between 0.5 and 1.5, corresponds to approximately the mean plus and minus one standard deviation. That range captures from 70 percent to 80 percent of all integrated mills each year (the remaining 20 to 30 percent of integrated mills operated at very low ratios of below 0.5 or very high ratios of above 1.5).[6]

These data suggest that most of the vertically integrated mills were not self-sufficient. Apparently, the majority of integrated mills continued to rely on market transactions to either supplement their pulp requirements or to sell excess pulp.[7] A comparison of the mills reporting equal pulp and paper capacities with mills that reported unequal pulp and paper capacities reveals several important differences (see Table 5–4). First, a larger proportion of the self-sufficient mills were located in the developing regions of the South and Pacific compared to the other integrated mills. In 1940, for example, 44 percent of self-sufficient integrated mills were located in the South or Pacific regions, compared to just 21 percent of the integrated mills that purchased market-pulp and 38 percent of integrated mills that sold market-pulp. This pattern is consistent with a transaction-cost theory that self-sufficient mills were vertically integrated to avoid market transactions, which would involve higher transaction costs in regions where the number of suppliers was relatively small and the potential for problems in negotiating therefore greater than in the older regions. This theory is supported by the fact that mills that supplemented their pulp requirements with market purchases (indicated by a pulp to paper ratio of less than 1.0) had the highest proportion of mills located in the established markets of the North and Lake regions compared to the other groups of integrated mills.

Second, the self-sufficient integrated mills were smaller than the other integrated mills in each sample year, except 1940. Most likely, this is because relatively few of the self-sufficient mills were newsprint mills, which operated at a significantly higher average scale than other grades. It turns out that paper capacity is shown to be positively associated with the extent of integration, after controlling for the grade of paper produced (see Chapter 6). Third, the proportion of self-sufficient mills (ratios equal to 1.0) that produced more than one grade of paper was lower than for the other integrated mills in three of the five sample years (1900, 1920, and 1940). Integrated mills may have been more likely to buy or sell pulp the more diversified their mix of paper grades. A diversified paper mix would have required more variety in the types of pulps used in production than if the mill produced just one grade.[8] Although the benefits of integration would lead mills to consider producing pulp internally, it may have been more economical to produce a large volume of one type of pulp rather than small batches of a variety of pulps. Mills would specialize in certain pulps and supplement their requirements with market purchases. In fact, less than one-third of integrated mills produced more than one type of pulp (usually a combination of groundwood and sulphite pulps used by newsprint mills), which was generally lower than the proportion that produced more than one grade of paper.

COMPARISON OF INTEGRATED VERSUS NONINTEGRATED MILLS

A statistical comparison of the integrated and nonintegrated paper mills is shown in Table 5–5. The differences between the two types of mills are striking. Integrated mills were significantly larger than the nonintegrated mills. Average capacity in the integrated mills was four times greater than for nonintegrated mills in 1900, more than double in 1910, about double in 1920 and 1930, and more than double in 1940. This evidence supports the notion that a minimum scale of operations was required before integration of paper and pulp was more economical than buying pulp from outside suppliers. The association between integration and firm size will be explored in the model for integration presented in Chapter 6.

Integrated mills on average were located in far less populated towns than independent paper mills (the difference was less pronounced in 1910, however). Integrated mills may have located in remote areas to be near sources of pulpwood, which was less economical to transport than pulp or paper due to its low ratio of value to weight. On the other hand, the direction of causation may have run the other way, if firms were more likely to integrate, the smaller the local market and the fewer the pulp suppliers. The potential for higher transaction costs in less developed regional markets due to the "small numbers bargaining problem" will be considered in the next chapter.

A larger percentage of integrated mills survived to 1940 compared to nonintegrated mills in the same sample year, although the survival-rate gap closed over the period.[9] A higher survival rate is consistent with higher rates of profit among integrated mills, which may have stemmed from the economies of vertical integration. The question remains whether integration itself led to survival, or whether superior management that chose to integrate (in addition to other successful strategies) was the key to survival. These and other determinants of survival will be discussed in greater detail in Chapter 7.

The share of mills that produced more than one type of paper was about double for integrated mills than for nonintegrated mills.[10] The association between multiple products and integration is likely due to the high share of newsprint and kraft mills among integrated mills because these products were more likely to be combined with other papers than the remaining product types. Newsprint mills probably diversified to offset the volatility of that declining market, while the diversified kraft producers gradually added that new and experimental paper to their established product mix. In fact, the share of kraft mills that produced multiple papers declined sharply as the market for kraft papers grew. Integrated mills adopted electricity sooner than nonintegrated mills. However, by 1930 a majority of mills in both groups used electric power.

The types of paper products made by integrated and nonintegrated mills also are summarized in Table 5–5. Mills producing a variety of papers are included in each of the categories of paper produced, so the total across all paper categories exceeds the actual total number of paper mills each year. The distribution of products made by the integrated and nonintegrated mills suggests that some types of paper, especially newsprint and kraft wrapping paper, were apparently better suited to integrated production. Among integrated mills, wrap and board mills dominated, followed in the early years by newsprint and book and writing mills. Kraft mills were the fourth largest category of integrated mills and replaced newsprint as the third largest category by 1940. Among nonintegrated mills, the distribution was even more concentrated in the category of wrap and board products than among the integrated mills. Wrap and board mills represented at least 60 percent of nonintegrated mills during this period. The other important categories among nonintegrated mills were book and writing and industrial papers. A very small percentage of nonintegrated mills produced newsprint and kraft papers.

The role of integration within each paper market is shown in Table 5–6. In two markets, newsprint and kraft papers, the majority of mills were integrated. In the declining newsprint segment, the share of integrated mills grew steadily as the number of integrated mills tapered off more slowly than nonintegrated mills. Integrated newsprint mills represented from 61 percent of mills in 1900 to 100 percent in 1940.[11] Kraft production was dominated by integrated mills in two sample years, 1920 and 1940, and the share of integrated mills in that market was significantly higher than in the rest of the markets in the other years. Integration among book and writing mills increased steadily from 19 percent in 1900 to 35 percent of mills in 1940. The growth in integration in the sanitary products market was even more remarkable, rising from no integrated mills in 1900 to 31 percent of mills by 1940. The largest absolute number of integrated mills was found in the wrap and board segment, but as a share of mills integration represented just 18 percent to 20 percent of mills. Finally, the proportion of integrated mills in the industrial papers market drifted upward over the period but remained a minority, from 11 percent of mills in 1900 to 15 percent in 1940.

The extent of integration in each product market corresponds to the average size of mills in those markets. The average and total daily capacities within each segment are summarized in Table 5–7. Average capacity is based on the total capacity of the mills producing a given product, although not all that capacity was used to produce that type of paper in the case where multiple products were made by the mill. Total capacities, on the other hand, are estimates of industry-wide capacity available for each type of paper. Because the directories do not report production or capacity data by paper type, it is assumed that capacity was divided proportionately among the different paper products.

Vertical integration and mill size are positively related across the product segments. The largest average mill size is found in the highly integrated newsprint segment, where average capacity is two to three times the size of mills in the other markets (except kraft). The next largest average capacity (between 1920 and 1940) is in the kraft segment, which also ranks second in proportion of integrated mills. Much smaller average sizes are found among the other less integrated markets. Total capacities do not suggest a relationship between integration and market growth, however. Where integration was high, growth was high in the kraft market but was low (even negative between 1930 and 1940) in the newsprint market. In the moderately integrated markets, growth was gradual in the book and wrap markets and quite high in the sanitary market. The least integrated market, industrial products, exhibited moderate growth but higher than that in the book and wrap markets.

INTEGRATION WITHIN CITIES

Patterns of vertical integration in single-mill towns and multiple-mill towns were explored by recording the number of integrated and nonintegrated mills found in each city or town listed in the 1941 edition of the directory. As noted in Chapter 1, as late as 1940 the majority of paper mills continued to operate as the only paper mill in town (57 percent of mills were in single-mill towns), which is consistent with the rural nature of this industry. Among the multiple-mill towns, the largest number found was eighteen, in Holyoke, Massachusetts (due largely to the many plants operated by the American Writing Paper Company at that location); most of these towns listed from two to five paper mills.

The proportion of paper mills that were vertically integrated was significantly higher among mills located in single-mill towns than the mills located in multiple-mill towns. Among the 436 mills in single-mill towns, 115 mills (26 percent) also produced pulp. By comparison, of the 307 mills in multiple-mill towns, only 49 mills (16 percent) were integrated. Of these 49 integrated mills, half operated in towns of all-integrated mills, and the other half were located in towns of mixed integrated and nonintegrated mills. Apparently, the factors that determined whether a mill integrated backwards to pulp production did not necessarily lead all mills in the same town to follow suit. When there were other mills in the same town to compare with a given integrated mill, the remaining mills were as likely to be integrated as they were to be nonintegrated. At least in the larger, multiple-mill towns, locational factors did not seem to play a critical role in the decision to integrate.

The role of location becomes clearer by sorting the statistics by integrated and nonintegrated mills, however. Among the 164 integrated paper mills in 1940, 115 mills (70 percent) were located in single-mill towns. This proportion is much higher than among the 579 nonintegrated mills, where 321 mills (55 percent) were found in single-mill towns. The finding that a much larger share of the integrated mills were operating in isolation (compared to the nonintegrated mills) is consistent with the argument that mills became self-sufficient when the number of pulp suppliers and buyers in the market was so few as to raise the costs associated with market transactions. Just as less developed regions were associated with integration among the paper mills, the smaller mill towns show a similar pattern where mills tended to integrate paper with pulp production. Perhaps when more than one paper mill operated in a close vicinity, outside pulp suppliers behaved more reliably or had more incentive to avoid opportunistic behavior than if the buyer was isolated. Alternatively, integrated mills may have tended to locate near remote timberland areas (to avoid shipping timber to the pulp facility), so were more likely to operate alone compared to a nonintegrated mill. However, both single-mill and multiple-mill towns were located in rural areas, and it seems that the location of all paper-mill towns favored proximity to timberlands (as well as water and transportation resources).

INTEGRATION IN MULTIPLANT FIRMS

Another interesting issue is whether firms that operated more than one paper mill consistently chose to integrate or not integrate all mills owned by the firm. If the preferences of each firm's management for reducing transaction costs or the risks of supply disruptions were the determining factors in the decision to integrate, perhaps all plants of a given firm would be integrated (or not) if controlled by the same management. Also, if a firm deals with an outside pulp producer to supply one paper mill, it may have been economical to arrange for the rest of the firm's paper mills to be supplied under the same contract terms. Once a firm incurs the costs of negotiating with a market-pulp producer, there may have been benefits to arranging for all paper mills to be supplied, and none of the firm's plants would be integrated.

To examine patterns of integration in multiplant paper firms, firms with five or more mills that were operating in 1940 were checked for the integrated status of their mills. Of the 15 firms in this group, 8 were uniformly integrated or not integrated across the mills owned by the same firm. However, 7 firms owned a mix of both integrated and nonintegrated mills. Apparently, the same management did not always choose to integrate either all or none of their plants.

Other factors besides management preferences for integration appeared to play a role in the decision to integrate a particular plant. One important variable was the grade of paper produced at the plant. Most of the firms that either integrated all or none of their mills also produced the same grade across all plants (for example, all of American Writing Paper's mills produced writing paper and none were integrated). In the eight firms with a uniform integrated status, only one produced different grades in its plants. If a firm produced different grades at different locations, the integrated status of each plant was consistent with the grade; newsprint and kraft mills tended to be integrated and the other grades not integrated. For example, in the 20 mills operated by International Paper, most of the plants of its subsidiary, the Southern Kraft Company, were integrated, while its board mills in the North and Lake regions were not integrated. Of the seven firms with mixed integration and nonintegration across plants, only two produced the same grade across all plants owned by the same company.

INTEGRATION AND DISINTEGRATION OVER TIME

Very few mills integrated a previously specialized mill or decided to disintegrate production to specialize in either pulp or paper production during any decade between 1900 and 1940. Apparently a firm decided to construct (or purchase) either an integrated or specialized mill upon entry to the industry and later was unlikely to dismantle either the upstream or downstream part of the integrated process, or to add pulp or paper facilities to create an integrated mill if the firm was originally specialized. However, integrated mills altered the proportions of pulp and paper capacities over the life cycle of the mill, measured by the ratio of pulp capacity to paper capacity. Because it was less costly and faster to expand an existing pulp or paper facility than construct a new one, mills exhibited greater flexibility in the extent of integration of pulp with paper production compared to their status as an integrated facility.

The changes in integration within the same mill over time are studied first by confining the sample to the 154 paper mills that survived the entire 40-year period between 1900 and 1940, the longest period of operation available from the directory data set.[12] Of the 154 mills, 38 remained integrated and 102 remained specialized in paper production over the entire period. Of the remaining 14 mills that experienced a change in integrated status over the period, most of these disintegrated rather than integrated. Between 1900 and 1910, 4 mills disintegrated, followed by 2 mills that disintegrated between 1910 and 1920, 3 mills that disintegrated between 1920 and 1930, and 3 mills that disintegrated in the last decade. Only 2 specialized paper mills integrated during the period, 1 between 1910 and 1920, and the other between 1920 and 1930.

Among the same group of survivors, about 70 percent of the mills maintained the same ratio of pulp capacity to paper capacity each year over the period 1900–1940 (most of these were the specialized mills that had ratios of 0). Of the mills that reported a change in their pulp to paper ratio, most reduced it. Mills that reduced their ratio of pulp to paper on average had a relatively high ratio of pulp to paper (near or above 1.0) in the beginning of each decade compared to mills that increased their pulp to paper ratios (and to those that kept the ratio constant). Among the mills with a negative change in the pulp-to-paper ratio, the ratio was above 1.0 before the change (except in 1920 when the average was 0.98) and dropped to about 0.70 by the end of the decade. Integrated mills with ratios below 1.0 tended to approach self-sufficiency up to 1930, by raising the ratio toward 1.0 during each decade; the average ratios for this group ranged from 0.98 to 1.20 after the ten-year period. The average pulp-to-paper ratios for all survivors each sample year declined from 0.33 in 1900 to 0.25 in 1940. Because this sample consists primarily of mills located in the North and Lake regions (only seven southern and one Pacific Coast surviving mills were operating as early as 1900), these changes in the extent of vertical integration probably reflect regional specialization away from newsprint and kraft grades and increased regional reliance on imported pulps from Europe and the Pacific Northwest.

The analysis of changes in integration may be expanded to consider all mills operating at decade intervals (see Table 5–8). When the sample of mills is extended to include any mills that existed during pairs of annual observations, the proportion of mills that switched between specialization and integration remained very small (although the number of mills switching increased by expanding the sample size).[13] Over the 40-year period, at most 11 mills integrated during any given decade, and at most 17 mills switched from integrated to specialized mills. As a measure of the small relative importance of these cases, integrating paper mills represented less than 1 percent of mills and disintegrating mills comprised at most 2 percent of mills. The number of integrating mills was highest in the first decade at 11 and then declined to 7 in the 1910s and to 5 each in the 1920s and 1930s. On the other hand, disintegration was more frequent in the 1920s and 1930s compared to the first two decades. Among disintegrating mills, most became specialized in paper production (and purchased pulp); only a total of 6 integrated mills became specialized in market-pulp production over the entire period.

Mills were much more likely to alter the ratio of pulp to paper capacities than to switch from integration altogether. Although the pulp-to-paper ratio of nonintegrated mills tended to remain 0 over decade-long periods (because most mills did not switch between integration and specialization), most integrated mills that survived a given decade reported different ratios of pulp to paper capacities between the beginning and end of the decade. Each decade, at least three-quarters of integrated mills that survived the decade (the share was as high as 90 percent in the first two decades of the study) chose to revise the ratio of pulp to paper capacities; the remaining mills maintained a constant pulp-to-paper ratio. More mills reduced their ratio of pulp to paper capacity than increased it; the mix was about even in the first decade, but about two-thirds of the adapting mills reduced their ratios in the following three decades. The reducing mills on average had ratios greater than 1.0 at the beginning of the decade, while the mills that raised their ratios started with average ratios below 1.0 each decade. The determinants of changes in the pulp-to-paper ratio over decade-long periods are explored in the statistical regression analysis presented in Chapter 6.

If a pattern can be discerned from these few examples, it appears that mills were on balance more actively disintegrating and reducing the extent of internal pulp production compared to the incidence of integration among established mills, particularly after 1920. Although the majority of mills maintained a consistent pattern of integration or specialization over the period, the small trend toward disintegration lends support to Stigler's argument that a maturing industry will disintegrate as the upstream and downstream markets grow (Stigler 1968a, 135–36). These examples also provide some evidence that the development of regional markets in the South and Pacific regions may have led to reduced self-reliance among paper mills as the number of pulp suppliers grew in these areas and the associated transaction costs declined.

ENTRANCE AND EXIT OF INTEGRATED MILLS EACH DECADE

Although an existing mill typically did not change its status as an integrated or specialized mill over its lifetime, vertical integration in papermaking was altered instead through changes in the patterns of integration among the new mills that entered the industry each decade. The entrance and exit of pulp and paper mills can be estimated by identifying the mills that existed at the beginning of each decade compared to the next. Following the analysis of entry and exit that was developed in Chapter 4, a mill is assumed to be new if it was not listed in the prior sample year in the same name and includes mills that were acquired by a new firm. Exit may be the result of a number of events, including failure or acquisition, which cause the old mill name to be absent in the following sample year. Because the sample years are at the beginning of each decade, this method documents the movements in and out of the industry over a ten-year period. This only approximates entry and exit, of course, because mills that enter and exit within a given decade (which operate a less than ten-year period) are not observed.

Table 5–9 shows the number of mills that entered and exited during each decade between 1900 and 1940. New mills that entered each decade were less integrated, as a share of total paper mill entrants, compared to the paper mills that had operated continuously during that decade. Of the new mills each decade, from 16 percent to 21 percent of paper mills were integrated, compared to 22 percent to 27 percent of the existing paper mills. The total number of entering paper mills that were integrated declined each decade; this contributed to the overall net decline in integrated mills each year, which was shown in Table 5–1. Failing mills had less tendency to be integrated compared to the decade-long survivors, however. Each decade period, integrated mills were a smaller proportion of mills that exited compared to the operating mills. The share of integrated mills ranged from 14 percent to 20 percent of mills that failed each decade, compared to rates that were 3 to 7 percentage points higher for all mills operating at the beginning of the decade. The underrepresentation of integrated mills among failing firms is consistent with the higher rate of survival among integrated mills, which was shown in Table 5–5.

Entrants also tended to be less integrated than existing mills within each of the regions (see Table 5–10). This decline is consistent with the growing dependence on imported pulp among mills located in the North and Lake regions and with the reduction in the concentration ratios found in the growing regions of the South and Pacific markets (discussed in greater detail in the next chapter). Particularly in the North, Lake, and Pacific regions, the proportion of entrants that were integrated was consistently lower than among the existing mills each decade. In the South, however, entrants were more likely to be integrated than existing mills in three out of four decades. This pattern is probably explained by the dominance of kraft mills among southern entrants and the tendency for this grade to be produced in large-scale, integrated plants.

In addition to the decline in the number of integrated firms entering each decade, the new mills tended to be less self-sufficient over time. The average pulp-to-paper ratio among entrants before 1920 was about 1.20; that ratio dropped to 1.00 in the 1920s and increased slightly to 1.06 in the 1930s (as the more highly integrated southern mills comprised a larger share of new mills). The average ratios of pulp to paper capacity among entering integrated mills in each region were lower in the 1920s and 1930s compared to previous decades; the decline was sharpest for mills entering the Pacific Coast region. Mills may have entered less dependent on internal pulp capacity because the regional markets, especially in the Pacific region, were becoming less concentrated as the number of suppliers increased with the growth in the local pulp and paper markets. At the same time, the integrated mills that exited each decade on average reported larger ratios of pulp to paper capacity than the entering mills (except for the first decade). This net decline in the average pulp to paper ratio among new and failing integrated mills reinforced the disintegration among existing mills in the later decades, and the average pulp-to-paper ratio declined from its peak of 1.11 in 1920 to 1.03 in 1940 among all integrated paper mills in each of these years.

VERTICAL INTEGRATION AND PAPER MILL SURVIVAL

The economic arguments for vertical integration assume that the objective of the firm is to maximize profits over the firm's lifetime. Evidence from the directories permits a test of whether integration by paper mills was indeed profit maximizing by analyzing whether survival was improved by the decision to integrate. Data presented in Table 5–5 showed that for a given sample year, integrated mills were more likely to survive to 1940 compared to nonintegrated paper mills. Also, a comparison of surviving mills to those that failed before 1940 shows a higher level of integration (measured by the average pulp capacity to paper capacity ratio) in each sample year (see Table 5–11).

The association between integration and survival can also be investigated by tracking the survival of a group of firms at the beginning of the period and by documenting how many of these original firms survived through the end of the period.[14] The approximate survival rates of integrated and nonintegrated paper mills that were listed in the 1900–1901 directory are shown in Table 5–12. By noting the number of mills that continued to be listed in subsequent directories, survival rates can be compared between the two types of mills each sample year. Unlike the approach shown earlier in Table 5–5, this method excludes mills that entered after 1900 in order to attempt to control for the age of the mill (although the dates of establishment for the 772 paper mills listed in 1900 varied). Limiting the sample to mills that were operating in 1900 helps to minimize differences in the age of equipment, technology used, and other factors that would differentiate the mills entering after 1900 from the sample group.[15]

Survival rates were significantly higher among the integrated mills each year. Moreover, the pace of mill failure was slower among the integrated mills each decade, until the 1930s. Although mill failures were higher for both groups in the first decade than any later decade, mill exits were more gradual among integrated mills than the nonintegrated mills. Higher survival rates suggest that integration was a profitable strategy that enhanced a paper mill's competitiveness. However, this positive association does not prove causation, and a more complete model of firm survival will be considered in Chapter 7.

SURVIVORSHIP TESTS

In Chapter 4, Stigler's survivorship test was used to determine the economies of scale in paper production. Following Stigler, the survivorship method can test the relationship between vertical integration and changes in the market share of firms over time (Stigler 1968b, 87). The survivorship test was conducted first for all paper grades combined. These initial results indicated that vertically integrated mills showed a small decline in total market share, which was gained by the nonintegrated mills. Integrated mills declined from 47 percent of capacity in 1900 to 44 percent by 1940. Within size categories, integrated mills gained market shares in most of the categories below 1 percent of the total industry capacity and lost market shares in two of the three largest categories. Nonintegrated mills gained market shares in the intermediate sizes that ranged from 0.2 percent to 1 percent of total industry capacity.

However, these results are biased by including the declining and highly integrated newsprint market with the other grades. It turns out that the decline observed in all integrated paper capacity can be attributed to the reduction in newsprint capacity over the period. When newsprint capacity is separated from the rest of the industry, the results of the survivorship test are reversed, and integration appears to promote survival.

The survivorship test for newsprint mills is based on the same size categories used in Chapter 4, which were defined here as percentages of newsprint capacity. Mill size was based on the portion of mill capacity assumed to be devoted to newsprint production. The survivorship test for integrated and nonintegrated newsprint mills illustrates the trend toward integration in that segment; by 1940, all newsprint mills were vertically integrated (see Table 5–13). Over time, the smallest size categories among the integrated newsprint mills lost market share, while mills larger than 2.5 percent of total newsprint capacity gained shares. In fact, by 1940 about 90 percent of newsprint mills ranged in size from 2.5 percent to 15 percent of that market. Nonintegrated newsprint mills had lost market shares across all size categories by the latter part of this period.

For nonnewsprint mills, the survivorship test shows that vertically integrated mills gained market share over the period (see Table 5–14). Integrated nonnewsprint mills represented 30 percent of nonnewsprint capacity in 1900; by 1940, that share had risen to 39 percent. The size-distribution of integrated nonnewsprint mills shifted slightly to the smallest and largest size categories over the period, and five of the nine categories exhibited growth in market shares between 1900 and 1940 (intermediate-size mills lost market share). In contrast, only two of the size categories gained market share among the nonintegrated mills, an intermediate and a large size range, which is consistent with the overall loss of market share for that group. It is also interesting to note that the integrated mills had larger market shares than the nonintegrated mills in the four largest size categories. As in the case of the newsprint mills, vertical integration in these other grades continued to be associated with larger mill sizes. These results also are consistent with the hypothesis that vertical integration was associated with paper mill survival in both the newsprint and nonnewsprint segments, particularly among the largest scale mills.

OWNERSHIP OF TIMBERLAND

Information about the integration of paper firms backwards into ownership of timberland was drawn from the 1931 and the 1941 issues of *Moody's Manual of Investments*. All pulp and paper firms listed in

Moody's in these two years were investigated; the few firms that could not be found in *Lockwood's Directory* data set were excluded. The Moody's sample consisted of 89 pulp and paper firms. Four of the firms were operating in 1931 but not 1941, 9 firms were operating in 1941 but not 1931, and the remaining 76 firms in the sample were operating in both years.

A firm was determined to have owned timberland if the financial statement that was summarized in Moody's either provided a description of the timberland that was owned or controlled by the firm, or if its balance sheet listed timberland assets. Occasionally the financial statement included a discussion of the proportion of pulpwood requirements that were met by the firm's own timber resources. Surprisingly, a firm might have owned timberland but still purchased all its pulpwood requirements; I continued to treat these firms as integrated into timberland, however. Guthrie notes that firms often bought wood even if timberland was owned by the firm to conserve their holdings (Guthrie 1950, 143, 183). The buy-or-cut decision depended on market prices and the expense of working their own timberland (Guthrie 1941, 134).

The information about timberland ownership was merged with other firm characteristics that were described in the directories of the corresponding years, including the location and paper capacities of all mills operated by each firm, grades of paper produced, and whether pulp was produced. Using this combined Moody's–Lockwood's data set, I compared the firms that owned timberland with those that did not to suggest what factors may have determined this form of backward integration. This comparison is summarized in Table 5–15.

Although less comprehensive than the directory data, the Moody's sample is representative of the population of firms in this period. Most of the Moody's firms were located in the North and Lake states, but a significant number of firms from the South and the Pacific Coast were included in the sample. Because almost half of the firms operated multiple plants (40 firms), location in more than one region has been accounted for; 16 firms operated in multiple regions. The distribution of grades also corresponds to that of the larger directory data set. The bulk of firms produced board and writing papers, followed in order of frequency by kraft, industrial, sanitary, and newsprint. The Moody's firms were far more likely to be vertically integrated with pulp, however. Almost 70 percent of the sample produced their own pulp, compared to about 20 percent in the industry as a whole in this period. The average mill size among the Moody's firms was also almost twice that of the industry-average mill size in 1940. The Moody's sample may be biased toward larger firms, since privately held firms were excluded from the investment publication. Given that size and integration are linked, it is not surprising that these firms were more likely to be integrated with pulp compared to the industry population.

The Moody's sample was almost evenly divided between firms that owned timberland and those without. Of the 89 firms, 43 owned or controlled their own timber resources, compared to 46 without timberland. (Because the Moody's sample is biased toward large, integrated firms, however, this sample proportion of nearly 50 percent ownership of timberland probably overstates the incidence of timberland integration among the industry population.) The South was the only region where a majority of firms owned timberland (17 out of 19 firms, including firms that had multiple-region locations). Timberland ownership was lowest, as a percentage of firms, among Lake and Pacific Coast firms, and almost equally divided among firms in the North. One explanation for this regional pattern may be the differences in the relative shares of private and public ownership of timberland across regions at this time. Federal- and state-owned land represented relatively small shares of timberland in the South and East compared to the rest of the nation (Guthrie 1941, 38). For example, 93 percent of southern acreage was privately owned, compared to a national average of 74 percent (Mouzon 1940, 81). As discussed below, other factors, such as firm size, integration into pulping, and grades produced may also have played a role in these regional patterns in timberland ownership.

Not surprisingly, integration with pulping was associated with timberland ownership. Only two firms that did not produce pulp were affiliated with timberland, indirectly through a subsidiary that owned the land. Among the integrated firms, two-thirds owned timberland, and all three specialized pulp firms owned timberland. The Moody's data appear to confirm that firms owned timberland to provide timber for their own pulping needs; with the two unusual exceptions noted, a firm did not own timberland without ownership of pulping facilities as well. Ownership of timberland represented a form of backward integration for paper firms (and in a few cases, pulp firms that did not produce paper), as opposed to other possible motives, such as for the sale of timber in the market or for investment purposes.

An analysis of timberland ownership across paper grades suggests a strong correlation between grade and land ownership. The majority of producers of newsprint (73 percent), kraft (69 percent), and sanitary (67 percent) papers owned timberland, compared to less than half of writing, board, and industrial grade producers. This association is probably explained by the greater likelihood that the producers of the standardized grades, especially newsprint and kraft, were vertically integrated with pulping (see Table 5–6), and therefore more likely to own timberland.

Finally, larger firms were more likely to be integrated with timberland. The average paper capacity of firms with timberland (including all mills owned by each firm) was 1.1 million pounds per day compared to an average 450 thousand pounds per day among firms without timberland. In a logit regression of the probability that a firm owns timberland as a function of the paper capacity of the firm, the coefficient of the size variable (whether measured as pounds or logarithm of pounds) was positive and statistically significant (see Table 5–16).

A profile of the firm that owns timberland can be summarized from these statistics. Large, integrated firms that produced standardized grades such as newsprint or kraft papers were typical of firms with timberland assets. The choice to own timberland may have been motivated by transaction-cost economies, to avoid the necessity of negotiating pulpwood prices and other contractual issues with an outside supplier, and to assure a supply of pulpwood.[16] In particular, the pulp mill is vulnerable to opportunistic behavior by a supplier if the timberland is specialized to the pulpwood requirements of that pulping facility (Globerman and Schwindt 1986, 203). Technological explanations for integration with timberland are less obvious than in the case of integration with pulping, since the process of bringing pulpwood to the pulping facility is not continuous (unlike pulp, which can be transferred directly to the paper mill more efficiently than from an outside supplier).

SUMMARY

The paper industry directories identify those mills that integrated pulp and paper production and allow a measure of the extent of integration by a comparison of the pulp and paper capacities of the integrated mills. About 20 percent of paper mills were integrated each year, although the proportion of pulp requirements that were produced within these integrated mills varied widely. Mills located in the developing regions of the South and Pacific were much more likely to be integrated, and the proportion of pulp supplied internally was higher than in the other regions. Integration also tended to be greater among mills that produced standardized grades, especially newsprint and kraft, in relatively large-scale plants. Once established, mills did not tend to either integrate backward to pulp production at a later date or disintegrate and become specialized paper mills. However, most of the integrated mills did adjust the ratio of pulp to paper capacities over time, and pulp-to-paper ratios converged toward 1.0 over the period. The pattern of integration also was affected by the entry and exit of mills each decade; fewer integrated mills entered each decade and the pulp-to-paper ratio among new mills gradually declined over time, which promoted the convergence in integration rates across regions over the 40-year period.

The discovery that integration was linked to higher survival rates in the paper industry is consistent with the theory that economies of integration motivate the decision to vertically integrate. This result for the paper industry is consistent with findings in other industries. Kane (1988, 56–57) found a higher rate of survival among integrated U.S. textile mills in the period 1885–1930, and Paskoff (1983, 86) reported that integrated rolling mills had the highest rate of survival among various types of facilities in the Pennsylvania iron industry between 1832 and 1850. A more complete investigation of paper mill survival is presented in Chapter 7.

Moody's Manual of Investments provided information about vertical integration backwards into ownership of timberland for a sample of 89 paper firms. This data was merged with the descriptions from the directories to compare the integrated and nonintegrated firms. Paper firms that owned timberland were found to be larger than the nonintegrated firms and were more likely to produce their own pulp and to produce standardized grades of paper (newsprint or kraft). Also, the southern firms in the sample were more likely to own timberland than firms in the other regions. Although the data are insufficient to test alternative hypotheses, the results are consistent with the view that large firms integrated backwards to avoid market transactions for the pulpwood that was needed in their pulping operations (the same motivation for integration into pulping). This transaction-cost approach to vertical integration is explored in greater detail in the following chapter.

NOTES

1. The analysis of the directory data set does not address other forms of integration, such as backward integration into ownership of forest lands or forward integration into converting and marketing activities, because this information is not provided by the directories. However, integration into timberland is analyzed for a smaller sample of firms at the end of this chapter. For a discussion of these other stages of integration, see Chandler (1977, 354) and Globerman and Schwindt (1986).

2. A relatively small number of paper firms operated pulp mills at a separate location, almost always in the same region as the paper mill. These special cases are not treated as vertical integration in this study because the usual advantages of avoiding transportation costs and the costs of drying the pulp do not apply if the pulp mill is located

some distance from the paper mill. In any event, because the number of firms in this category is so small (for example, 8 in 1900, 20 in 1920, and 12 in 1940), and because most operated vertically integrated paper mills in addition to these separate pulp mills (4 in 1900, 13 in 1920, and 10 in 1940), the statistical analysis of vertical integration would be little changed if these separate pulp mills were treated as vertically integrated with the paper mills operated by the same firm.

3. Levy (1984) argues that industry-level data are appropriate to test Stigler's theory. However, Wilder and Tucker (1984, 391) argue that Stigler's comments apply to the firm as well as the industry and defend their use of firm-level data (across industries) in their earlier work (Tucker and Wilder 1977).

4. Levy (1984, 378) and Perry (1989, 232) discuss the difficulty of Stigler's model, which is not explicit about the conditions leading to increasing and decreasing costs and specialization.

5. Alternatively, the regional markets may be thought of as separate industries that were in different stages of an industry life cycle, following Stigler (1968a). The relatively low rate of integration among paper mills in the North and Lake regions is consistent with markets that had reached a later stage of maturity during this period, where firms disintegrated (specialized) as the markets expanded.

6. This description was based on histograms of the distributions, not shown here. The number of mills with pulp to paper ratios equal to 1.0 was: 19 in 1900, 28 in 1910, 18 in 1920, 19 in 1930, and 18 in 1940. A more tolerant range of pulp to paper ratios between 0.9 and 1.1 included only between 21 percent and 35 percent of integrated mills in any given year. Outliers in 1920 were removed from the results discussed here and in the linear regressions. The first, the New York and Pennsylvania Co.'s Lock Haven, Pennsylvania, mill, reported a ratio of 10.0, which was inconsistent with that mill's ratio in other sample years and may have been due to a reporting error. The second, the Champion Fibre Co.'s Canton, North Carolina, mill, reported a ratio of 17.5. Judging from other sample years, this mill was in the process of introducing paper to its established pulp capacity in 1920. In later years, paper capacity had increased to more than 50 percent of pulp capacity.

7. This assumes that mills supplemented their pulp requirements with market pulp when the ratio of pulp to paper capacities was less than 1.0 and sold excess pulp when that ratio was greater than 1.0. In the pulp and paper industry, market transactions usually involved the negotiation of short-term contracts rather than spot sales (U.S. Tariff Commission 1938, 190).

8. The pulp-mill equipment was not interchangeable between different types of pulps (U.S. Tariff Commission 1938, 92).

9. The difference in the survival rates was statistically significant at the 1 percent level in 1900, 1910, and 1920 and at the 6 percent level in 1930.

10. The number of papers produced by each mill was also calculated. The average number of papers produced by integrated mills ranged from 1.38 to 1.64 over the period, compared to 1.18 to 1.26 among the nonintegrated mills, which is consistent with the diversification dummy variable.

11. In 1940, all Canadian newsprint mills were vertically integrated with pulp, so this was not a characteristic of only U.S. mills. The fact that mills in two different national markets were similar also lends support for a technological explanation for integration among paper mills of this grade.

12. The sample excludes 11 mills that survived the 1900–1940 period but were specialized in pulp production during at least one sample year (4 mills were specialized in pulp throughout the period, 3 mills began as specialized pulp mills and later specialized in pulp, and 4 paper mills later switched to pulp specialization). The sample includes only mills that produced paper each year in order to concentrate on their decision whether to "buy or make" pulp (upstream integration, rather than downstream).

13. This analysis does not measure the process of integration/disintegration among mills that did not survive to the end of the given decade, that entered during that decade, or that entered and exited during that decade. Mills that only temporarily switched to a new strategy within that decade also would not be observed.

14. A comparison of the survival rates of firms by certain attributes was suggested by Paskoff (1983, 86) in his study of the Pennsylvania iron industry and by McGaw (1987, 401–6) in her study of early Berkshire papermaking.

15. Although the older mills may modernize, new and old mills each approach the decision to switch to new equipment and technology differently because the established mill's capital costs are sunk costs. See Kane (1988, 49–50) and Feller (1966) for a discussion of the role of mill age and sunk costs in the decision to adopt the new ring spinning technology in the cotton textile industry before 1930.

16. McLaughlin and Robuck allude to these problems in their 1949 study of southern manufacturing. They note that southern paper firms tended to own enough timberland in close proximity to their mills to supply about half of their pulpwood requirements, to avoid becoming "a big factor in the open market" (McLaughlin and Robock 1949, 61).

Table 5-1
Vertical Integration in U.S. Paper Industry: 1900–1940

	1900	1910	1920	1930	1940
Total No. Paper Mills	772	802	810	819	743
Total No. Pulp Mills	253	247	250	240	210
No. Integrated Mills	148	175	184	182	164
% of paper mills	19%	22%	23%	22%	22%
% of pulp mills	58%	71%	74%	76%	78%
Integrated Paper Capacity (% total paper capacity)	47%	46%	39%	38%	44%
Integrated Pulp Capacity (% total pulp capacity)	64%	73%	80%	83%	83%

Source: Compiled by the author from Lockwood's Directory of the Paper and Allied Trades.

Table 5-2
Vertical Integration by Region: 1900–1940
(Percent of Paper Mills Integrated with Pulp)

Region	1900	1910	1920	1930	1940
North	17%	20%	21%	19%	17%
Lake	21	21	20	19	18
South	44	42	41	47	52
Pacific Coast	44	62	50	49	49

Source: Compiled by the author from Lockwood's Directory of the Paper and Allied Trades.

Table 5–3
Integrated Mills: Distribution of the Ratio of Pulp Capacity to Paper Capacity
(Number of Integrated Mills in Each Range)

Year	Average (Pulp/Paper)	(Pulp/Paper)<.5	.5≤(Pulp/Paper)≤1.5	(Pulp/Paper)>1.5
1900	0.94 (.55)	25	102	16
1910	1.06 (.62)	17	126	21
1920	1.11 (.62)	19	123	29
1930	1.06 (.45)	15	144	20
1940	1.03 (.50)	18	123	13

Source: Compiled by the author from Lockwood's Directory of the Paper and Allied Trades.
Notes: Standard deviations of the distributions are reported in parentheses. In 1920, the statistics exclude two mills that reported pulp to paper ratios of 10.0 and 17.5, respectively.

Table 5–4
Comparison of Self-Sufficient and Other Integrated Mills

	Percent of Mills Operating in South or Pacific Regions		
	(Pulp/Paper)<1	(Pulp/Paper)=1	(Pulp/Paper)>1
1900	8%	11%	16%
1910	4	29	14
1920	9	28	15
1930	15	37	29
1940	21	44	38

	Average Paper Mill Capacity (Thousand pounds per day)		
	(Pulp/Paper)<1	(Pulp/Paper)=1	(Pulp/Paper)>1
1900	73.4	52.3	71.4
1910	112.5	82.1	119.6
1920	134.3	99.3	147.9
1930	231.3	162.9	203.2
1940	321.4	333.3	350.8

	Percent of Mills Producing Multiple Paper Products		
	(Pulp/Paper)<1	(Pulp/Paper)=1	(Pulp/Paper)>1
1900	34%	22%	31%
1910	32	39	30
1920	33	22	47
1930	44	53	44
1940	51	39	47

Source: Compiled by the author from <u>Lockwood's Directory of the Paper and Allied Trades</u>.

Table 5–5
Comparison of Integrated versus Nonintegrated Paper Mills: 1900–1940

	1900		1910		1920		1930		1940	
	Integrated	Only Paper	Integrated	Only Paper	Integrated	Only Paper	Integrated	Only Paper	Integrated	Only Paper
No. Mills	148	624	175	627	184	626	182	636	164	579
Average Capacity (thou. lb./day)	69.4	19.0	109.4	36.9	135.3	62.3	209.3	98.5	336.5	121.0
Ave. Population (thou.)	32.7	45.8	33.6	36.4	17.2	33.1	19.8	81.4	24.7	129.0
Percent of Mills:										
Survived to 1940	.36	.17	.42	.27	.54	.42	.70	.64	--	--
Diversified	.32	.16	.32	.17	.39	.16	.44	.22	.45	.19
Electricity	.02	.00	.14	.08	.38	.30	.65	.54	.73	.69
Newsprint	.37	.06	.39	.02	.31	.02	.27	.01	.16	.00
Book & Writing	.29	.28	.29	.27	.40	.26	.42	.26	.44	.23
Wrap & Board	.69	.72	.53	.69	.50	.63	.49	.60	.52	.60
Kraft	--	--	.04	.01	.14	.03	.22	.07	.24	.07
Sanitary	.00	.01	.02	.03	.04	.05	.06	.08	.14	.09
Industrial	.06	.12	.11	.17	.09	.18	.16	.24	.15	.23

Source: Compiled by the author from Lockwood's Directory of the Paper and Allied Trades.

Table 5–6

Number of Integrated and Nonintegrated Mills in Various Paper Markets: 1900–1940

	1900	1910	1920	1930	1940
Newsprint					
Integrated	54	67	57	48	25
Nonintegrated	35	10	12	6	0
(% Integrated)	(61%)	(87%)	(83%)	(89%)	(100%)
Book & Writing					
Integrated	41	50	74	76	70
Nonintegrated	174	165	158	165	132
(% Integrated)	(19%)	(23%)	(32%)	(32%)	(35%)
Wrap & Board					
Integrated	99	91	89	90	83
Nonintegrated	449	428	389	378	341
(% Integrated)	(18%)	(18%)	(19%)	(19%)	(20%)
Kraft					
Integrated	–	7	23	39	39
Nonintegrated	–	9	20	45	37
(% Integrated)		(44%)	(53%)	(46%)	(51%)
Sanitary					
Integrated	0	3	7	11	23
Nonintegrated	8	20	31	48	52
(% Integrated)	(0%)	(13%)	(18%)	(19%)	(31%)
Industrial					
Integrated	9	18	17	28	24
Nonintegrated	75	104	112	154	132
(% Integrated)	(11%)	(15%)	(13%)	(15%)	(15%)

Source: Compiled by the author from Lockwood's Directory of the Paper and Allied Trades.

Table 5–7
Average and Total Capacities in Various Paper Markets: 1900–1940
(Thousands of Pounds per 24 Hours)

	1900	1910	1920	1930	1940
Average Capacity of Mills Producing:					
Newsprint	77.4	137.7	178.3	253.1	375.4
Book & Writing	28.7	52.2	78.8	114.6	162.2
Wrap & Board	25.3	45.4	80.5	128.8	180.0
Kraft	–	48.4	125.4	182.2	304.7
Sanitary	7.1	13.3	33.2	60.5	102.0
Industrial	31.1	49.9	74.3	111.8	125.8
Total Capacity Devoted to:					
Newsprint	5,062.3	8,147.3	7,507.0	8,805.8	5,868.0
Book & Writing	4,579.6	9,151.9	14,132.3	19,760.8	21,978.3
Wrap & Board	10,654.5	18,703.8	29,638.8	45,348.5	58,216.7
Kraft	–	442.2	2,680.8	9,452.8	15,514.8
Sanitary	33.0	160.6	791.6	1,938.8	3,744.1
Industrial	1,542.6	3,885.7	6,538.4	12,995.3	13,139.1

Source: Compiled by the author from Lockwood's Directory of the Paper and Allied Trades.
Notes: Average capacity represents mill size and includes capacity of all types of paper produced by the mill. Total capacity by type of paper assumes a proportionate share of capacity was used for each type of paper made in the mills that produced more than one type of paper.

Table 5–8
Switching Between Integration and Specialization Each Decade

| Decade | Became Integrated | | Disintegrated | |
	From Paper Mill	From Pulp Mill	Became Paper Mill	Became Pulp Mill
1900-1910	5	6	6	1
1910-1920	4[a]	3	3	1
1920-1930	2	3	16	1
1930-1940	4	1	9	3

Source: Compiled by the author from Lockwood's Directory of the Paper and Allied Trades.
[a] Includes two mills that later returned to paper specialization, one in the 1920s and the other in the 1930s.

Table 5–9
Entrance and Exit of Integrated Mills vs. Specialized Mills Each Decade

Decade	Total New	Integrated	Paper Only	Pulp Only
1900-1910	400	72	291	37
1910-1920	358	52	274	32
1920-1930	329	56	247	26
1930-1940	229	44	166	19

Decade	Total Exit	Integrated	Paper Only	Pulp Only
1900-1910	405	49	289	67
1910-1920	355	46	274	35
1920-1930	332	46	252	34
1930-1940	314	55	228	31

Source: Compiled by the author from Lockwood's Directory of the Paper and Allied Trades.

Table 5–10
Integrated Mills: Entrants and Established Mills Each Decade, by Region

Decade and Region	Integrated Entrants (% Entering Paper Mills)	Integrated Established Mills (% Mills Operating Entire Decade)
1900-1910		
U.S.	19.8%	22.4%
North	19.1	21.0
Lake	19.2	23.3
South	46.7	36.4
Pacific	55.6	75.0
1910-1920		
U.S.	16.0%	26.8%
North	13.9	26.3
Lake	12.2	25.5
South	38.1	43.8
Pacific	50.0	50.0
1920-1930		
U.S.	18.5%	24.0%
North	14.9	20.8
Lake	9.7	24.2
South	51.4	40.0
Pacific	36.0	75.0
1930-1940		
U.S.	21.0%	22.2%
North	12.0	18.3
Lake	8.5	21.4
South	71.0	38.1
Pacific	42.9	52.4

Source: Compiled by the author from Lockwood's Directory of the Paper and Allied Trades.

Table 5–11
Comparison of Pulp to Paper Ratio Between Surviving and Failing Mills

Year	Mills Surviving to 1940 Average (Pulp/Paper)	Mills Failing Before 1940 Average (Pulp/Paper)
1900	36%	14%
1910	30%	19%
1920	32%	25%
1930	26%	20%

Source: Compiled by the author from Lockwood's Directory of the Paper and Allied Trades.
Note: The difference in the means was statistically significant at the 1% level in 1900, 1910, and 1920, and at the 2% level in 1930.

Table 5–12
Vertical Integration and Mill Survival

Type	No. Mills Listed in 1900	Number of Mills That Continued to be Listed in:			
		1910	1920	1930	1940
Integrated	148	98	83	71	49
Survival Rate[a]		66%	56%	48%	33%
Paper Only	624	335	226	156	105
Survival Rate[a]		54%	36%	25%	17%

Source: Compiled by the author from Lockwood's Directory of the Paper and Allied Trades.
[a] Reported as a percentage of the original number of mills listed in 1900.

Table 5–13

Newsprint Mills: Survivorship Test of Integrated and Nonintegrated Mills
(Percent of Newsprint Capacity)

Mill Size (Percent of Newsprint Capacity)	Integrated Newsprint Mills					Nonintegrated Newsprint Mills				
	1900	1910	1920	1930	1940	1900	1910	1920	1930	1940
Under 0.1	.3	–	–	–	–	.4	.2	.1	–	–
0.1 to 0.2	.5	.7	.1	–	–	1.0	.4	–	.2	–
0.2 to 0.3	.7	1.6	.5	.5	–	1.6	.3	–	–	–
0.3 to 0.4	.6	2.1	.7	1.4	–	.3	.4	.4	–	–
0.4 to 0.5	3.0	1.4	3.5	–	.9	1.6	.4	.4	–	–
0.5 to 0.75	2.4	7.3	2.6	3.8	–	1.7	–	.7	.7	–
0.75 to 1.0	6.5	6.9	11.0	5.6	2.7	1.9	–	1.6	–	–
1.0 to 1.5	7.5	12.1	12.7	9.2	2.6	1.4	1.4	5.0	3.6	–
1.5 to 2.5	17.7	7.8	12.0	17.1	3.2	3.2	–	–	2.4	–
2.5 to 5.0	18.2	26.9	22.8	29.0	24.7	–	–	5.7	–	–
5.0 to 10.0	17.8	30.1	20.1	26.4	31.7	–	–	–	–	–
10.0 to 15.0	11.9	–	–	–	34.3	–	–	–	–	–
Total	87.1	96.9	86.0	93.0	100.0	13.1	3.1	13.9	6.9	0.0

Source: Compiled by the author from Lockwood's Directory of the Paper and Allied Trades.

124

Table 5–14
Nonnewsprint Mills: Survivorship Test of Integrated and Nonintegrated Mills
(Percent of Capacity of Nonnewsprint Mills)

Mill Size (Percent of Total Paper Capacity of Nonnewsprint Mills)	Integrated Nonnewsprint Mills					Nonintegrated Nonnewsprint Mills				
	1900	1910	1920	1930	1940	1900	1910	1920	1930	1940
Under 0.1	1.0	.8	1.8	2.2	2.1	15.8	14.1	14.7	16.2	14.4
0.1 to 0.2	2.7	5.6	6.0	6.9	5.4	17.6	22.4	15.0	14.2	13.6
0.2 to 0.3	4.9	5.1	5.3	5.1	4.2	14.8	9.1	12.1	9.9	9.4
0.3 to 0.4	5.9	5.2	3.0	2.4	4.9	4.8	7.4	5.5	8.3	7.7
0.4 to 0.5	3.9	2.8	2.9	5.2	2.7	7.1	3.7	9.5	5.3	5.3
0.5 to 0.75	3.7	4.9	4.6	2.3	7.3	7.1	6.7	5.2	7.7	5.8
0.75 to 1.0	0.8	2.8	3.4	1.6	4.3	2.6	5.4	3.3	4.3	2.6
1.0 to 1.5	5.5	1.1	1.0	3.7	4.6	–	1.3	6.7	4.7	2.0
1.5 to 2.5	1.9	1.7	–	–	3.7	–	–	–	–	–
Total	30.3	30.0	28.0	29.4	39.2	69.8	70.1	72.0	70.6	60.8

Source: Compiled by the author from Lockwood's Directory of the Paper and Allied Trades.

Table 5–15
Timberland Ownership: 1930–1940 (89 U.S. Paper Firms)

	Own Timberland	No Timberland
Number of Firms	43	46
Region		
North	12	15
Lake	9	18
South	9	2
Pacific	3	5
North & Lake	1	3
North & South	3	0
North & Pacific	1	0
Lake & South	1	1
Lake & Pacific	0	1
South & Pacific	1	0
Three regions	3	1
Pulp Integration		
Pulp	41	20
No Pulp	2	26
Grade[a]		
Newsprint	11	4
Book & Writing	21	22
Wrap & Board	29	32
Kraft	20	9
Sanitary	10	5
Industrial	11	2
Average Capacity (thou. lbs./day)	1,106	451

Source: Moody's Manual of Investments, 1931 and 1941; Lockwood's Directory of the Paper and Allied Trades.

[a] Totals exceed number of firms due to production of multiple grades.

Table 5–16
Logit Regression of Timberland Ownership: 1940

	Model 1	Model 2
Constant	-.92	-5.62
	(-2.55)	(-3.13)
Capacity	.13	
	(2.58)	
Capacity^2		.90
		(3.08)
Number of obs.	83	83

Note: The asymptotic t-statistics are reported in parentheses. The dependent variable is the natural log of $[p/(1-p)]$, where p is the probability that a firm owns timberland.

6

Regression Analysis of Pulp and Paper Integration

This chapter draws from the extensive literature on vertical integration to explain the patterns of integration observed in the U.S. pulp and paper industry in this period. Directory data are used to provide a formal test of the determinants of vertical integration that have been proposed by others in previous research of the pulp and paper industry. Factors such as mill size, paper grades produced, and location are evaluated in connection with vertical integration. A model of integration based on the transaction-cost approach is developed. The model is estimated by regression analysis, first with a logit-regression model of the probability of integration, and then with a truncated (Tobit) regression model of the extent of firm integration, measured by the ratio of pulp capacity to paper capacity. Regression analysis of changes in the extent of integration over decade-long periods is also presented.

In the final section of this chapter, the logit-regression model of integration is estimated separately for entrants and established mills in each sample year. Because the established mills generally remained either integrated or not integrated once the plant was built (see Chapter 5), the entrants are shown to have been more sensitive to the determinants of integration than the established mills in a given year. These results suggest that economists are advised to investigate the differences between new and old firms and to account for firm or plant age in conducting empirical research of vertical integration and other issues in firm behavior.

MODEL OF VERTICAL INTEGRATION

The following model of integration in the paper industry is based on the transaction-cost approach. Transaction-cost models typically include variables that are thought to indicate opportunities for bilateral bargaining problems and increased costs of external exchanges, by measuring the number of traders in the market with market concentration ratios (e.g., Caves and Bradburd 1988; Hennart 1988; Levy 1985).[1] Most studies have addressed interindustry differences in vertical integration or have examined the general level of integration in an industry in light of the costs of transactions in that industry. This model, on the other hand, explains the variation in the decision to integrate and the extent of integration across firms in the same industry.

The transaction-cost approach suggests that paper mills will be more likely to integrate, as the costs of purchasing market pulp (relative to the costs of producing the pulp internally) increase. The aspects of transaction costs that are measurable based on the directory data include the following independent variables: the product of the concentration ratios for the top four paper mills and the top four market-pulp mills in each region, mill size, and dummy variables for newsprint and kraft paper production.

The regional market concentration is measured by the product of the pulp and paper concentration ratios (CRPROD). Each concentration ratio is the share of total regional paper capacity or market-pulp capacity held by the top four mills in each market. The product of these concentration ratios may be interpreted as an indirect measure of the threat of bilateral monopoly exchange problems in that regional market. As discussed in the previous chapter, a regional measure is appropriate because most grades of pulp and paper were traded within the producing region during this period (Guthrie 1950, 86–89). Markets in the developing regions of the South and Pacific were characterized by relatively few mills and significantly higher measures of concentration than the other regional markets (see Chapter 4). The relatively high concentration found in the pulp and paper markets of the South and the Pacific Coast suggests that firms in these regions may have integrated to a greater extent than in the older regions to avoid negotiation costs, potential supply disruptions, or opportunistic behavior due to the small numbers of local buyers and sellers. This theory implies that the concentration-ratio product will be positively associated with vertical integration in the regressions that follow.[2]

Firm size is estimated by the paper capacity (pounds per 24 hours) of the paper mill. The logarithm of capacity (LOGCAP) is used in the regression analysis. Paper capacity is a proxy for firm size because data such as firm sales or assets are not available for the full sample of firms listed in the directory. Also, because at least 85 percent of pulp and paper firms operated just one mill in each sample year (representing at least 50 percent of paper capacity), observations of individual mills are treated as firm observations.[3] Firm size is expected to be positively associated with the decision to integrate and with the extent of vertical integration because the transaction-costs savings will be greater compared to a smaller firm (all else equal). As Temin notes, larger firms are more likely to assure a steady supply of inputs through integration, because the costs of a supply disruption will be greater than for a smaller firm (Temin 1988, 902). A larger firm will also be more likely to integrate if economies of scale in the upstream process result in lower costs for the large firm's own production compared to a small firm (Williamson 1985, 94). Also, if the frequency of transactions rises with firm size, a greater frequency of transactions will raise the benefits to integration and may justify the costs of internal organization (Williamson 1985, 60). Others hypothesize a negative association between firm size and vertical integration, due to managerial diseconomies of scale (Blair and Kaserman 1985, 294; Levy 1985, 439). However, these authors have not suggested at what size these diseconomies set in.

The final variables, NEWS and KRAFT, are dummy variables that indicate the production of newsprint or kraft papers. Integration is expected to be a positive function of the production of these grades. Mills that produced these papers were more likely to be integrated because the products were standardized and could be produced on a larger scale than the more specialized papers in other categories. Integrated pulp production was more economical for these large paper mills because a large enough volume of one type of pulp (sometimes two) was required by the mill to take advantage of economies of scale in pulp production. Other grades of paper were produced in smaller batches (to order) and required a wider range of grades of pulp. Therefore, the coefficients of the dummy variables for newsprint and kraft papers are expected to be positive.

REGRESSION RESULTS

The model is estimated first by logit and Tobit (truncated) regression analysis. The data source was *Lockwood's Directory of the Paper and Allied Trades*. The data were collected at decade intervals from the 1901, 1911, 1921, 1931, and 1941 editions and included all U.S. pulp and paper mills listed each sample year. The same set variables—the product of the regional pulp and paper concentration ratios, the logarithm of paper capacity, a newsprint dummy, a kraft dummy, and a constant term—were included in the model that was estimated in each sample year, with the exception that the dummy variable for kraft production was omitted from both the logit and Tobit regressions in 1900 (because this grade was not produced commercially until 1910) and the newsprint dummy variable was omitted in 1940 in the logit estimation (because all newsprint mills were integrated that year). Because the number of mills operating each year varied with entry and exit of mills, the sample size ranges from 697 to 792 paper mills over the period. (In fact, only 154 paper mills survived the entire period, so the composition of the sample changed significantly each sample year.)

The logit model treats the dependent variable as the odds that a mill will integrate, or

$$\ln[p/(1-p)],$$

where p is the probability of integration, and the dependent variables include a constant and the variables discussed above. The question of what determines the decision to integrate will be simplified by assuming all firms in the sample entered the market integrated or specialized and remained so until exiting the market. As discussed below, this assumption is consistent with the data that reveals that very few mills changed between integration and specialization during any of the decades studied.

The results of the logit regressions for each sample year are reported in Table 6–1, with t-statistics shown in parentheses. The decision to integrate is shown to be positively associated each sample year with the concentration of the regional pulp and paper markets, the logarithm of mill capacity, and whether a mill produced newsprint or kraft paper, as hypothesized.[4] All of the coefficients for these variables were highly statistically significant each year. Statistical tests find that the coefficients were not stable over time, however.[5] A number of trends cause the coefficients to rise or decline over time: capacity growth, redistribution of mills to the relatively more concentrated regions of the South and Pacific Coast, the decline in U.S. newsprint production, and growth of kraft mills (introduced in 1910).

The elasticity of the probability that a mill vertically integrates (p) with respect to changes in each independent variable was calculated by the following formula:

(logit regression coefficient) (independent variable) $(1-p)$, evaluated at the sample means.[6] The range of elasticities found over the period 1900–1940 are reported in Table 6–1. The elasticities were highest for the dummy variables, NEWS and KRAFT; these values measure the percentage change in the probability to integrate if either grade is produced. Smaller elasticities were calculated for the effect of a 1 percent rise in mill capacity, followed by the range reported for the concentration-ratio product.

The same logit model was estimated for a sample of mills that excluded all newsprint mills (any mill that produced newsprint), to check that the previous results were not determined by the highly integrated newsprint sector. The independent variables included in the model were a constant term, the product of pulp and paper concentration ratios, and the logarithm of paper capacity (no grade dummy variables were necessary). The results of the regression analysis are shown in Table 6–2. The coefficients and the statistical significance of the variables were changed little by this experiment. Among the nonnewsprint mills, the probability of integration was higher, the larger the mill size and the greater the product of pulp and paper market concentration ratios in each mill's region. Another set of regressions that excluded all newsprint and kraft mills, the two most integrated sectors of the industry, produced similar statistics (not shown here). As a result, the regressions based on all paper mills that identified the newsprint and kraft mills by dummy variables appear to be reliable estimates of this vertical integration model.

The second method of estimating the model treats vertical integration as a continuous variable, where integration is defined as pulp capacity expressed as a ratio of paper capacity. Because the dependent variable is truncated below the value zero, a Tobit regression is estimated. The results of the Tobit regression are reported in Table 6–3. These regression estimates are consistent with the earlier logit results. The extent of vertical integration was positively associated with the concentration of the regional pulp and paper markets, the logarithm of mill capacity, and whether the mill produced newsprint or kraft papers. All of these coefficients were highly statistically significant in each sample year. The coefficients were not stable over time and follow the same temporal patterns seen in the logit results.

The elasticity of the ratio of pulp to paper capacities with respect to changes in each independent variable was determined by:

(linear regression coefficient) (mean value of independent variable) / (mean value of the dependent variable).

These elasticities are reported in Table 6–3. Changes in the independent variables had a larger effect on percentage changes in the pulp-to-paper ratio compared to percentage changes in the probability to integrate, but the elasticities are ranked as in the logit regressions.

The finding that vertical integration is associated with the joint concentration ratios in the regional paper and pulp markets is strong support for the transaction-cost view and is consistent with previous research. Concentration was positively related to vertical integration in the study by Levy (1985) of 37 industries (69 firms), where concentration was measured by the weighted-average, four-firm concentration ratio of the industries in which the integrated firm produced. In their interindustry studies of vertical integration, both MacDonald (1985) and Caves and Bradburd (1988) use three variables to measure the relevant concentration: the four-firm concentration ratio of the supplying industry, an average four-firm concentration ratio of buyer concentration, and a Herfindahl index over the supplying industry shipments to the customer industries. MacDonald (1985) finds that the first two concentration variables are significantly and positively associated with industry-level vertical integration (MacDonald 1985, 330). Caves and Bradburd define a composite variable to represent concentration as the product of these three measures of concentration; this variable was positively related to vertical integration in regression analysis (Caves and Bradburd 1988, 276).

The positive relationship between integration and firm size in both models supports Williamson's hypothesis that larger firms will be more likely to realize economies of scale in upstream production and to vertically integrate compared to smaller firms (Williamson 1985, 94). This result confirms the observation by Globerman and Schwindt (1986), who report that larger firms (measured by sales) were more likely to integrate in the Canadian paper industry, and they explain this association by the higher frequency of transactions among larger firms compared to smaller firms (Globerman and Schwindt 1986, 208–9). Moreover, the association between firm size and vertical integration has been found in other industries. For example, in a logit regression of vertical integration in the early nineteenth-century cotton textile industry, Temin finds that integration of spinning and weaving was positively associated with the size of the mill (measured by the number of spinners). He argues that large firms had a greater incentive to integrate because they "stood to lose more from a temporary interruption in supply or demand" (Temin 1988, 902). Similarly, Kane observes that the average spindleage capacity of integrated textile mills was significantly larger than in specialized spinning mills in the early twentieth-century U.S. cotton textile industry (Kane 1988, 56–57).[7]

The regression results for the newsprint and kraft dummy variables clarify the relationship between these paper grades and vertical integration. Although the higher incidence of integration among newsprint and kraft mills is well known, most observers have attributed this to a combination of economies of scale in paper production (larger runs of a standardized grade) and homogeneous pulp requirements (e.g., OECD 1982, 7). The result that integration is associated with production of these grades after controlling for the size of the paper mill suggests that other factors besides economies of scale in the production of these grades plays a role in the decision to integrate these mills. Thus, the hypothesis that a mill is more likely to integrate the fewer the grades of pulp required for production is indirectly supported by these results.

CHANGES IN EXTENT OF INTEGRATION OVER TIME

The focus of this section is the mill's decision to become either more or less dependent on market pulp over time, measured by changes in the ratio of pulp capacity to paper capacity among integrated mills. Given that the initial decision to integrate was associated with mill location, mill size, and grades produced, the analysis can be extended to ask if these factors played a role in the decision to alter the mix of purchased and internally produced pulp over the life cycle of the mill.

As discussed in Chapter 5, although it was uncommon for mills to switch between integration and specialization over time, the majority of integrated mills were found to alter their ratio of pulp to paper capacities over decade intervals. Of the integrated mills that survived during each decade of the study, the share of mills that kept a constant ratio of pulp to paper capacities ranged from 10 percent in the first two decades (1900–1910, 1910–1920), 15 percent in the 1920s, and 25 percent in the 1930s. Of the remaining integrated mills that did alter the pulp-to-paper ratio, a somewhat larger number of mills decreased the ratio (increased their reliance on market pulp) than mills that increased the ratio.

The mills included in the regression analysis that follows satisfied the conditions that the mill survived from the beginning to the end of the selected decade and that the mill reported a positive ratio of pulp to paper capacities (in other words, the mill was integrated throughout the decade and the respective capacities were known). Changes in the ratios of pulp and paper capacities over the decade period are calculated as

(the end of decade pulp-to-paper ratio) / (the beginning of decade pulp-to-paper ratio)

As a result, the dependent variable in the following regressions is positive and ranges from below 1.0 for mills that decreased their pulp-to-paper ratio over the decade, to above 1.0 for mills that raised the ratio. The sample excludes mills that switched between integrated and nonintegrated status because the change in the pulp-to-paper ratio is not meaningful for these few cases (the value of the ratio is 0 in one year).

The independent variables that are considered in the regression analysis of changes in the extent of integration include a constant term and the beginning of decade values of the following variables: the pulp-to-paper ratio, the logarithm of paper capacity, dummy variables for production of newsprint and kraft papers, and the product of the regional pulp and paper, four-firm concentration ratios. These independent variables are the same as those considered in the previous regression models of the mill's decision to integrate, plus a variable to measure the initial value of the extent of integration.[8] The statistics discussed in Chapter 5 suggested that mills with relatively high beginning values of the pulp-to-paper ratio tended to reduce the ratio over the following decade, whereas mills with low initial ratios tended to raise their ratios.

The results of the regression analysis for each of the four decades of the study are shown in Table 6–4. Integrated mills that survived the decade that is identified in the top row of the table are included in the data set for each regression. For the most part, the composition of the sample varied with each regression, since only a portion of the mills survived consecutive decades. Nevertheless, the sample size is adequate to find reliable statistical results.

The most consistent result of the regressions over the entire period was the negative and statistically significant relationship between the beginning-of-period pulp-to-paper ratio and the subsequent change in that ratio. As suspected, the change in the extent of integration was higher, the lower the initial measure of integration. Some possible explanations for this result may include the theories that a mill became more self-reliant as management gained experience with pulping operations, or that mills that were "partially" integrated sought to avoid market purchases of pulp after early reliance on outside suppliers. Since the results of the previous section suggested that mills integrate for efficiency reasons, perhaps the less integrated mills are "catching-up" to an efficient ratio of pulp-to-paper capacities of near 1.0 (and the mills with "excess pulp" are approaching the efficient ratio from above). One could argue that these mills are converging on the efficient ratio because only the surviving mills are observed in the analysis (changes in the ratio could not be observed for mills that exited before the end of the decade).

The role of the remaining independent variables in the decision to change the pulp-to-paper ratio is ambiguous. The size of the paper mill (logarithm of paper capacity) at the beginning of the decade appeared to be negatively associated with changes in the pulp-to-paper ratio of integrated mills (in three of the four decades), but the coefficient of this variable was not statistically significant in any of the regressions. There is some evidence that newsprint mills in the 1920s and 1930s were more likely to raise the ratio of pulp-to-paper capacities, relative to other grades, based on positive and statistically significant coefficients for the newsprint dummy variable in the last two regressions. This result is consistent with the strong association between newsprint production and vertical integration in general. Kraft production also was associated with a rise in the pulp-to-paper ratio, but only in the regression for the 1920s.

The local concentration of pulp and paper mills seemed to play a role in changes in the extent of integration only in the last regression. A separate set of regressions that include dummy variables for each region (not shown here) reveals that location in the South was associated with an increased pulp-to-paper ratio in the 1930s, which probably explains the results seen for the concentration-ratio product (since the southern concentration ratios were high compared to the other regions). Thus the concentration ratio may have influenced growth in the pulp-to-paper ratio by promoting greater self-sufficiency among mills located in a region where the cost of dealing with outside pulp suppliers was higher than in other regions. However, the coefficient for the concentration-ratio variable was statistically significant only in the 1930s, so the results are difficult to generalize for the entire period.

COMPARISON OF ENTRANTS VERSUS ESTABLISHED MILLS

An additional issue that I explore in this chapter is whether the vertical integration behavior of entering mills differed from established mills. Because mills were observed only at decade intervals, entry is approximated by mills that were operating in a given sample year but not the prior sample year (I assume they entered during that decade). Established mills were operating both in the current year and the prior sample year. Table 6–5 presents the results of logit analysis of the probability to integrate for new and established firms operating in 1920, 1930, and 1940.[9]

The regression coefficients suggest that established mills were less responsive to regional concentration ratios than entering mills each year. In addition, the coefficient for CRPROD rises sharply in 1930 and 1940 for entering mills, but declines in 1940 following a weaker increase in 1930 for the established mills. Moreover, the CRPROD coefficients in 1920 and 1940 are not statistically significant for established mills. The jump in the CRPROD coefficient seen in Table 6–1 in 1930 and 1940, based on new and old mills combined, can be attributed to the relatively large effect changes in concentration had on new mills after 1920, which were entering the South and Pacific regions in greater proportions each year.

The statistical analysis of the directory data discussed in Chapter 5 revealed that once a mill was built as integrated or specialized, few mills changed that status. Over decade-long intervals, at most 18 paper mills (out of the 400–500 mills that survived a given decade) chose to switch, most by disintegrating.[10] As a result, most established mills did not adapt to changes in the determinants of integration over time. Rather than add or dismantle pulp facilities, established mills were flexible only to the extent that integrated mills changed their ratio of pulp capacity to paper capacity each decade.

By contrast, entrants to each region were less likely to be integrated over time (except entrants to the South in 1930 and 1940, due to the predominance of kraft mills), and the average ratio of pulp-to-paper capacity also was declining for these mills compared to previous entrants. The large coefficient for the concentration ratio for entrants is consistent with their adaptation to the drop in regional concentration in the developing regions. The results for a Tobit regression of the ratio of pulp-to-paper, not shown here, show distinctions between entrants and established mills that are similar to the logit regression of the probability of integration shown in Table 6–5.

SUMMARY

This historical case study of vertical integration of pulp and paper production brings further evidence of transaction-cost economies in vertical integration. Paper firms were more likely to integrate (and the extent of integration was higher) in regions where the market concentration of pulp and paper producers was higher, and this result was consistent over a 40-year period of observations. The influence of market concentration was more pronounced among entrants each year compared to established mills that did not alter their integrated status once a plant was built. The empirical model also confirmed that vertical integration of pulp and paper is positively associated with the capacity of the paper mill and is more likely in the production of standardized grades, such as newsprint and kraft, than in other paper grades.

An integrated mill was shown to be more likely to increase its ratio of pulp capacity to paper capacity, the lower the initial ratio of pulp-to-paper capacities and if standardized grades (newsprint or kraft) were produced. However, there was little evidence that location or mill size played a role in the integrated mill's decision to become more (or less) dependent on market pulp over the life cycle of the mill (once the initial decision to integrate had been made).

NOTES

1. The transactional economies explanation for vertical integration is difficult to distinguish from the market imperfections explanation in empirical tests, because indicators such as high market concentration are consistent with either the small numbers bargaining problem or monopoly (monopsony) (see MacDonald 1985, 327; Levy 1985, 439; Caves and Bradburd 1988, 269–70). However, the competitive nature of the pulp and paper markets, discussed in Chapter 4, makes the issue of market power less of a concern than the problems involved in negotiating and enforcing a market contract in this industry.

2. Tests of alternative measures of market concentration, using either the local pulp or paper concentration ratios separately, were similar to the results reported for the product of the two concentration ratios, because it turns out that both were either high or low in the same regional market.

3. See the discussion of multiplant operations in Chapter 4.

4. Alternative measures of market concentration also were tested. Regional dummy variables for the Lake, South, and Pacific regions (location in the North was the excluded dummy variable) resulted in positive and significant coefficients for the South and Pacific dummy variables, but negative and insignificant coefficients for the Lake region dummy.

5. A likelihood-ratio test based on a logit regression of the pooled data rejected a null hypothesis of coefficient stability at the 5 percent level.

6. See Kane (1988, 92) for the derivation of this elasticity calculation.

7. The relationship between firm size and integration is less certain in studies of interindustry comparisons of vertical integration, however. Levy (1985) found a negative association between average firm size and industry integration (measured by the ratio of value added to sales), which he attributed to internal costs that rise with firm size. However, Caves and Bradburd argue that Levy's result is "implausible on the evidence that most small firms operate in single industries" and is explained by multicollinearity problems with the use of the value added divided by sales measure of integration and concentration measures (Caves and Bradburd 1988, 266). They explain that "heavy" industries will result in high concentration (due to economies of scale) and high ratios of value added to sales. Because these industries will also exhibit positive correlations between concentration and firm size, the inclusion of both of these variables in the regressions estimated by Levy could explain the misleading negative coefficient for firm size. Other interindustry studies have failed to discover a strong relationship between size and integration (Adelman 1955; Gort 1962; Livesay and Porter 1969; Tucker and Wilder 1977).

8. Despite the previous finding that these variables were associated with the pulp-to-paper ratio among all U.S. mills in a given year, in a separate regression based on this sample (of only integrated mills), I did not find an association and therefore do not suspect multicollinearity here.

9. The null hypothesis that the coefficients are the same for both entering and established mills is rejected at the 5 percent level.

10. See Chapter 5 for more details about the switching between integration and specialization.

Table 6–1
Logit Regression of Vertical Integration in U.S. Paper Industry: 1900–1940

	1900	1910	1920	1930	1940
Constant	-6.18	-6.22	-4.75	-5.40	-6.55
	(-12.29)	(-11.31)	(-10.29)	(-10.75)	(-11.40)
CRPROD	4.31	2.28	2.95	9.74	8.59
	(3.43)	(2.29)	(2.56)	(3.91)	(2.78)
LOGCAP	1.36	1.18	.74	.72	.96
	(9.73)	(8.85)	(6.95)	(7.04)	(8.74)
NEWS	1.36	2.96	2.69	3.40	(a)
	(4.72)	(7.80)	(7.67)	(7.38)	
KRAFT	(b)	1.37	1.63	1.07	1.01
		(2.47)	(4.59)	(3.85)	(3.44)
Number of obs.	759	768	768	792	698

Range of elasticities of probability of vertical integration:

CRPROD	.07	to	.38
CAP	.55	to	1.10
NEWS	1.10	to	2.62
KRAFT	.79	to	1.26

Note: The asymptotic t-statistics are reported in parentheses. The dependent variable is the natural log of [p/(1-p)], where p is the probability that a mill is vertically integrated, defined as producing both pulp and paper.

a All newsprint mills were vertically integrated in 1940.

b Kraft was not produced in 1900.

Table 6–2
Logit Regression of Vertical Integration Without Newsprint Mills

	1900	1910	1920	1930	1940
Constant	-6.22	-6.06	-4.96	-5.50	-6.48
	(-11.11)	(-10.97)	(-10.45)	(-10.93)	(-11.21)
CRPROD	3.34	3.17	3.06	11.09	11.30
	(2.31)	(3.00)	(2.62)	(4.62)	(3.72)
LOGCAP	1.39	1.15	.82	.76	.92
	(8.80)	(8.50)	(7.52)	(7.48)	(8.26)
Number of obs.	670	698	710	744	682

Note: The asymptotic t-statistics are reported in parentheses. The dependent variable is the natural log of [p/(1-p)], where p is the probability that a mill is vertically integrated, defined as producing both pulp and paper.

Table 6–3
Truncated Regression of Vertical Integration in U.S. Paper Industry: 1900–1940

	1900	1910	1920	1930	1940
Constant	-3.51	-3.51	-3.32	-3.24	-3.62
	(-14.64)	(-12.19)	(-13.29)	(-13.49)	(-13.07)
CRPROD	2.50	1.65	2.00	5.02	4.51
	(3.98)	(2.72)	(2.51)	(3.49)	(2.51)
LOGCAP	.73	.62	.49	.43	.49
	(10.55)	(8.62)	(7.97)	(8.35)	(8.66)
NEWS	.71	1.38	1.59	1.61	1.64
	(4.15)	(9.36)	(9.34)	(11.07)	(9.27)
KRAFT	(a)	1.08	1.10	.65	.72
		(2.95)	(4.01)	(4.14)	(4.39)
R^2	.60	.58	.47	.49	.50
Number of mills	756	761	760	791	697

Range of elasticities of dependent variable with respect to changes in:

CRPROD	.30	to	1.09
CAP	1.81	to	4.06
NEWS	3.94	to	7.45
KRAFT	2.71	to	4.70

Notes: The dependent variable is the ratio of pulp capacity to paper capacity. The t-statistics are reported in parentheses. In 1920, the regression excludes two mills that reported pulp to paper ratios of 10.0 and 17.5, respectively.
a Kraft was not produced in 1900.

Table 6–4
Linear Regression of Changes in Extent of Integration, by Decade

	1900-1910	1910-1920	1920-1930	1930-1940
Constant	.93	1.57	-1.46	1.92
	(1.15)	(5.28)	(-4.96)	(4.50)
Beginning of Decade Values of:				
PULP/PAPER	-.83	-.14	-.31	-.51
	(-3.40)	(-1.42)	(-3.81)	(-3.92)
LOGCAP	.29	-.06	-.03	-.12
	(1.59)	(-1.01)	(-.60)	(-1.67)
NEWS	-.10	-.07	.19	.33
	(-.32)	(-.72)	(2.04)	(2.35)
KRAFT	(a)	-.32	.31	-.08
		(-1.47)	(2.44)	(-.52)
CRPROD	.10	-.41	-.12	3.98
	(.07)	(-1.06)	(-.36)	(2.94)
R^2	.17	.07	.17	.19
No. mills	87	114	113	113

Note: The t-statistics are reported in parentheses. The dependent variable is the ratio of the end of decade (pulp capacity / paper capacity) to the beginning of decade (pulp capacity / paper capacity).
[a] Kraft was not produced in 1900.

Table 6–5
Logit Regression of Vertical Integration: Entrants vs. Established Mills

	Entrants			Established		
	1920	1930	1940	1920	1930	1940
Constant	-4.42	-5.43	-7.89	-4.97	-5.54	-6.04
	(-5.73)	(-5.93)	(-5.97)	(-8.38)	(-8.84)	(-9.43)
CRPROD	3.90	15.99	16.28	3.23	8.93	5.77
	(2.87)	(4.09)	(2.80)	(1.52)	(2.41)	(1.54)
LOGCAP	.56	.48	1.07	.84	.82	.91
	(3.10)	(2.51)	(4.10)	(6.18)	(6.52)	(7.47)
NEWS	1.78	4.43	(a)	3.63	3.01	(a)
	(3.47)	(5.35)		(5.83)	(5.36)	
KRAFT	1.48	2.04	1.16	1.72	.51	.99
	(2.63)	(4.56)	(1.93)	(3.67)	(1.33)	(2.89)
Number obs.	307	290	188	461	502	510

Note: The asymptotic t-statistics are reported in parentheses. The dependent variable is the natural log of [p/(1-p)], where p is the probability that a mill is vertically integrated, defined as producing both pulp and paper.
a All newsprint mills were vertically integrated in 1940.

7

Mill Survival to 1940

This chapter investigates the dynamics of entry, exit, and growth in the paper industry during the first four decades of the twentieth century. While economists have long been interested in firm survival and growth, these topics have only recently been addressed within the context of dynamic equilibrium models (Jovanovic 1982; Pakes and Ericson 1990). The objective of much empirical work in this area has been to test whether these new theoretical models are consistent with actual firm behavior (Evans 1987a and 1987b; Dunne, Roberts, and Samuelson 1989). This study of the paper industry adds to the recent empirical literature by detailing the determinants of firm survival and growth among a complete size and age distribution of firms in the same industry. Moreover, the timing of each firm's entrance, exit, and length of life cycle is studied.

The life cycles of individual paper mills are estimated from observations taken from *Lockwood's Directory of the Paper and Allied Trades* at decade intervals between 1900 and 1940. Three approaches to survival analysis have been taken: first, by considering the mills that survived to 1940 compared to those that failed before the end of the period; second, by identifying mills that survived during decade intervals over the period; and third, by estimating the length of mill lifetimes. The study of mill growth examines the change in mill capacity for mills that survived decade-long intervals between 1900 and 1940. Both mill survival and mill growth are analyzed in relationship to mill size, mill age, location, and the types of diversity and paper grades that were produced each year.

The study of survival and growth begins with a discussion of the models that underlie the statistical work in this chapter. Next, the directory data for surviving and failing firms are summarized, including analysis of the role of mill age and location in relation to mill survival. A logit regression of the probability of long-term and short-term survival is presented, followed by an analysis of the number of decades a mill operated. Mill growth is analyzed by finding the distribution of mill growth statistics from the directory evidence and by a regression model of mill growth by decade. The chapter concludes with a review of what these results imply about firm survival and growth and the relevance of alternative models of firm behavior.

MODEL OF MILL SURVIVAL AND GROWTH

Mills are assumed to behave according to the traditional model of profit maximization, where firms maximize the expected present value of a stream of future profits. Mills remain open as long as this value is greater than the expected sale price of the firm (liquidation value); otherwise, the mill exits. Mill survival is a function of economic profits, which in turn are determined by a number of unobserved variables, including local factor prices, product prices, and managerial ability.[1] In place of direct measures of profits and these other variables, this study relies on evidence about the size, age, location, and type of products made by the mills to shed light on the determinants of profits and survival.

An influential model of firm growth has been developed by Jovanovic (1982) and has been empirically implemented in a number of studies, including Evans (1987a and 1987b) and Dunne, Roberts, and Samuelson (1989). Jovanovic's model assumes that an industry is composed of heterogeneous firms that learn about their individual efficiency over time. As a firm ages, it learns about its "true costs" and updates its prior belief that the distribution of costs was random. Firms that learn they are efficient will grow and survive, while inefficient firms fail. The learning model implies that the probability of failure and firm growth will decline with age but is independent of mill size.[2]

Given the important role that age plays in Jovanovic's theoretical model, mill age is included in all the regressions presented in this chapter. Since previous studies of firm growth have found that the probability of failure and firm growth are negatively related to firm size, mill size is also included in the models that are estimated below.

In addition to mill age and size, industry-specific variables are considered. Because import competition and demand growth varied across the markets for different paper grades, the model accounts for the types of paper products made by the mill. In particular, one would expect that production of newsprint would reduce the probability of survival and mill growth because domestic producers were gradually displaced by imported Canadian newsprint in this period.

Other variables used in the models for survival and growth are substitutes for unobserved mill profits, and include location, which is a proxy for local factor prices and other regional factors (such as transportation costs), and diversification across different product markets. Location in the newer regions of the South and Pacific Coast is expected to be positively related to survival and growth (after accounting for mill age) because production costs (especially pulpwood and labor costs) were known to be lower in these regions (see Chapter 3). Diversification is expected to be associated with a higher probability of survival because mills would be able to offset demand cycles in one market against another. However, the effect of diversification on growth is uncertain. Mills that are producing for a slow-growing market will probably grow faster if production is diversified (such as International Paper's diversification away from newsprint), but growth may be maximized if the mill produces a single, fast-growing grade. Location is indicated by one of four regions (defined in Chapter 1), and diversification is measured by the number of paper grades a mill produced, as defined by the six grade categories used in this study.

SURVIVAL TO 1940

Among the mills operating each year, each mill has been identified as a survivor if it was listed in the 1941 edition of the directory, or as a failure if it exited sometime prior to 1940.[3] As shown in Table 7–1, only 19 percent of mills operating in 1900 survived to 1940. A larger share of mills were survivors as the sample year approaches 1940 (and the period of survival shortens). For example, from 1920, 43 percent of mills were still operating in 1940, and 64 percent of mills operating in 1930 survived to 1940. Table 7–1 also shows the proportion of mills in each sample year that survived to the next decade. Because the survival period is shortened to just ten years, the decade-to-decade survival rates far exceed the share of mills that survived to 1940.

Table 7–2 presents the average values in each year for a variety of descriptive features of mills that survived compared to mills that failed before 1940. This statistical summary highlights the main differences between surviving and failing mills as a prelude to the regression analysis that follows. Until 1930, failures far outnumbered survivors; by 1930, there were more survivors than failures because the period of survival had been shortened to 10 years (compared to 40 years for the mills operating in 1900, for example). These statistics suggest that vertical integration was associated with survival (as was shown in Chapter 5). When categorized as integrated or specialized, a larger proportion of integrated mills survived (and survivors outnumbered failures as early as 1920), compared to specialized paper or pulp mills.

Surviving mills consistently were larger than failing mills, whether measured by average paper capacity or by average pulp capacity. While survival may have led to relatively larger mills, the association between size and survival (to 1940) in operating years as early as 1900 instead suggests that survival was a function of initial mill size. One advantage of size may have been economies of scale, which reduce a mill's average costs as mill size increases. Because integration and size were correlated (see Chapter 6), the association between size and survival also may indirectly reflect the benefits of integration. A comparison of the average size of mill towns between survivors and failures suggests no pattern; surviving mills were located in smaller towns than the failing mills in three out of the four sample years, but the annual differences in the mean populations of each group were not great.

A larger share of surviving mills produced newsprint and book and writing paper compared to mills that failed (except in 1930, when survivors produced a smaller share of newsprint). Although the majority of mills in both categories produced wrap and board papers, a larger share of failing mills produced these grades than surviving mills. Among the pulp grades, a larger share of surviving mills produced soda (required for book and writing papers), sulphite, and sulphate (in 1930) compared to failing mills. A larger share of failing mills produced groundwood than surviving mills, which is consistent with the shift in demand away from the weak groundwood pulp in favor of sulphite pulps in this period. There is some evidence that production of more than one grade of paper was associated with mill survival; the share of paper mills that were diversified was higher among surviving mills in three out of four sample years (but the shares were similar in 1930, and higher among failing mills than survivors in 1910).

The surviving mills that were operating in 1900 are of special interest, because these mills survived the entire 40-year period of the study. As shown in Table 7–2, 165 mills in 1900 survived to 1940; only 7 of these were specialized pulp mills. The regional distribution of these mills was as follows: 103 in the North, 43 in the Lake region, 7 in the South, and 1 in the Pacific Coast region. Two trends appear as these mills are observed over the period: disintegration and a shift away from newsprint in favor of writing and kraft papers.[4] In 1900, about one-third of these surviving paper mills were vertically integrated, and the average ratio of pulp-to-paper capacity was 0.33. By 1940, the share of vertically integrated mills had dropped to about one-fourth (12 mills became specialized and only 2 specialized mills became integrated), and the average pulp-to-paper ratio dropped to 0.25. The surviving mills also were shifting away from news-print production toward other grades, especially book and writing papers. In 1900, 16 percent of these mills produced newsprint; that share dropped to just 4 percent by 1940. The share of mills producing book and writing papers increased from 44 percent in 1900 to 55 percent by 1940. Produc-tion of kraft paper also increased among these mills, from 3 percent in 1910 to 8 percent in 1940.

SURVIVAL EACH DECADE

To extend this analysis, survival over decade-long periods has been documented. One shortcoming of the previous definition of survival is the equal treatment of mills that fail any time during the 40-year period. Instead, mills can be identified by the decade in which failure occurs. Each year, the mills that were known to have failed prior to the next sample year were identified as "exits" and were compared to the mills that survived that same decade (see Table 7–3). Over time a larger number of mills survived through the next decade and the number of exits steadily declined, which resulted in a rising share of mills that survived each decade. Integrated mills fared better each decade than specialized mills. From two-thirds to three-fourths of integrated mills survived to the following decade, compared to just over half of the specialized paper mills and less than half of the specialized pulp mills. In fact, exits outnumbered survivors for the pulp mills in each decade except the 1910s. This relatively high failure rate may be explained by the growth of imported pulp, which displaced pulp produced in specialized domestic pulp mills.

Mills classified as "exits" each decade tended to be smaller than the firms that failed before 1940. Thus a relatively small size appears to contribute to earlier failure among pulp and paper mills. Similarly, mills surviving to the next decade were on average smaller than the mills known to have survived to 1940 (comparing average capacities in the same years), which suggests that mill size contributed positively to the duration of survival. As was the case for mills surviving to 1940, the survivors of each decade were more likely to produce newsprint and writing papers than the mills that failed during each decade.

MILL AGE AND SURVIVAL

The youngest mills in any given year appeared to be at the highest risk for failure in the subsequent decade in the period 1900–1940. Among mills exiting each decade, the bulk had been new entrants in the preceding decade. The relationship between date of entry and mill exit is shown in Table 7–4. The period of entry is estimated by the first year in which the mill was listed in the directories. Because the directories were consulted at decade-long intervals, the exact date of entry is not known. Also, the entry date for mills that appear in the 1900 directory was not identified. The top row indicates the number of paper mills in each entry cohort. Each column of the table shows when the mills of a given entry cohort exited over the decades that followed the period of entry. The number of exits in each column sum to the total number of mills that failed before 1940 from the same group of entrants. The final row indicates the number of mills that survived to 1940, by entry date.

The data shown in the columns in Table 7–4 reveal that about half of all new mills failed in their first decade of operation. The failure rate slowed with experience, as fewer mills from an original group of entrants failed over subsequent decades (this pattern is clearest for mills entering before 1900). The youngest firms each year also accounted for at least 45 percent of the mills that exited each decade. However, the oldest firms in the 1920s and 1930s, those that entered before 1900, had the second-highest number of exits in those two decades. While inexperience may have put new mills at a disadvantage, the oldest firms may have been handicapped with less efficient equipment if the pre-1900 plants had not been modernized. The favorable combination of experience and twentieth-century equipment likely explains the relative success of mills that entered between 1901 and 1920 (among the mills operating before 1940).

Table 7–5 presents additional measures of the postentry performance of each group of entrants over the period. Mills are identified by date of entry, which serves as a proxy for mill age during each decade.[5] The first section of Table 7–5 shows the number of mills operating each year by entry cohort and the percentage of mills within each cohort that survived to the following decade. The bulk of mills operating each year were new entrants, and the older the entry date, the fewer the number of mills belonging to that entry-cohort (except for mills that entered before 1900, which could not be distinguished by entry date or mill age). The survival rates among the mills belonging to each entry cohort were lowest in their first decade of operations (looking across each row in Table 7–5). Also, among mills operating in a given year, survival rates were lowest for the youngest mills (looking down each column in Table 7–5). This latter relationship between mill age and survival is analyzed in the regressions below.

The middle section of Table 7–5 presents the share of total paper capacity represented by the mills belonging to each entry cohort. Over time, attrition led to declining market shares for each of the entry cohorts. Growth of the surviving mills did not compensate for the decline in the number of mills in each cohort. The market share of new entrants declined each decade as well, as the number of encumbents increased and number of entrants declined each decade.

The last section of Table 7–5 reports the relative size of the mills belonging to each entry cohort by year. The oldest mills, those that entered before 1900, became steadily smaller than the average paper mill each year. Although the oldest mills became larger on average throughout the period, mill growth was slower than the industry average. By contrast, the relative size of other entry cohorts increased over time (and later declined, for the 1910 and 1920 cohorts). These observations are consistent with the well-known negative relationship between firm growth and age that has been documented in several studies and is consistent with Jovanovic's learning model. In the paper industry, this relationship may also have a technological explanation. One reason the newer mills were larger than the pre-1900 mills may have been the result of technological improvements in the size and speed of paper machinery after 1900, which allowed new firms to enter with larger mill capacities than older mills. The older mills may have been slower to rebuild or replace their smaller equipment because it may have been profitable to operate with depreciated equipment that had become a sunk cost rather than purchase the new models.[6]

REGIONAL DISTRIBUTION OF ENTRY AND EXIT

The relocation of pulp and paper production was accomplished through the growth of the industry in the South and Pacific regions and the attrition of producers in the North and Lake regions. The process of relocation can be illustrated by comparing the rates of entry, exit, and survival in each region. Table 7–6 presents the number of mills entering, surviving, and failing over each decade between 1900 and 1940. Entrants are defined as mills that were not listed at the beginning of the decade but were listed at the end of that decade. Although the specific date of entry is not known, it is assumed that these mills entered some time during the decade. Exits are mills that were listed at the beginning of the decade, but not at the end of that decade. Stays are defined as mills that were listed at both the beginning and end of each decade. These statistics refer only to paper mills and exclude specialized pulp mills.[7]

The entry and exit data shown in Table 7–6 reveal a generally higher rate of net entry to the South and Pacific regions compared to the North and Lake regions, especially during the 1920s and 1930s. First, entry to the North and Lake regions slowed by about half from the beginning to the end of the period. Although entry to the South and Pacific regions remained below that of the older regions, the number of entrants to the new regions grew dramatically to the 1920s and then dropped in the 1930s (during the Great Depression). Second, the North experienced a net loss of paper mills in all but the first decade, and the net loss climbed throughout the period. During the 1920s, net entry was highest in the South and Pacific regions, and by the 1930s, the Lake region experienced a significant net loss of mills. These statistics reflect the greater tendency for entering firms to take over existing plants in the older regions (resulting in the turnover of regional capacity) compared to the newer regions, as discussed in Chapter 3 (and shown in Table 3–7). Finally, the number of mills surviving during subsequent decades declined in the North, less than doubled in the Lake region, and grew fastest in the new regions. Although the total number of surviving mills remained highest in the established regions, the early stages of the relocation to the new regions are evident as early as the 1920s.

These statistics also suggest that paper mills survived better in the South compared to the Pacific Coast. Mill exits were relatively higher in the Pacific region, accounting for the smaller number of mills operating in that region. In the first two decades, only about one-quarter of Pacific mills survived the decade, compared to about 60 percent of southern mills; in the last two decades, the decade-survival rate was about 60 percent for Pacific mills, compared to about 70 percent for the southern mills. However, a large part of the apparently poor record of the Pacific mills is accounted for by the series of mergers leading to the creation of the Crown Zellerbach Corporation in 1928.[8]

LOGIT REGRESSION OF MILL SURVIVAL

The first regression is a logit model survival to 1940, based on observations of paper mills operating in 1900, 1910, 1920, and 1930, based on the directories for each year indicated. The dependent variable is defined as the odds that a mill will survive to 1940 (from the current year of operation), or $\ln [p/(1-p)]$, where p is the probability of survival to 1940. The independent variables are measures of mill size, age, location, and type and number of paper grades produced. The specific variables that are included in the model are the logarithm of paper capacity, mill age, dummy variables for location in the Lake, South, and Pacific regions (location in the North was excluded), dummy variables for the production of newsprint, writing, wrap, and kraft papers (production of sanitary or industrial papers was excluded), and the number of papers produced. Mill capacity was measured by the pounds of daily paper capacity of each mill, for all grades combined. Mill age was estimated by appearances in previous directories and was measured in number of decades of prior operation. All mills were treated as entrants (with the same age) for the first directory in 1900, because previous directories were not consulted. Mill location was indicated by the four regions as defined in this study. The last variable, the number of papers, refers to the production of more than one of the six paper grades defined in this study (actual values ranged from one to four) and serves as an indicator of mill diversification across paper markets.

Although vertical integration was statistically associated with survival in the comparison of integrated and specialized mills, a dummy variable for integration was not included in the regression model. Because the independent variables that may be related to survival, such as capacity and mill age, are the same variables that were associated with vertical integration (see Chapter 6), a dummy variable for integration does not provide additional information to the survival model that includes those other variables. With the limited number of characteristics available from the directories, it is difficult to augment the survival model with variables that are independent of integration. When a dummy variable for vertical integration was included in the survival models just described, the coefficient for integration was not statistically significant.[9]

The results of the logit regression of the probability of survival to 1940 are reported in Table 7-7, with t-statistics reported in parentheses. Each year, survival was positively associated with mill size and age, and these coefficients were statistically significant throughout the period. The coefficient for mill capacity remained fairly stable each year, but the coefficient for mill age decreased with time. The downward trend in the age coefficient likely is explained by the greater diversity in mill age each year. In 1910, only two mill ages were defined, depending on whether a mill was an entrant or had survived from 1900. The coefficient for mill age indicates the effect of being an established mill rather than an entrant. By 1930, four mill ages were possible, ranging from 0 for mills entering in 1930 to 4 for those that were operating in 1900. In the years after 1910, the coefficient for mill age indicates the marginal effect that a 1-percent increase in age had on the probability of survival, which was lower than the effect of simply being an encumbant.

The coefficients for the regional dummy variables indicate that only location in the South was positively correlated to survival (relative to location in the North). The coefficient for location in the South is positive each year but statistically significant only in 1900. Surprisingly, the coefficient for location in the Pacific region was negative each year but was never statistically significant. This result may reflect the inferior survival statistics for the Pacific mills relative to the North; mill failures from the Pacific region were a larger share of mills operating each decade compared to those in the North (see Table 7–6). However, the significant decline in the sizes of the regional dummy variables by 1930 suggests that location played a smaller role in survival than in earlier decades.

Mills that produced newsprint appeared to have reduced their chances for survival, especially for mills operating in 1930. The coefficient for the newsprint dummy variable was negative in three out of four regressions and was statistically significant for mills operating in 1930. These results are consistent with the gradual displacement of domestic newsprint production by imported newsprint from Canada in the early twentieth century. Production of book and writing papers, which include fine papers, was positively associated with survival among mills operating in the first three decades, and the coefficient for that dummy variable was statistically significant for mills operating in 1900 and 1910.[10] The coefficients for the dummy variables for wrap and kraft papers were generally negative but were not statistically significant. Writing paper appears to be the only paper market that was relatively more profitable than the sanitary or industrial markets. There was some evidence that diversification detracted from survival. The coefficient for the dummy variable that indicated the production of more than one grade of paper was statistically significant in only one year, 1910, when it was negative; the coefficient was positive in the other regressions but not statistically significant.

The elasticity of the probability of survival to 1940 (p) with respect to changes in each independent variable was calculated by the following formula:

(logit regression coefficient) (independent variable) $(1 - p)$.

This elasticity was evaluated by using the sample proportion of mills that survived to 1940 and the sample means for each of the independent variables each year (see Table 7–8).[11] Location in the Pacific region had the largest elasticity among the independent variables; location in the Pacific would reduce the probability of survival to 1940 in the range from 0.1 to 1.15 percent. Location in the South had the next highest range of elasticities (positive), followed by mill size (positive), and mill age (positive). The remaining elasticities ranged from positive to negative values, which indicates that a null hypothesis of a zero elasticity (the independent variable has no association with the probability of survival) cannot be rejected.

The second regression is a logit model of the probability of survival to the next decade (instead survival to the end of the period, 1940). Table 7–9 reports the regression results for mills operating in 1900, 1910, and 1920, and the period of survival is the decade following each of these sample years. (A regression for the period 1930–1940 was already reported in Table 7–7.) The independent variables and the models estimated are the same as those used for the regression of survival to 1940: the logarithm of mill capacity, mill age, location, grades of paper, and diversification. However, the value of the coefficients varied from the previous regressions because the sample of survivors was expanded considerably to include mills that survived at least one decade in addition to those mills that remained through 1940. Again, size and age were positively associated with mill survival, and the coefficients for these variables were statistically significant each year (except the coefficient for size was negative in 1900). The coefficients for size were stable in the 1910 and 1920 regressions and were similar to those found in the earlier regressions. The coefficients for mill age were somewhat larger compared to the previous regressions, however. It seems that mill age had a larger impact on survival over a ten-year period than for longer-term survival among mills that were operating in the same year. As for long-term survival, the coefficient for mill age was smaller as the range of possible ages increased each decade.

Survival by decade initially was positively associated with location in all regions outside the North, particularly in the Pacific region. Through the next two decades, however, only the coefficient for location in the South remained positive (but was not statistically significant). This pattern suggests that the marginal impact of a southern location (relative to the North) was improving as production in that region expanded. The coefficient for the Pacific dummy variable was negative in the second and third decades, but the size of the coefficient diminished over time and was not statistically significant these years.

The regression results concerning the paper grades were mixed. The only statistically significant coefficients were found in the case of writing and wrap dummy variables, in 1910 and 1900, respectively. Production of newsprint appeared to contribute to survival (relative to the excluded grades) for the short term, at least until 1920. By the 1920s, however, the coefficient for the newsprint dummy variable became negative. These results help to specify when production of newsprint became a liability—not until the 1920s. Diversification was negatively associated with survival and statistically significant only in the first decade; the sign of the coefficient was mixed and not significant in the remaining decades.

The elasticities of the probability of survival during each decade with respect to changes in each independent variable, shown in Table 7–10, reveal that a null hypothesis of a zero elasticity could not be rejected for most of the variables. Among the nonzero elasticities, mill age had the greatest impact on survival compared to the other variables. A 1-percent increase in mill age was associated with a 0.15 to 0.23 percent increase in the probability of survival to the next decade, a range that was fairly close to the impact on the probability of survival to 1940. The next highest elasticities were for location in the South (positive) and production of kraft paper (negative). The remaining elasticities ranged over both positive and negative values.

LENGTH OF MILL LIFETIME

A third approach to the analysis of survival is a regression model of the length of a paper mill's lifetime, measured by the total number of sample years in which a mill operated (regardless the date of entry). Mill lifetime ranged from one (for mills operating just one sample year) to five (for mills that operated from 1900 to 1940, or five sample years). The average lifetime for all mills operating anytime during the period 1900–1940 was two sample years, or at least one full decade. The average lifetime among the mills operating at the beginning of each decade is reported by region in Table 7–11 (the number of mills operating in each region is shown in parentheses). In 1900, the average lifetime of mills operating in the South exceeded that of the other regions because mills in the North and Lake regions were more likely to exit over the ensuing years than the relatively more successful southern mills. In later years, however, the average lifetimes of mills operating in the South and Pacific regions were below that of the older regions, because a larger share of mills in the new regions were entrants (with shorter lifetimes) compared to the North and Lake regions.

The regression of lifetime as a function of selected variables was evaluated for mills operating in 1900, 1910, and 1920, to capture the relationship between characteristics of the mills early in the life cycle and subsequent length of the life cycle (see Table 7–12). Ideally one would observe entrants or young mills in order to measure the initial conditions that determined subsequent mill lifetimes. The regressions in this study necessarily mix mills of all ages becasue the true mill age has not been identified. However, to the extent entrants comprised a large share of mills operating in the early decades (see Table 7–5), these regressions are reasonable tests of the relationship between early mill parameters and lifetimes.

The first regression tests the association between each independent variable—mill size, location, grades produced, and diversity—and the subsequent lifetime of the mills that were operating in 1900. The model included the following independent variables: the logarithm of mill capacity; dummy variables for location in the Lake, South, or Pacific regions; dummy variables for the production of newsprint, writing, wrap, or kraft papers; and the number of paper grades produced. The dummy variables measure the marginal effect of location relative to the North and the marginal effect of grades relative to sanitary or industrial grades. The regression results suggest that mill lifetime was longer the larger the mill, if the mill was located in the South, if the mill produced writing paper, and the greater the number of grades produced; lifetime was shorter if the mill was located in the Lake or Pacific regions or produced newsprint or wrap grades. The coefficients for mill size and the Lake, Pacific, and wrap paper dummy variables were statistically significant.

The regressions that are based on data observed in 1910 and 1920 indicated that the coefficients for the logarithm of capacity, and the Lake, Pacific, and writing paper dummy variables were of the same sign (and statistically significant for all but the Lake dummy variable) as found in 1900. However, the coefficient for the mill size was much smaller than in the first regression. Perhaps mill size had a smaller impact on the length of a mill's lifetime when the distribution of mill sizes had shifted above a minimum efficient scale, beyond which larger capacities no longer contributed to relative success.[12] The coefficients for the remaining variables switched signs over the period and generally were not statistically significant. The coefficient for location in the South became negative by 1920, most likely because the average age of southern mills in the later years was younger than in the established regions. (This complication was avoided in the first regression because all mills were treated as entrants in 1900.)

The elasticities based on these regression results are shown in Table 7–13. For the ordinary least squares method of regression, elasticities are calculated by:

(regression coefficient) (sample mean of independent variable) / (sample mean of mill lifetime).

The elasticities were highest for location in the Pacific region (negative), followed by production of writing paper (positive), production of wrap (negative), mill size (positive), and location in the Lake region (negative), in descending order. The remaining elasticities ranged from negative to positive values, so the null hypothesis that the independent variable had no effect on mill lifetime could not be rejected.

MILL GROWTH

Mill growth may be measured by the percentage change in paper capacity over time.[13] Mill growth over decade intervals was estimated by the ratio of the paper capacity at the end of the decade relative to capacity at the beginning of the decade. Because mill growth can be calculated only for mills that have survived each decade, the sample is about half the size of the total population of mills that operated in each sample year. Moreover, since only surviving mills can be used in this analysis, the regression estimates may reflect a sample-selection bias due to the exclusion of mills that failed each decade. Because failure rates were higher the younger and smaller the mill, data drawn from survivors may underrepresent relatively new, small mills and bias the findings of mill growth in relation to mill age and mill size. Correction for a censored sample requires a two-stage estimation that accounts for the probability of remaining in the sample (Maddala 1983). However, estimating the model with standard sample-selection model techniques was not successful due to numerical difficulties.[14]

The distribution of decade growth rates is shown in Table 7–14 for the four decades between 1900 and 1940. The average decade growth was highest in the first decade (up 70 percent), then stabilized at between 40 and 50 percent each decade during the 1910s and 1920s, and then fell to 19 percent during the 1930s. The total number of mills that were included in the statistics ranged from 422 during 1900–1910 to 514 during 1930–1940.

The bulk of surviving mills each decade increased paper capacity over the ten-year period. From 50 to 66 percent of mills reported higher capacities at the end of a given decade. The next largest group of mills were those that made no change in capacity between sample years; from 20 to 40 percent of mills reported no growth in capacity over a given decade. Finally, about 10 percent of mills reduced capacity over a given decade (usually by dismantling equipment from the mill, but in some cases, separate plants at the same site were closed). Table 7–14 also reports the average paper capacity at the beginning of each decade for each category of mills. Mills that maintained capacity were the smallest on average of the three groups of mills each decade. In three of the four decades examined, the growing mills on average were smaller than the mills that had cut capacity during the same decade. (During the 1920s, the average sizes of the growing and the shrinking mills were nearly equal at the beginning of the decade.)

Table 7–15 summarizes the results of a linear regression model (ordinary least squares) of mill growth as a function of mill size, age, location, grades of paper produced, and diversity. The model includes the logarithm of paper capacity; age; dummy variables for all regions except the North; dummy variables for newsprint, writing, wrap, and kraft papers (excluding sanitary and industrial grades); and the number of grades produced.[15]

Mill growth was negatively associated with mill size and mill age each year (coefficients were statistically significant in the first two decades for mill size, and in the second and fourth decades for mill age). The size of the coefficients for size and age declined over the period, possibly because of the effect of a shift in the distribution of mills above the minimum efficient scale over time and because the range of the mill age estimates widened over the period.

Dummy variables were included for mills located in the Lake, South, and Pacific regions, and the coefficients for these variables can be interpreted as marginal effects of location in each of these regions relative to location in the North (the excluded dummy variable). Almost all of these regional coefficients were positive, which indicates that growth was higher if mills were located outside the North. The coefficients generally were higher for locations in the South and Pacific regions than for the Lake region, in all decades except 1910–1920 (when the coefficient for the South was negative but not statistically significant). The generally higher coefficients for the new regions are consistent with the emergence of these regions in this period, when mill growth was more rapid than in the established regions.

Dummy variables for four paper grades were included in the regressions, and the coefficients indicate the marginal effect of these grades on growth relative to production of the excluded grades (sanitary and industrial papers). Production of newsprint had a negative contribution to growth, as did writing paper in the last three decades, but only one coefficient for each of these grades was statistically significant. Slower growth among newsprint mills was consistent with the displacement of domestic production by imported newsprint. The coefficient for wrap and board grades initially was positive for two decades and then negative but was never statistically significant. Production of kraft paper had a positive coefficient in two out of three regressions but was statistically significant only in the 1910s.

The coefficient for the number of papers produced was positive in three of the four decades (and statistically significant during the 1920s). This suggests that diversification contributed to faster growth, possibly because these mills could anticipate more stable future production if sales of different grades of paper were offsetting (negatively correlated).

The elasticities that are reported in Table 7–16 reveal that location in the Pacific had the greatest impact on mill growth (positive), followed by mill age (negative), production of newsprint (negative), mill size (negative), and location in the Lake region (positive). The remaining elastistics were inconclusive because of mixed negative and positive coefficients.

SUMMARY

The study of mill entry, exit, and survival provides insight into the process of industry growth and relocation during the period 1900–1940. Failure rates for mills entering each decade were highest during their first decade of operations. The number of entrants during each decade declined over time, especially following the Great Depression. As a result, entrants comprised a declining share of industry capacity over the period. Although the number of entrants to the North remained the highest of all the regions, entry to the region slowed over time. The relocation of the industry was accomplished by the net exit of northern mills (and Lake region mills during the 1930s), while the Southern and Pacific regions experienced net entry.

The statistical analysis of survival and growth shows that the probability of failure and mill growth generally were negatively associated with mill size and age. In addition, the length of a mill's lifetime increased with mill size. These results are consistent with a number of empirical studies that report that survival rates increased with firm age and firm size in large interindustry samples (e.g., Churchill 1955; Evans 1987a and 1987b; Dunne, Roberts, and Samuelson 1989). Moreover, these results contribute an industry case study of the importance of firm size and age, based on a complete size distribution of firms.

These results concerning age and size effects have important implications for both recent dynamic models of firm growth as well as traditional models. The finding that the probability of survival increased with age is consistent with the theory of firm learning developed by Jovanovic (1982). The role of firm size in survival is indirect support for hypotheses of the efficiency of large-scale plants (Caves and Barton 1990). The observed correlation between growth and size contradicts stochastic models of firm growth, which view differences in firm size to be determined by random factors (Scherer and Ross 1990, 141–46). These models assume that firm growth will be independent of firm size, known as Gibrat's Law, because each firm faces the same probability distribution of growth rates. However, the directory data are insufficient to distinguish alternative hypotheses for size effects, such as the migration of profitable firms to larger sizes, differences in managerial ability, or a higher cost of capital for small firms (Marcus 1967; Keeley 1984; Caves and Barton 1990; Scherer and Ross 1990).

The study also contributes results that are specific to the paper industry. Paper mill survival was positively associated with location in the South in both the short-term and long-term survival regressions. This finding is consistent with the claim that favorable southern wages and pulpwood prices explain the relocation of production to that region once pulping technology enabled the use of the southern pine. Production of newsprint appeared to reduce the chance of survival in the second half of the period studied, probably because domestic producers were being displaced by imported Canadian newsprint at that time. There was some evidence that diversification in paper grades reduced the probability of survival and the length of a mill's lifetime (after controlling for mill size), which points to the potential risks of spreading resources (managerial and marketing) across more than one market.

Mill growth was positively associated with location outside the North, and the marginal effect of location in the South was greater than in the other non-North locations by the second half of the period. Production of newsprint was associated with slower growth (the evidence was strongest in the 1920s), but the results concerning paper grades were generally inconclusive. Diversification promoted growth in the regression results for the 1920s, but the results for other years were inconclusive.

NOTES

1. Limited information on accounting profits from other sources, such as annual reports or *Moody's Manual of Investments*, has not been included in the study because it is available for only a small sample of firms in this period and because it would require an adjustment for the measurement of accounting and economic profits (e.g., see Stigler 1963).

2. In alternative models of firm growth, growth is not a function of age; growth may be random, or in response to action by management, where in either case time (age) is not relevant to the firm's performance.

3. No distinction has been made between liquidations and mills that changed ownership following merger or acquisition. In the latter case, a plant may remain open;

since it is operated under new management, however, this study defines that event as an exit. Other cases that were treated as exits included mills destroyed by fire, converted to other uses, or leased out to other firms. Idle mills were not considered exits because the interruption in production may have been temporary.

4. For a more detailed discussion of changes in vertical integration over the period see Chapter 5, especially Table 5–8.

5. This analysis follows Dunne, Roberts, and Samuelson (1988, 502–3).

6. Feller offers this explanation for the case of slower diffusion of new cotton textile technology among northern firms (Feller 1966).

7. The few mills that switched between vertical integration and specialization were treated as entrants (if they were pulp mills in the previous decade) or exits (if they became pulp mills) because specialized pulp mills were excluded from the analysis. However, the impact on the statistics was negligible. For statistics of entry and exit that include pulp mills, see Table 4–15.

8. Nine of the exits in the Pacific during the period 1900–1940 (one in 1905, five in 1914, and five in the 1930s) are explained by the following mergers: the Crown Paper Co. and the Columbia River Paper Co. merged to form the Crown Columbia River Paper Co. in 1905; the Crown Columbia Pulp and Paper Co. absorbed the Floriston Pulp and Paper Co. in 1912 (and changed the corporate name to the Crown Columbia Paper Co.); the Crown Columbia Paper Co., the Lebanon Paper Co., and the Willamette Pulp and Paper Co. merged to form the Crown Willamette Paper Co. in 1914, which became a subsidiary of the Crown Zellerbach Corp. in 1928 (see Lockwood, *250 Years of Papermaking in America*, 1940, 89–90).

9. This result suggests that the error term from the regression model for vertical integration was not associated with survival, because the error term was the information from the vertical integration variable not accounted for by the other independent variables.

10. Exclusion of the many American Writing Paper mills each year had little effect on the results, so this one company did not dominate the association between writing papers and survival.

11. For the derivation of this elasticity calculation, see Kane (1988, 92).

12. The role of a threshold size in the decision to vertically integrate was discussed in Chapter 6.

13. Only internal growth is considered; external growth would include the acquisition of new or existing facilities at other sites. This section could be expanded to account for mills that experienced changes in their multiple-plant status (and the amount of capacity added in this manner), which was analyzed in Chapter 4.

14. The sample-selection model was not reported because of numerical problems with the computation of standard errors.

15. Models that included squared terms for mill size and age and an interactive term between the two variables were investigated, following Evans (1987a and 1987b). However, these non-linear models did not produce statistically significant results, possibly because the range of mill age was limited to estimates of the number of decades in operation instead of number of years.

Table 7–1
Survival Rates of Pulp and Paper Mills by Decade

	1900	1910	1920	1930	1940
No. mills	879	874	877	874	789
Integrated	148	175	184	182	164
Paper only	624	627	626	636	579
Pulp only	107	72	67	56	46
Survived to 1940	19%	29%	43%	64%	100%
Survived to following decade	54%	59%	62%	64%	n.a.

Source: Compiled by the author from Lockwood's Directory of the Paper and Allied Trades.

Table 7–2
Comparison of Mills That Survived and Failed Before 1940, by Decade

	1900		1910		1920		1930	
	Survivors	Failures	Survivors	Failures	Survivors	Failures	Survivors	Failures
No. mills	165	714	252	622	375	502	560	314
Integrated	53	95	74	101	99	85	127	55
Paper only	105	519	168	459	261	365	408	228
Pulp only	7	100	10	62	15	52	25	31
Ave. paper capacity (thou. lbs/day)	43.4	25.0	71.9	44.5	96.0	65.2	141.5	89.0
Ave. pulp capacity (thou. lbs/day)	79.6	47.9	133.5	87.2	163.5	99.1	216.1	157.6
Ave. population (thou.)	29.0	40.8	32.3	33.5	34.9	22.3	53.7	85.1
Percent of mills:								
Newsprint	16%	11%	12%	9%	10%	8%	6%	9%
Book & writing	43	24	39	22	35	25	32	26
Wrap & board	56	75	53	71	58	62	58	58
Kraft	0	0	2	2	6	5	10	11
Sanitary	2	1	3	3	4	5	7	7
Industrial	11	11	9	18	15	17	21	24
Groundwood pulp	66%	78%	63%	80%	58%	74%	48%	67%
Soda pulp	20	9	21	8	20	8	15	8
Sulphite pulp	39	25	45	32	47	31	43	33
Sulphate pulp	0	0	1	2	8	8	19	13
Diversified product	24%	17%	17%	22%	24%	18%	28%	26%

Table 7-3

Comparison of Mills That Survived and Failed During Each Decade
(Mean Values at Beginning of Each Decade)

| | 1900-1910 | | 1910-1920 | | 1920-1930 | | 1930-1940 | |
	Survived Decade	Exits	Survived Decade	Exits	Survived Decade	Exits	Survived Decade	Exits
No. mills	474	405	519	355	545	332	560	314
Integrated	99	49	129	46	138	46	127	55
Paper Only	335	289	353	274	374	252	408	228
Pulp Only	39	67	37	35	33	34	25	31
Ave. paper capacity (thou. lbs/day)	34.0	22.0	62.2	38.8	88.3	62.9	141.5	89.0
Percent of paper mills:								
Newsprint	14%	9%	12%	6%	10%	7%	6%	9%
Book & writing	35	19	36	14	33	22	32	26
Wrap & board	63	82	58	77	58	64	58	58
Kraft	0	0	2	3	6	5	10	11
Sanitary	2	0	2	4	4	6	7	7
Industrial	13	9	14	17	17	16	21	24
Vertically integrated	23%	14%	27%	14%	27%	15%	24%	19%

Source: Compiled by the author from Lockwood's Directory of the Paper and Allied Trades.

Table 7–4

Number of Paper Mills Started and Subsequent Failures by Decade

	Period of Entry					
	Before 1900	1910 Cohort	1920 Cohort	1930 Cohort	1940 Cohort	
Paper mills entering:	772	369	329	306	210	
Mills exiting during each decade:						Total Exits
1900-1910	339	--	--	--	--	339
1910-1920	119	202	--	--	--	321
1920-1930	85	58	155	--	--	298
1930-1940	75	24	58	128	--	285
Total exits before 1940:	618	284	213	128	--	
Operating in 1940:	154	85	116	178	210	

Source: Compiled by the author from Lockwood's Directory of the Paper and Allied Trades.

Table 7–5

Survival Rates, Market Shares, and Average Mill Sizes of Entry Cohorts by Decade

	1900	1910	1920	1930	1940
Number of Paper Mills and Percent Surviving to Next Decade					
1900 Mills	772	433	314	229	154
	(.56)	(.73)	(.73)	(.67)	
1910 Entry Cohorts		369	167	109	85
		(.45)	(.65)	(.78)	
1920 Entry Cohorts			329	174	116
			(.53)	(.67)	
1930 Entry Cohorts				306	178
				(.58)	
1940 Entry Cohorts					210
Market Shares					
1900 Mills	1.00	.52	.36	.22	.16
1910 Entry Cohorts		.48	.26	.20	.14
1920 Entry Cohorts			.38	.22	.15
1930 Entry Cohorts				.36	.26
1940 Entry Cohorts					.29
Ave. Size of Surviving Mills Relative to Industry Average					
1900 Mills	1.00	.95	.92	.78	.77
1910 Entry Cohorts		1.06	1.26	1.45	1.18
1920 Entry Cohorts			.95	1.05	.94
1930 Entry Cohorts				.97	1.09
1940 Entry Cohorts					1.05

Source: Compiled by the author from Lockwood's Directory of the Paper and Allied Trades.

Table 7–6

Regional Entry, Exit, and Survival of Paper Mills by Decade

	1900-1910	1910-1920	1920-1930	1930-1940
Entrants (by end of decade)				
North	225	202	153	107
Lake	120	90	93	59
South	15	21	35	31
Pacific	9	16	25	13
Exits (before end of decade)				
North	219	224	196	173
Lake	101	78	82	78
South	7	10	12	18
Pacific	12	9	8	15
Stays (entire decade)				
North	315	316	322	301
Lake	103	145	153	168
South	11	16	25	42
Pacific	4	4	12	22

Source: Compiled by the author from Lockwood's Directory of the Paper and Allied Trades.

Table 7–7
Logit Regression of Probability of Survival to 1940

	1900	1910	1920	1930
Constant	-2.59***	-1.85***	-2.07***	-1.22***
	(-6.69)	(-4.61)	(-5.75)	(-3.48)
Log(Cap)	.44***	.36***	.38***	.41***
	(4.66)	(4.37)	(5.08)	(5.67)
Age	(a)	.63***	.30***	.21***
		(3.58)	(3.36)	(3.11)
Lake	-.14	.11	-.07	-.01
	(-.64)	(.60)	(.41)	(-.06)
South	.93*	.65	.44	.34
	(1.79)	(1.43)	(1.22)	(1.00)
Pacific	-1.42	-.60	-.82	-.29
	(-1.34)	(-.70)	(-1.47)	(-.77)
News	-.10	.55	-.29	-1.05***
	(-.24)	(1.44)	(-.86)	(-3.01)
Writing	.60*	.98***	.27	-.01
	(1.77)	(3.42)	(1.18)	(-.04)
Wrap	-.36	.11	-.03	-.21
	(-1.05)	(.39)	(-.11)	(-.99)
Kraft	(b)	.71	-.08	-.42
		(1.15)	(-.21)	(-1.37)
No. of Papers	.04	-.87***	.09	.13
	(.12)	(-3.18)	(.44)	(.71)
No. obs.	759	768	768	798

Notes: The dependent variable is the natural log of [p/(1-p)], where p is the probability that a paper mill survives to 1940. The asymptotic t-statistics are reported in parentheses.
a Estimated age was the same for all mills in 1900.
b Kraft was not produced in 1900.

* Significant at the 10 percent level.
** Significant at the 5 percent level.
*** Significant at the 1 percent level.

169

Table 7–8
Elasticities from Logit Regression of Probability of Survival to 1940

Variable	Range of Elasticities		
Capacity	.148	to	.356
Age	.098	to	.250
Lake	-.113	to	.078
South	.753	to	.915
Pacific	-1.150	to	-.104
News	-.081	to	.775
Writing	-.004	to	.741
Wrap	-.444	to	.078
Kraft	-.151	to	.011
No. of Papers	-.757	to	.064

Notes: The elasticities represent the percentage change in the probability of survival to 1940 with respect to a 1 percent increase in the independent variable (or presence of, in the case of dummy variables). Calculated from regression coefficients shown in Table 7-7 and evaluated at the sample means.

Table 7–9
Logit Regression of Probability of Survival to Next Decade

	1900-1910	1910-1920	1920-1930
Constant	.22	-1.20***	-1.36***
	(.68)	(-3.18)	(-3.64)
Log(Cap)	-.29***	.34***	.35***
	(-3.71)	(4.24)	(4.49)
Age	(a)	.99***	.41***
		(5.92)	(4.39)
Lake	.54***	.21	-.15
	(2.96)	(1.10)	(-.83)
South	.08	.62	.38
	(.16)	(1.29)	(.98)
Pacific	1.58***	-1.17*	-.33
	(2.61)	(-1.67)	(-.63)
News	.33	.62	-.40
	(.91)	(1.58)	(-1.14)
Writing	-.13	.95***	.18
	(-.04)	(3.51)	(.72)
Wrap	.95***	-.23	-.10
	(3.19)	(-.94)	(-.45)
Kraft	(b)	-.48	-.20
		(-.83)	(-.50)
No. of Papers	-.48*	-.16	.28
	(-1.88)	(-.67)	(1.24)
No. obs.	759	768	769

Notes: The dependent variable is the natural log of $[p/(1-p)]$, where p is the probability that a paper mill survives to the next decade. The asymptotic t-statistics are reported in parentheses.
[a] Estimated age was the same for all mills in 1900.
[b] Kraft was not produced in 1900.

* Significant at the 10 percent level.
** Significant at the 5 percent level.
*** Significant at the 1 percent level.

Table 7–10
Elasticities from Logit Regression of Probability of Survival to Next Decade

Variable	Range of Elasticities		
Capacity	-.133	to	.140
Age	.151	to	.227
Lake	-.023	to	.248
South	.037	to	.254
Pacific	-.480	to	.727
News	-.152	to	.254
Writing	-.060	to	.390
Wrap	-.094	to	.437
Kraft	-.197	to	-.076
No. of Papers	-.271	to	.133

Notes: The elasticities represent the percentage change in the probability of survival to next decade with respect to a 1 percent increase in the independent variable (or presence of, in the case of dummy variables). Calculated from regression coefficients shown in Table 7-9 and evaluated at the sample means.

Table 7–11
Mill Lifetime by Region
(Average Number of Sample Years Mill Operated)

	Average Lifetime Among Mills Operating In:				
	1900	1910	1920	1930	1940
NORTH					
Ave. lifetime	2.487	2.852	3.073	3.101	2.897
No. mills	(534)	(540)	(519)	(476)	(408)
LAKE					
Ave. lifetime	2.397	2.901	3.085	2.951	2.758
No. mills	(204)	(223)	(235)	(246)	(227)
SOUTH					
Ave. lifetime	2.889	2.923	2.838	2.450	2.055
No. mills	(18)	(26)	(37)	(60)	(73)
PACIFIC					
Ave. lifetime	1.563	2.000	2.200	2.054	1.886
No. mills	(16)	(13)	(20)	(37)	(35)

Source: Compiled by the author from Lockwood's Directory of the Paper and Allied Trades.

Table 7–12
Linear Regression of Length of Paper Mill Lifetime

Variables	Mills Operating in: 1900	1910	1920
Constant	1.83***	2.36***	2.51**
	(8.24)	(10.68)	(11.94)
Log(Cap)	.29***	.18***	.10**
	(5.42)	(3.65)	(2.20)
Lake	-.27**	-.06	-.10
	(-2.09)	(-.54)	(-.88)
South	.26	.30	-.11
	(.73)	(1.03)	(-.45)
Pacific	-.95***	-.73*	-.96***
	(-2.49)	(-1.77)	(-2.92)
News	-.11	.41*	.08
	(-.45)	(1.79)	(.38)
Writing	.22	1.01***	.73***
	(1.05)	(6.15)	(5.14)
Wrap	-.66***	.000	-.001
	(-3.22)	(.003)	(-.01)
Kraft	(a)	-.19	.11
		(-.52)	(.47)
No. of Papers	.26	-.30**	.01
	(1.53)	(-2.04)	(.10)
R^2	.12	.12	.08
No. observations	759	768	769

Notes: The dependent variable is the number of sample years (at decade intervals) in which mill operated. The t-statistics are reported in parentheses.
a Kraft was not produced in 1900.

* Significant at the 10 percent level.
** Significant at the 5 percent level.
*** Significant at the 1 percent level.

Table 7–13
Elasticities from Linear Regression of Mill Lifetime

Variable	Range of Elasticities		
Capacity	.033	to	.118
Lake	-.110	to	-.021
South	-.036	to	.106
Pacific	-.387	to	-.256
News	-.045	to	.144
Writing	.090	to	.354
Wrap	-.269	to	-.000
Kraft	-.067	to	.036
No. of Papers	-.129	to	.130

Notes: The elasticities represent the percentage change in mill lifetime with respect to a 1 percent increase in the independent variable (or presence of, in the case of dummy variables). Calculated from regression coefficients shown in Table 7-12 and evaluated at the sample means.

Table 7–14
Distribution of Decade Paper Capacity Growth Rate
(End of Decade Capacity/Beginning of Decade Capacity)

Decade	Ave. Capacity Growth	Total Mills	Increased Capacity		No Change		Decreased Capacity	
			No. Mills	Ave. Capacity	No. Mills	Ave. Capacity	No. Mills	Ave. Capacity
1900-10	1.70	422	280	33.2	86	18.3	56	63.6
1910-20	1.42	463	262	68.1	155	44.8	46	88.1
1920-30	1.48	497	305	103.8	145	51.3	47	102.5
1930-40	1.19	514	258	161.1	213	107.4	43	201.6

Source: Compiled by the author from Lockwood's Directory of the Paper and Allied Trades.
Note: Average capcacity is thousands of pounds per day at the beginning of each decade.

173

Table 7–15
Linear Regression of Paper Mill Growth

	1900-1910	1910-1920	1920-1930	1930-1940
Constant	1.56***	2.19***	1.29***	1.30***
	(5.73)	(10.19)	(4.91)	(17.45)
Log(Cap)	-.15***	-.16***	-.06	-.02
	(-2.25)	(-3.72)	(-1.10)	(-1.24)
Age	(a)	-.26***	-.10	-.04***
		(-2.65)	(-1.45)	(-2.64)
Lake	.18	.11	.29***	.01
	(1.08)	(1.10)	(2.39)	(.30)
South	.26	-.10	.68***	.18***
	(.62)	(-.38)	(2.73)	(2.99)
Pacific	.43	1.54***	.79**	.14*
	(.61)	(3.18)	(2.04)	(1.71)
News	-.27	-.05	-.61***	-.11
	(-.95)	(-.28)	(-2.54)	(-1.52)
Writing	.02	-.08	-.22	-.09**
	(.08)	(-.54)	(-1.31)	(-1.99)
Wrap	.21	.002	-.13	-.05
	(.89)	(.02)	(-.80)	(-1.24)
Kraft	(b)	.78**	-.36	.03
		(2.04)	(-1.34)	(.44)
No. of Papers	.32	-.04	.48***	.04
	(1.58)	(-.29)	(3.13)	(1.19)
R²	.04	.08	.05	.08
No. obs.	421	458	493	512

Notes: The dependent variable is growth in paper capacity, measured by the ratio of the end of decade and beginning of decade capacities. The t-statistics are reported in parentheses.
a Estimated mill age was the same for all mills in 1900.
b Kraft was not produced in 1900.

* Significant at the 10 percent level.
** Significant at the 5 percent level.
*** Significant at the 1 percent level.

Table 7–16
Elasticities from Linear Regression of Mill Growth

Variable	Range of Elasticities		
Capacity	-.113	to	-.017
Age	-.456	to	-.048
Lake	.008	to	.195
South	-.070	to	.458
Pacific	.118	to	1.083
News	-.411	to	-.035
Writing	-.148	to	.118
Wrap	-.088	to	.124
Kraft	-.243	to	.549
No. of Papers	-.035	to	.413

Notes: The elasticities represent the percentage change in capacity between the beginning and end of each decade with respect to a 1 percent increase in the independent variable (or presence of, in the case of dummy variables). Calculated from regression coefficients shown in Table 7-15 and evaluated at the sample means.

8

Conclusion

This study of the U.S. pulp and paper industry during the period 1900–1940 has contributed insight into many of the issues that have been raised by previous pulp and paper industry analysts. As one of the oldest and most competitive of U.S. manufacturing sectors, the paper industry has received much attention by business historians and economists. One of the most striking features of this industry's history is the relocation of production from the North to the South during this period, which is recognized as second in magnitude only to the well-known cotton textile relocation of about the same period. New data and modern methods of economic analysis have been applied to this important period of industry relocation to learn how production shifts from one region to another, why firms choose different forms of organization, and what contributes to firm survival in this period of transition.

In particular, use of *Lockwood's Directory of the Paper and Allied Trades* to identify each pulp and paper mill operating in this period has advanced our understanding of the process of relocation of the industry to the South and Pacific Coast, the structure of the industry, and various aspects of paper firm behavior. Although other studies have utilized the directories, this research is unique in that individual mills are followed over time to create a data base that allows both cross-section and time-series analysis. One of the most powerful features of this approach is that firm entry and exit, as well as the life cycles of firms, can be measured. Common assumptions about the pulp and paper industry are evaluated in light of these measures, especially by analysis of paper mill entry and survival. This research also has application to broader issues of industrial organization because it provides a case study that addresses general questions about firm behavior, including industry relocation, entry and exit, vertical integration, and firm survival and growth.

The study also offers original statistics that have been calculated from government sources, primarily the *Census of Manufactures* of the period. These statistics complement the directory data with information about regional production, capacity utilization, and cost data, which were not available from the directories. The census data were shown to be consistent with the directory data by comparing aggregated industry figures, such as number of mills or total capacity; this provided a check of the reliability of the directory data base. Data collected from issues of *Moody's Manual of Investments* provided additional details about selected firms that enhanced the evidence gathered from the directories.

The focus of the study is the process of relocation of the industry. The question of relocation was approached a number of ways. The directories were used to identify entrants to each region during the height of the relocation, the 1920s and 1930s. Entrants that built new mills were distinguished from those that took over existsing plants, and entrants that were branches of established firms were identified. Entry to the new regions, especially the South, was characterized by building of new plants (addition of capacity) and by a larger role for branch plants compared to the established regions. Entry and exit statistics for each decade also showed a higher rate of net exit of mills in the older regions, especially the North, than in the expanding regions. I was able to confirm Fuchs' (1962) observation that industry relocation is generally a matter of faster growth in the new region rather than a physical transfer of capacity from the old to the new region.

Other relocation issues were addressed by summarizing the directory data and other statistics to compare the regional pulp and paper industries each decade. Product specialization, rate of capacity and mill growth, vertical integration, and market concentration were compared across regions to measure the evolution of the industry in each region. The directory-based profiles of each region were consistent with a technology-induced relocation, since the regions specialized in paper grades that utilized local timber resources. Specialization in high grades by mills in the older regions as opposed to southern specialization in kraft grades, a twentieth-century pulping process, marked this period of relocation.

A number of traditional assumptions about the pulp and paper industry were not well supported by data drawn from the directories. Market concentration ratios were generally low, whether based on national, regional, or product markets (with the exception of early regional markets in the South and Pacific regions prior to relocation of the industry to these areas). Although a relatively high level of concentration was found in newsprint production, the significant import competition in this market mitigates concerns about market power. Moreover, evidence of firm conduct, which was drawn from secondary sources, is consistent with competitive markets in this industry. Assertions by many economists that high barriers to entry characterize the industry were shown to be mistakenly based on net entry figures. Instead, the data reveal a high rate of firm turnover each decade and vigorous entry and exit rates that are inconsistent with barriers to entry. The survivorship technique suggests that economies of scale were achieved at plant sizes that represented small shares of the market each decade. On balance, there is little support for the traditional oligopoly view of this industry.

Other structural issues that were documented by the directories include the shift to the corporate form over the period (in contrast to the continued importance of individual ownership among U.S. manufacturing sectors), the incidence of multiplant ownership, and accounting for multiple-mill ownership in measures of top-firm concentration ratios. Control of large market shares by consolidations such as International Paper and American Writing Paper Co. are shown to have been temporary at best; multiplant firms generally represented small market shares when measured in the context of appropriate industry or paper market definitions.

The directories provide an unambiguous measure of vertical integration of pulp and paper production processes. Integration was identified by reports of pulp and paper capacity in each mill's directory entry. The data were used to analyze the decision to integrate pulp with paper production, as well as the extent of integration, measured by the ratio of pulp-to-paper capacities at each mill. The probability that a mill would integrate and the ratio of pulp-to-paper capacities were positively associated with the regional concentration of pulp and paper markets, mill size, and the production of standardized grades (newsprint and kraft papers). Support was found for a transaction-cost explanation for vertical integration, based on the role of regional market concentration. Mills located in the South and the West were more likely to integrate in order to avoid the costs of market transactions in these developing regions, where bargaining problems associated with exchanges among a small number of traders were likely to be greater than in the established regions. These results are consistent with the growing number of modern studies of transaction-cost models of vertical integration.

Moreover, the analysis indicated that once established, few mills altered their integrated status. Instead, adaptation to the decline in southern and western concentration ratios over time occurred through a lower propensity to integrate pulp and paper production among new entrants to these regions, rather than through changes in encumbent mills. Entrants also reported lower average ratios of pulp-to-paper capacity each decade. However, once established, integrated mills did alter the ratio of pulp-to-paper capacities over decade-long periods of operation. The pulp-to-paper ratio was more likely to rise the lower the initial ratio at the beginning of the decade. Thus, mills appeared to be adapting over time by approaching self-sufficiency in pulp production, once the mill had entered as an integrated plant.

Integration into the ownership of timberland was documented for a sample of paper firms that reported timberland assets in the financial reports found in *Moody's Manual of Investments* of the 1930s. The data from Moody's was merged with directory information to analyze the decision to integrate backwards into timberland. Timberland ownership was shown to be associated with integration with pulping, which suggests that firms owned timberland to supply timber for their own pulping needs (and avoid market transactions for pulpwood). Other features of timberland owners included production of standardized grades and paper mill size, both factors that are also associated with integration into pulping.

Other aspects of vertical integration in paper mills that provided insight into that form of ownership were found by comparing integration between one-mill and multiple-mill towns, integration in multiplant firms, and survival between integrated and specialized mills. A higher share of integrated mills were located in single-mill towns compared to nonintegrated mills. Isolation appeared to promote vertical integration, which is consistent with the transaction-cost view that mills were self-sufficient when the number of traders in the local market were few. Interestingly, the mills of multiplant firms were not necessarily uniformly integrated or nonintegrated. Instead, integration of the individual mills of a given firm was associated with the grade produced by each mill. Multiplant firms with a diversified product chose to integrate the mills that produced standardized grades (newsprint and kraft) and purchased market pulp for the higher-grade mils. Finally, integrated mills revealed higher rates of survival than nonintegrated mills, according to simple statistics of survival as well as survivorship tests. However, the reasons for better survival of integrated mills could not be investigated in the regression analysis of firm survival, because the same set of independent variables in the models of mill survival were those that were associated with vertical integration (mill size, grade, and location).

The observations of mill life cycles that were drawn from the directories permitted an analysis of mill survival and growth during each decade between 1900 and 1940. The probability of mill failure and the growth of mill capacity were found to be negatively associated with mill age and mill size, which is consistent with many previous studies of interindustry samples. These results provide a case study that lends support for recent models of firm survival and growth (e.g., Jovanovic 1982) and provide little confirmation of older stochastic models based on Gibrat's Law.

The analysis of mill survival and growth was also relevant to the issue of relocation. In addition to age and size effects, survival and growth was found to be associated with location in the South (and more generally, location outside the North). This result is consistent with a neoclassical model of relocation, in which the relocation is explained by conditions that promote greater profitability in the new regions. In the absence of information about profits, however, observed survival and growth are taken as indirect measures of firm viability. (Balance sheet and income statements were available only for the relatively small sample of firms listed in Moody's; the directories did not provide cost or profit data.) The association between survival (and growth) and location in the South lends support to the argument that southern advantages, such as lower factor costs (documented by secondary sources) led to the migration of production to the South. The continued shift of production to the South that is revealed in current industry statistics confirms the economic advantages of that region; today southern mills produce the majority of domestic pulp, paper, and paperboard.

While the specific results of this study apply to the pulp and paper industry, the findings have application to general theories of industry relocation and issues in industrial organization. Use of industry directories provides the opportunity to extend this research to other industries and to contribute to our understanding of the process of industry relocation. This case study points to the importance of considering highly disaggregated data, such as information from directories, rather than relying on possibly misleading traditional sources of aggregated industry information. Individual firm or plant data are required to address issues of entry and survival and to analyze how relocation proceeds. The study of differences across firms in a given industry, and how these differences evolve over time, seems critical in gaining a better understanding of firm behavior.

Appendix A: Papermaking Technology

This appendix reviews the technology of papermaking from both a historical and modern perspective. It is designed for the reader who is unacquainted with how paper is made and requires a general background to aid in understanding the economics of the twentieth-century pulp and paper industry.

The basic method of papermaking involves passing a solution of paper stock (pulp) through a screen, which forms a mat of fibers as the water is removed. The fibers of the pulp stock will bond because of the properties of cellulose molecules, which form hydrogen bonds when the fibers are mixed with water and allowed to dry. The cellulose fibers that have been used to create paper include wood, cotton, flax, straw, and other types of vegetation. Fiber is also recycled from old newspapers, magazines, and other waste papers. Pulp and paper mills operate on a continuous, 24-hour basis.

This appendix summarizes a brief history of papermaking and describes the technical aspects of pulp and paper technology. This summary is based on sections from the Lockwood Trade Journal's study, *250 Years of Papermaking in America* (1940), the studies of the paper industry by the economists Stevenson (1940) and Guthrie (1950), and technical reference books by Whitney (1984) and Weidenmuller (1984). The specific references to these works are omitted in the following discussion. I also benefitted from "hands-on" experience in handmade papermaking with Professor Joe Brown in his laboratories at the Rochester Institute of Technology in Rochester, New York, and from a tour of the Flower City Tissue Mills in Rochester, New York, guided by owner Bill Shafer.

THE HISTORY OF PAPERMAKING

The origin of modern papermaking has been traced to China in the year 105 A.D. (The earlier development of papyrus by the Egyptians is not considered a form of paper because it is built up of layers rather than a bonding of discrete fibers. Another early nonpaper writing paper, pergament, was made from untanned animal skins and continues to be produced in limited quantities today.) The earliest papermaking materials were vegetable fibers, especially the inner bark of the mulberry tree. The pulp stock was prepared by cooking and beating the fibers in water. The first papers were made by hand, by dipping a wooden "forming frame" screen box (made from bamboo strips) into a vat of the prepared pulp stock. As the frame was lifted from the vat, the water ran off and the remaining thin layer of matted fibers created a sheet of paper. The paper was then lifted from the screen and dried, and the papermaker dipped the empty screen into the paper stock to form the next sheet of paper. Over time, the process was improved by laying each sheet of paper on a piece of wool felt, and then pressing and drying stacks of the felts on a hot surface. These steps remain the basis for the art of hand papermaking today.

By the early fifteenth century, papermaking had spread from China through Asia, Persia, Egypt, Morocco, and Europe. (The Mayans and South Sea Islanders also developed papermaking, but their discoveries never spread to other regions.) Standardized paper formats were developed and there were many paper grades in use. Old cotton and linen rags had become the main fibers used in papermaking, especially in Europe. Papermaking was finally introduced to the United States in 1690, when a German immigrant, Wilhelm Rittinghausen, built the Rittenhouse Mill in Germantown, Pennsylvania (near Philadelphia).

The development of printing in the fifteenth century caused a surge in the demand for paper, which put pressure on the limited supplies of used rags and the slow handmade method of paper production. These problems were solved centuries later with the development of the first continuous paper machine in 1799 and with the discovery of wood pulping techniques in the following century. The next sections describe each of these inventions.

INVENTION OF THE PAPER MACHINE

The first papermaking machine was invented by Nicholas Louis Robert in France in 1799. The machine was later named after the two English brothers in the stationery business, Henry and Sealy Fourdrinier, who eventually obtained the rights to the machine in return for financing its commercial development. The Fourdriniers patented an improved version of Robert's machine in England in 1807. The Fourdrinier carried pulp over an endless traveling wire screen that was mounted on a horizontal table. The fibers were matted as the water drained from the moving screen and the wet sheet was removed at the other end of the machine. The Fourdrinier was first installed in an American mill in 1827, and the first U.S.-made Fourdrinier was built in 1829. Although the basic principle of the machine has not changed since its invention, numerous improvements have been made in the Fourdrinier, primarily by increasing the width and speed of the machine. Over the past two hundred years, the widths of the largest machines have increased tenfold to about 30 feet (the largest Fourdriniers are over 30 feet long), and machine speeds have increased from 1 to 2 feet per minute on the earliest machines to 200 feet per minute by the late nineteenth century, to 1,000 feet per minute by 1940, and to more than 3,000 feet per minute today.

A second paper machine, the cylinder, was patented in England by John Dickinson in 1809. The cylinder replaced the flat wire-screen belt of the Fourdrinier with cylinders that were covered with a similar screen material. The cylinders revolved in vats of pulp, and suction forced the pulp fibers to create a sheet of paper as the water from the pulp solution passed through the screen. The wet sheet of paper was drawn on to another cylinder covered with woolen felt and then dried. Single-cylinder machines were used in the production of light-weight papers. Multi-cylinder machines, which were several cylinders operating in a series, each depositing a sheet of paper on the same woolen felt, were advantageous in the production of heavy-weight papers and paperboard. Although a lower-quality paper was produced by a cylinder machine, it was less expensive than the Fourdrinier and was competitive in the production of lower-grade papers through the twentieth century. In the first half of the twentieth century, the period studied in this book, most paperboard was produced on cylinder machines, and other grades of paper were produced on Fourdriniers. Later, the Fourdrinier dominated all grades as improvements in its design outpaced that of the cylinder. In particular, the speed of the cylinder was limited because of the centrifugal force of the revolving cylinders, while the horizontal design of the Fourdrinier avoided this constraint.

DISCOVERY OF WOOD PULPING METHODS

The earliest improvements in the preparation of pulp involved the mechanization of pulping the rags that were the primary source of fiber well into the eighteenth century. The first was the development of water-powered stampers (or hammers) that tore and washed the rags to create a pulp solution. In 1750, the Dutch introduced a cylinder beater, known as the Hollander. The Hollander beater consisted of a tub with a metal shaft fitted with knives that tore the rags. The Hollander was introduced to America in 1775; modern beaters are built on the same general principle of this early machine.

Meanwhile scientists searched for an alternative to the increasingly scarce rag as a source of pulp material. The discovery of wood pulp was instigated by the French physicist Reaumur's observations of the paperlike nests built by wasps, which led to the scientific study of wood and plant fibers used by these insects. The first commercial use of wood in paper-making was the development of groundwood pulp by the German artisan Keller in 1844. In this process, pulpwood is pressed against a grinding stone to mechanically reduce the wood to pulp fibers. Groundwood is a relatively short-fiber pulp and contains all the substances originally present in the wood, including lignin, sap, and resin. Groundwood pulp offers the advantage of a high yield (about 90 percent of the original weight of the pulpwood is contained in the pulp), but the paper produced is relatively weak because the lignin interferes with the bonding of the cellulose fibers of the pulp. Groundwood pulp is best suited to low-quality papers that are used for a short duration, such as newspaper.

To improve the quality of pulp made from wood, chemical pulping processes were developed. Chemists discovered that wood consisted of cellulose, which are the wood fibers, and lignin, which cements the fibers. The chemical processes dissolve the lignin and resins in the wood to release the fibers that are retained for the pulp stock. Chemical pulping creates a stronger paper, due to the improved bonding once the lignin is removed but at the cost of a lower yield (less than 50 percent of the original weight of the pulpwood).

Three chemical processes—soda, sulphite, and sulphate (or kraft)—were discovered in the midnineteenth century. For each of these methods, the pulpwood is first chipped (rather than ground) and then cooked or digested for several hours in a chemical solution. The oldest, the soda process, was patented by Hugh Burgess in England in 1852 and in America in 1854. The first U.S.-made soda pulp was produced by Burgess in 1855; the process was commercially viable in the United States by 1866. The wood chips were cooked in a solution of soda ash and lime dissolved in water. The soda process was named for the sodium hydroxide, or caustic soda, that was created in the cooking stage. Soda pulp was made primarily from short-fibered hardwoods, such as poplar, cottonwood gum, beech, birch, and maple. However, the harsh solution resulted in a relatively weak paper and a yield of only about 40 percent. The pulp usually was bleached and used as a filler with stronger pulps in high grades of writing and book papers.

The sulphite process digests wood chips in a solution of sulphur dioxide and calcium bisulphite. The first patent for sulphite wood pulp was awarded to an American chemist, Tilghman, in 1867 (however, earlier patents had been granted in France and the United States for sulphite straw pulping methods). The first commercial use of the sulphite process was in 1882. The sulphite process was best suited to nonresinous, long-fibered softwoods such as hemlock, spruce, balsam, and white fir; the pulp produced is light in color and easily bleached. By varying the length of the cooking period and the strength of the chemical liquor, pulps of different strengths and purity could be produced. Unbleached sulphite pulp was used in newsprint (mixed with groundwood pulp), wrapping, tissue, and paperboards. Bleached sulphite was used in high-grade papers, and a highly purified grade was used in the production of rayon and various compounds of cellulose in the twentieth century.

Sulphate is a modified version of the soda process that was developed during the 1880s by the German chemist Dahl. Sulphate mills were built in Europe in the 1880s, but sulphate pulp was not produced in America until 1909. The cooking liquor in the sulphate process is a mixture of sodium hydroxide (caustic soda) and sodium sulfide; sodium sulphate or salt cake is used in the preparation of the liquor. This process is suitable to most types of wood, including resinous varieties; southern pine, Jack pine, Douglas fir, hemlock, and spruce are used for this method. The presence of sodium sulfide shortens the cooking period and buffers the system to produce a stronger pulp. In fact, sulphate is commonly known as kraft, the German word for strong. However, the shorter cooking time leaves impurities that give the pulp a brownish color that was more difficult to bleach than the soda and sulphite pulps. Because bleaching the sulphate pulp was an expensive procedure that also weakened the fibers, most sulphate pulp was left unbleached and was restricted to use in papers where strength rather than color was most important. In the first half of the twentieth century, sulphate pulp generally was used alone to produce wrapping paper, bags, container boards, and towels, and was used with repulped wastepaper to produce other kinds of paperboards. When improvements in the bleaching of sulphate pulp became commercial, bleached sulphate was used in the manufacture of food container boards, printing and fine papers, and many other kinds of paper. Today, about 80 percent of U.S. pulp is sulphate, and about half of sulphate pulp is bleached or semibleached.

In the 1920s, a semichemical process was developed that produced a higher-yield pulp (between 60 and 90 percent) suitable for newsprint, wrapping, board and other low-grade papers. After chemical treatment (sulphite process), the softened chips are mechanically disintegrated to produce a pulp. The semichemical process is less costly than the sulphite process due to a reduced cooking time, and a stronger pulp is produced. However, sulphate was a less expensive process that offered these advantages plus wider use of wood varieties, and semichemical pulp never represented a very large share of U.S. pulp production.

STEPS IN MODERN PAPERMAKING

Preparation of pulpwood. The lumber received by the mill must be debarked in an automatic barking drum and then either ground by grinding wheels for groundwood pulp or chipped for chemical pulping. (Bark and other waste products generated at mills provide about 15 percent of the energy used in pulp and paper industry.) Pulpwood is a small-diameter wood that is too small for use as sawn timber. Both softwoods (coniferous), such as southern pine and spruce, and hardwoods (deciduous), such as birch, are used in papermaking. The softwoods have longer fibers but are more resinous; the papermaker may use a combination of both types to achieve the desired properties of paper strength and printability. The softwood fibers make the paper strong, while the hardwood fibers create a smoother finish.

In the United States, a small proportion of pulp is derived from nonwood sources, including rag, cotton, straw, and sugarcane bagasse (an important pulp fiber in India, the Philippines, and the West Indies). These raw materials, in addition to wastepaper, must be sorted and washed in preparation for pulping.

Pulping. The ground pulpwood for groundwood pulp is sorted to remove splinters and fine particles and may be bleached (but not to the same brightness as chemical pulps). Most groundwood is used at the same site and is transferred in slush form to the paper machine. For chemical grades of pulp, the chipped pulpwood must be cooked under high temperatures in a large vat known as a digester, which operates as a large steam pressure cooker. The chemicals in the cooking liquor depend on the desired properties of the pulp for papermaking. The cooking process removes the lignin, rosins, and other unwanted materials from the wood, which are washed away. The remaining cellulose fibers may be bleached in a solution of lime and chlorine, and these bleaching chemicals are then washed away. Next, pulp is mixed in a beating machine, where the fibers are "fibrillated" and "hydrated" to cause them to hang together to form paper. Other materials may be added at the beating stage, such as clay, starch, or dyes, depending on the type of paper produced. If the pulp is used on site to make paper, it is transferred to the paper mill. If the pulp is to be transported to another location or sold, it is dried and cut into sheets for shipping. Pulp is marketed and measured by weight on an "air-dry" basis, which assumes a 10 percent moisture content and a 90 percent fiber content (U.S. Tariff Commission 1938, 43).

One important aspect of the pulping stage is the recovery of chemicals that are present in the cooking liquor. The liquor is drained and condensed in evaporators, where the lignin is burned to release energy that can be utilized by the mill. (About 35 percent of all energy used in the pulp and paper industry is self-generated by mills from spent liquor.) The remaining chemicals are recovered as salts to be reused in the cooking process. Mills that utilize wastepaper recycle the old paper in various ways, depending on the type of wastepaper and the product that is produced (usually newsprint or paperboard). Recycling often requires a deinking process, to remove the ink from old newsprint or magazines.

Papermaking. The pulp stock is diluted to about 99 percent water and only about 1 percent fiber when it is dispersed across the moving screen of the paper machine. In the Fourdrinier, the pulp solution is pumped from the headbox onto a continuous moving wire mesh belt that is supported by a series of table rolls. Water is drained from the mat of fibers as the wire screen passes over rolls and suction boxes; the water is collected from below and recycled. The half-dried paper is picked off the screen and fed into a series of presses that squeeze out more water. Drying is completed by passing the sheet of paper through a series of heated cylinders. (When dried, paper still contains about 5 percent water; otherwise, paper is too brittle to handle.) Depending on the grade, the paper may be sized, coated, or calendared to smooth the paper and to achieve a desired finish. The completely formed paper is wound on a reel at the end of the machine. Operators remove the full reels, and the large rolls of finished paper are rewound and trimmed into smaller reels. The paper may be shipped in that form or may be fed to a rotary cutter where the paper is cut into sheets and packaged for shipment.

Differences in the grades of paper produced on the Fourdrinier are due primarily to the use of different types of pulp stock and to variations in the preparation of the stock. Low-grade papers and paperboard utilize un-bleached sulphate (kraft), groundwood, and wastepaper, whereas high-grade papers require bleached sulphate, sulphite, and additives such as sizing (rag pulp may be used in the finest specialty papers). Within limits, the mill can vary the grade of paper produced by altering the composition of the pulp stock and adjusting the paper machine (however, a board mill could not easily shift to the production of fine writing paper). For example, the Flower City Tissue Mills in Rochester, New York, produces different grades of wrapping tissue with the same Fourdrinier, including a high-grade jeweler's wrapping tissue that requires a carefully controlled and purified pulp stock.

Converting. Most paper is converted before it is used by the consumer. The paper mills or independent converters treat the surface of the paper by coating, embossing, or gumming, and then shape the paper into constructed products such as envelopes, bags, or container boxes. Special equipment is used to manufacture the converted products, and the process is usually completed in a single operation.

NEW TECHNOLOGY

Although the basic methods of modern papermaking have remained unchanged in over two centuries, a tremendous amount of chemical and mechanical improvements have been developed. Technological innovations today are centered on a number of issues: limited woodlands, toxic emissions, mechanical pulping techniques, recycling methods, development of alkaline papers, and improvements in paper machinery. Limited forest resources are being extended through the development of genetically improved trees, which have faster growth rates and greater resistance to disease and drought. Today four genetically superior trees are planted for every one tree that is cut down. The use of wastepaper will also help extend future sources of wood fiber. (Biotechnology is also involved in the search for microbes that can hasten the decomposition of wastepaper in landfills.)

The industry today is spending millions of dollars to research new bleaching chemistry that will reduce or avoid the creation of dioxin, a byproduct of chlorine bleaching methods. One promising alternative is the use of hydrogen peroxide instead of chlorine; another uses oxygen instead of chlorine. In an effort to reduce other chemical emissions, an alcohol-based pulping process is being developed that eliminates sulfur-containing compounds and elemental chlorine. Stricter environmental regulations will spur the industry to continue to find new methods of reducing chemical effluent. (However, at its Ticonderoga, New York, mill, International Paper is resisting efforts by environmentalists to stop chlorine bleaching. Company officials argue that dioxin and other by-products have not been proven to cause cancer, and that switching would "price their products out of the market" ["Border War Breaks Out" 1991, 5B].)

One area where the United States lags foreign producers is in the discovery of "alphabet" mechanical grades of wood pulp that are cheaper than chemical grades and less harmful to the environment. These new grades include chemi-thermomechanical pulp (CTMP), stone ground-wood (SGW), refiner mechanical pulp (RMP), and pressurized ground-wood (PGW). The new technology produces mechanical grades that are appropriate for printing and packaging grades, whereas earlier ground-wood pulp was limited to use in newsprint and other low-grade papers. Currently mechanical pulping is concentrated in Canada and Scandinavia, but U.S. mills are scheduled for operation by the end of 1990. U.S. entry into this new market is important because of the apparent advantages of these grades compared to traditional chemical grades.

Experiments with new papermaking techniques that utilize recycled wastepaper are underway. Attention is centered on newsprint and paper-board technology, because old newsprint and corrugated boxes are two of the easiest papers to recycle. A recent U.S.-Canadian joint venture between Chesapeake Corp. and Stake Technology Ltd. developed a new process known as steam explosion that is simpler and cheaper than conventional methods (Holusha 1991). The usual method of recycling wastepaper involves six separate steps that reduce the wastepaper to slush and remove the ink, before going to the bleaching and storage stages. The steam explosion method involves just one process that shreds the wastepaper and forces the material into a pressurized chamber at high heat. This treatment is enough to reduce the wastepaper to pulp. In addition, any ink becomes so dispersed that the process eliminates the deinking and bleach stages. This new method has not yet been tested in large-scale operations, however.

Another important pulping trend is the emergence of alkaline-based pulp to replace the long-dominant, acid-based methods (Evans 1985, Appendix A: 70–73). Alkaline papermaking involves the use of a neutral sizing agent with calcium carbonate as a filler instead of the traditional rosen and alum sizing system. Alkaline-based paper helps avoid a number of problems associated with alum sizing, including machine corrosion, water pollution, and poor aging qualities of the paper. The short life span of papers made with alum sizing has become a serious problem for libraries, which are coping with the yellowing and deterioration of old books that were printed on acid-based paper. The alkaline method also has improved drying properties that save energy costs for the mills. Altogether, the switch to alkaline papermaking can save from $20 to $70 per ton, depending on the mill and grade of paper produced (Westmoreland and Majmudar 1985, Appendix A: 99). *Pulp & Paper* reports that 43 paper mills are now producing alkaline-based papers, and the number is expected to keep growing ("U.S. Paper Industry" 1991, 60; Evans 1985, Appendix A: 70).

Innovations in paper machinery have focused on raising production through higher speeds rather than creating wider machinery and are available to papermakers through machine rebuilding. The most prominent technological improvement in paper machinery is the development of twin wire forming that increases the drainage capacity and speed of the Fourdrinier (OECD 1988, 220; York 1985, Appendix B: 45). Changes in headbox design (from which the pulp stock flows to the forming section) have created greater stability and contributed to higher machine speeds. Other improvements include spoiler bars inside dryers (which break up condensation that forms on the inner surface of the drums), new felt fabrics that improve the mechanics of drying the paper, and centralized control systems.

Appendix B: Methodology of Data Collection

DIRECTORY DATA

The primary data source for the book is *Lockwood's Directory of the Paper and Allied Trades*, which has been published annually since 1873 by the Lockwood Trade Journal Company. (Earlier editions were issued under alternative titles that included *Lockwood's Directory of the Paper Trade*, from 1873 through the 1880s, and *Lockwood's Directory of the Paper, Stationery and Allied Trades* from the 1890s through the 1920s.) In 1987, *Lockwood's Directory* was merged with *Post's Pulp and Paper Directory* (established in 1884) and is now published as *Lockwood-Post's Directory of the Pulp, Paper and Allied Trades*. The directory is available in two formats: a regular edition and an abbreviated traveler's edition containing only the pulp and paper mill sections.

The directories were issued in September, and the edition was dated by the year following the copyright and issue year. To collect data for mills operating at ten-year intervals from 1900 to 1940, I used the 1900–01, 1911, 1921, 1931, and 1941 editions of the directory. These editions were found at the New York Public Library, which holds a continuous series of the directories beginning with the 1900–01 edition. (After a search for nineteenth-century editions I found only two: the 1883 edition is available on microfilm from the Center for Research Libraries in Chicago and the 1886–87 edition is available at UCLA.)

The directory lists all North American pulp and paper mills that existed each year, whether operating or not. The study includes all mainland U.S.

pulp and paper mills that were operating or idle, but excludes mills that were reported to be dismantled, burned, or experimental mills. Idle mills were included to avoid treating surviving mills as failures when the mill closed temporarily. However, it turns out that only a few idle mills survived to the next decade, so that most of the idle mills were treated as failures in the analysis (except for mills that were idle in 1940). The number of idle mills varied widely with the sample year: 51 in 1900, 12 in 1910, 5 in 1920, 60 in 1930 (reflecting the Great Depression), and 50 in 1940. Of these idle mills, one in 1900 survived to the next period (1910), and 5 mills that were idle in 1930 survived to 1940; all other idle mills in the years 1900 through 1930 failed to survive to the next decade (I did not check whether the mills that were idle in 1940 survived to a later date). The study excludes the mills operating in Alaska (one operated in 1920) and Hawaii (one operated in 1930 and 1940), because these environments were unique and the number of mills were too few to warrant special treatment.

Beginning with the 1941 edition of the directory, the pulp and paper mills were individually coded. If a firm operated both a pulp and a paper mill at the same location, these vertically integrated mills were treated as a single code. If a firm operated multiple paper mills at the same location but listed a single combined capacity for the group, this was treated as a single code. If the directory entry described separate capacities for a group of paper mills (or group of pulp mills) at the same location, each was identified by a separate code. Vertically integrated pairs of paper and pulp mills within these groups were given the same code; usually these were identified in the directories by pulp-mill names that matched one of the paper-mill names among the group of paper mills.

The mill codes served a number of different purposes. Besides identifying the mill, the code was used to indicate whether the mill was a surviving or failing mill and its location. All mills operating in 1940 were treated as surviving mills in the study, so survival was indicated by codes that ranged from one to the last value assigned in the 1940 sample. The next directory that was coded was the 1931 directory. The mills that were listed in both the 1941 and 1931 directories were given the same code (and thus identified as survivors) and mills listed in the 1931 but not the 1941 directory were assigned new codes. This process continued for the 1921, 1911, and 1901 directories. The codes were allocated first to the 1940 mills, then to the 1930 mills, 1920, 1910, and finally to the 1900 mills not already identified in any subsequent years. Because the mills were coded in this "backward" fashion, the range of codes assigned each year were used to identify the last directory in which each mill appeared. The mill codes were also divided into four series to identify the region (North, Lake, South or Pacific, defined below). Each series began at 1000-point intervals to separate the regions (beginning at 1 for northern mills, 1000 for Lake mills, 2000 for southern mills, and 3000 for Pacific mills).

Working from the 1941 to the 1901 directories, mills that were listed by the same name at the same location were assigned the same code year to year. Occasionally it was difficult to determine if a mill in a given location was owned by the same firm year to year, however, due to discrepancies in the mill name or other inconsistencies. In a relatively small group of entries, a judgement was made whether to change the mill code between editions of the directories. The codes were kept the same if (1) the firm added an "Inc." or "Co." following incorporation, (2) the names of the mill's officers were the same following a minor modification in the mill name, or (3) the town name was different but the mill was the same (usually because the mill was in a rural location that was near more than one town, or because the town name was modified by an "East" or "South"). The number of cases where mill names were not identical from one year to the next for the reasons described above, but the code was kept the same, was as follows: 30 between 1900 and 1910, 21 between 1910 and 1920, 52 between 1920 and 1930, and 38 between 1930 and 1940. A few of these cases were checked against the company histories listed in *Moody's Manual of Investments* of this period to confirm that the mills had not changed hands year to year. (For example, the Hoberg Paper & Fibre Co. changed its name to Hoberg Paper Mills in 1936, according to Moody's, and was treated as the same company in the study.)

Mills located at the same plant were assigned new codes if (1) the name and management of the mill changed (the listing often indicated that a new firm succeeded the old one), (2) the mill became a division or subsidiary of another firm, or (3) the mill was leased to another firm. Although the decision to keep or change the code for an existing plant when the listing was modified in subsequent directories was subject to error, the number of cases involving judgement on my part was relatively small (the cases were ambiguous, lacking details outside the directory entries, in less than 10 percent of total observations in any given year). Takeover of existing plants by new firms was discussed in detail in Chapter 3.

In cases where a firm owned more than one mill at different locations, or reported separate capacities for mills at the same location, the mills were identified by different codes. As a result, the number of coded mills exceeds the number of firms in this study. The distinction between firm and plant observations was made throughout the study, however. For the data collected for 1900, 1920, and 1940, multiple plant ownership was accounted for by use of the index of firms that was included in each directory. In these years, the number of mills operated by the firm that owned each mill was recorded for each mill code. The statistics concerning the number of firms and multiplant ownership are reported in Chapter 4. In addition, firms that owned several mills (such as International Paper) were analyzed separately and discussed throughout the book.

All states engaged in pulp and paper production were organized into the following four regions: the North includes Connecticut, Delaware, Maine, Maryland, Massachusetts, New Hampshire, New Jersey, New York, Pennsylvania, Rhode Island, and Vermont; the Lake and Central region includes Illinois, Indiana, Iowa, Kansas, Michigan, Minnesota, Missouri, Ohio, and Wisconsin; the South includes Alabama, Arkansas, Florida, Georgia, Louisiana, Mississippi, North Carolina, South Carolina, Tennessee, Texas, Virginia, and West Virginia; the Pacific includes California, Oregon, and Washington. These groups are consistent with the divisions commonly used in other reports, including the U.S. Tariff Commission's *Report on Wood Pulp and Pulpwood* (U.S. Tariff Commission 1938, 9–10) and Mouzon's study of the southern pulp and paper industry (Mouzon 1940, 61). Besides conforming with generally accepted regional definitions, these groups distinguish the primary forest regions of the United States (for example, see the maps provided in the modern editions of *Lockwood-Post's Directory of the Pulp, Paper and Allied Trades*).

The directory entries usually described the specific type of pulp and paper produced at the mill. These products were coded by five pulp grades and six paper grades. The pulp varieties were classified as groundwood (or mechanical pulp), soda, sulphite, sulphate (or kraft), and semichemical. Miscellaneous pulps, such as cotton linter pulp, esparto (grass), or other nonwood pulps were coded by a missing value; the mill was still classified as a pulp mill and the pulp capacity was recorded. The entries sometimes indicated whether the pulp was bleached or unbleached, wet or dry, but this information was not utilized in this study.

Paper grades were classified as newsprint, book and writing, wrap and board, kraft, sanitary, and industrial papers. Although a wide variety of papers were made in this period, each with distinct characteristics, these six categories are based on the broad classifications found in the *Census of Manufactures* of this period. The categories also correspond to the major differences in the functions and uses of each paper grade (see the discussions in Guthrie 1950, 51–54; Stevenson 1940, 132–35; Sutermeister 1954, 199–209). Two directories of paper terms were used to classify the papers listed in the directories, and the most common varieties include the following:

1. Newsprint: newspaper or "news" (at least 70 percent groundwood pulp), groundwood papers (from 20 to 75 percent groundwood pulp);

2. Book and writing: includes sulphite papers, rag paper, fine papers, onion skin, thin paper, flats, typewriter paper, papers used for coated, carbon, manifold, and envelope papers;

3. Wrap and board: includes fibre, screenings, express, mill blanks and mill wrappers, middles, liners, twisting, rope paper, tag, tissue wrap, crepe, fruit wrap;

4. Kraft: includes all boards modified by the word kraft (kraft was not double-counted as board);

5. Sanitary: includes toilet tissue, facial tissue, napkins, paper towels, wadding;

6. Industrial: includes felt, asbestos, insulation, sheathing, roofing, hanging, absorbent, blotting, filter, matrix.

A few grades, especially manila, were difficult to classify because the name did not distinguish its use in any single category. Manila, a common early twentieth century term, refers to paper made from manila hemp (rope) stock that was used for a variety of papers, including writing, wrapping, and tissue papers. Manila also referred to the color of the paper, which was not necessarily made from manila stock. When manila was listed as the only grade produced, I classified it as wrapping paper (following the *Census of Manufactures* of this period); if more than one grade was listed, I grouped manila to be consistent with the rest of papers produced by the mill (usually the other papers were wrapping papers). Otherwise, I assigned missing values for the product categories in the cases where the variety was not listed in a dictionary or not well defined.

The information from the directory listings was recorded as quantitative or qualitative variables, depending on the nature of the data. If the listing was incomplete, a missing value was assigned to that variable. The quantitative variables were the capacity data and the population statistics. Pulp and paper capacity was measured by the pounds of production per 24-hour periods, because mills were operated on a continuous basis. Mills reported the "rated" capacity, which represents the capacity at normal operating speeds for the heaviest weight of pulp or paper grade produced (Stevenson 1940, 102). The population of the mill town was based on census figures, and the publishers note that there was sometimes a lag between the last census report and the directory information (in the 1921 edition, for example, the most recent census data were not available at press time, so the population figures given were the "old ones"). Other directory information about the number and sizes of machines is available but was not used for this study.

The rest of the information was recorded by using qualitative "dummy" variables, which measure whether certain characteristics existed or not. Each of the paper and pulp grades were identified by dummy variables that indicated whether the grade was produced or not; the advantage of this approach is that a mill that produced a variety of grades was represented by a series of grade variables with the value 1. The descriptions of the types of power used were recorded by dummy variables for steam, water, and electrical power sources. Mills using a combination of power sources were indicated by dummy variables equal to 1 for each source.

From these basic data a number of variables were calculated. The codes were used to identify mills that survived to 1940, and a dummy variable for survival was equal to 1 if the mill code was known to exist in the 1941 directory. Regional dummy variables were defined by the mill code, as described above. The extent of vertical integration was measured by the ratio of the pulp capacity divided by the paper capacity at each mill. A dummy variable for vertical integration was measured by whether a mill reported both pulp and paper production (either by listing an amount of capacity for both pulp and paper production or descriptions of grades of both pulp and paper products). A dummy variable indicating whether the mill produced more than one grade of paper product was defined by the presence of more than one paper grade dummy variable with a value of 1; a variable counting the number of paper grades produced by each mill was defined as the sum of the paper grade dummy variables.

The directory listings were fairly complete and the number of cases included in the analysis of each variable was high (and far in excess of the number required for the statistical methods used). As an indication of the magnitude of the missing value problem, the range of the number of missing values recorded for each variable in any given year was as follows: paper capacity missing values ranged from 11 cases (in 1900) to 36 cases (in 1940); pulp capacity missing values ranged from 2 (in 1930) to 9 (in 1910); population missing values ranged from 12 (in 1940) to 85 (in 1910); the type of paper grade was missing in from 1 (in 1900) to 16 cases (in 1920); the type of pulp grade was missing in from 2 (in 1910) to 11 cases (in 1930); the type of power used in the paper mill was missing in from 12 (in 1900) to 59 cases (in 1930); the type of power used in the pulp mill was missing in from 25 (in 1910) to 44 cases (in 1940). Relative to the number of observations each year, which ranged from 789 to 879 over the period, the number of missing values was not significant and posed no special problems for the study. None of the remaining dummy variables used in the study were reported as missing values, because these derived variables were equal to zero when the underlying characteristics used to define the variable was not reported in the directory.

CENSUS OF MANUFACTURES DATA

The data reported from the *Census of Manufactures* that are discussed in Chapter 2 of the book were aggregated according to the product categories that were defined for the directory data. The definitions of paper grades reported in the *Census of Manufactures* between 1899 and 1947 varied over the period, but it was possible to aggregate the data to conform generally to the six categories used for the directory data. Newsprint was reported as a separate grade in the census reports each year. Writing and book papers included these various grades: fine, cover, groundwood paper, poster paper, catalog, and tablet. Wrapping and paperboard included the census categories of manila, kraft, bag paper, tag, cardboard, and categories of tissue paper defined as high grade or waxing. Sanitary papers included categories of tissue papers defined as toilet tissue, towel, and napkins. Industrial papers included blotting paper, building paper, and hanging papers. The census category "Miscellaneous" or "Other" included plate, lithograph, map, and woodcut papers and categories not shown separately to avoid disclosing data for individual establishments, and was reported as "Other" in Table 2–4. (Converted paper products, also known as manufactures of paper, were not included in the pulp and paper statistics shown in Table 2–4.) The only difficulty in using the census data involved the treatment of "tissue," because the census reports between 1899 and 1914 did not distinguish wrapping and sanitary tissues. As a result, the data shown in Table 2–4 treat all tissue produced in 1899 and 1909 as "Sanitary" and exclude tissue production from "Wrap" in these years. This probably overestimates the production of sanitary papers and underestimates the production of wrapping papers in these years.

The regional census data that were reported in Chapter 3 were aggregated according to the regional definitions that were defined for the directory data. However, state production was incomplete in the census reports between 1909 and 1923 because only the production of the leading states was included in this period. A small share of production was not classified in any of the four regions each year, because state production was too small to be listed separately or was not reported to avoid disclosure of an individual establishment. Also, when the census data were reported by region, sometimes there were minor variations between the regional definitions used in this research and those used by the *Census of Manufac-*

tures of this period, and adjustments were made to the census data to assure consistency across the study. For example, in the 1937 *Census of Manufactures*, the North included Ohio, Tennessee, and West Virginia; in the 1947 *Census of Manufactures*, Delaware and Maryland were included with the southern states (as part of the "South Atlantic" region).

Appendix C: Concentration Ratios in Regional Product Markets

This appendix presents additional measures of market concentration to supplement the discussion of industrial structure in Chapter 4. Tables C–1 through C–4 summarize the share of the regional market for each grade of paper and pulp produced by the four largest individual mills in the period 1900–1940. The concentration ratios for each of the six categories of paper markets are based on daily paper-mill capacities reported in the directories. In mills that produced more than one grade of paper, the total paper capacity was allocated proportionately across each grade produced. The pulp concentration measures reflect pulp production for market. Market pulp was defined as the total pulp capacity of specialized pulp mills and the pulp capacity in excess of paper capacity of the integrated mills.

These concentration ratios are based on a narrow market definition and so are higher than the concentration ratios discussed in Chapter 4. The regional product markets may be the most accurate basis for measures of concentration in the early twentieth century paper industry, before developments in transportation facilitated interregional trade. Because of high transportation costs in this period, most products were shipped within the four broadly defined regions of the North, Lake, South and Pacific Coast areas. In addition to transportation costs, interregional shipping of pulp and paper products also raised the risk of interrupted supplies and the costs of transacting between the buyer and seller. Most mills tended to locate near markets, such as newsprint and book paper mills that supplied local publishers. The exceptions where interregional trade was important included sulphite pulp from the Pacific, which was exported to the North and abroad, northern sanitary paper, which was shipped to the Pacific region, and southern kraft board, which was sold in markets in the Pacific and the North (U.S. Tariff Commission 1938, 11; Guthrie 1950, 86–89).

The regional concentration ratios for the North are reported in Table C–1. Concentration was low in the northern book and writing, wrap and board, and industrial paper markets. Newsprint was somewhat more concentrated than these other products, and that concentration rose to 62 percent by 1940 as northern newsprint capacity declined due to competition from Canadian newsprint. The smaller kraft wrapping and sanitary markets were highly concentrated in 1900 and 1910, but concentration declined as the number of mills producing these products increased in the North. Among the market-pulp mills in the North, concentration was fairly low in the market for groundwood. As groundwood capacity declined in the North (due to less newsprint capacity), concentration gradually increased to over 50 percent by 1940. Sulphite concentration also increased over the period. Because of relatively little capacity, concentration in the soda and sulphate markets was quite high. However, imported pulp represented a significant share of the northern pulp market, so these concentration ratios overestimate the potential market power of the northern market-pulp mills.

The trends in market concentration in the Lake region were similar to those found in the North (see Table C–2). Concentration tended to rise sharply in the newsprint market as Lake newsprint mills shifted to other products with the general decline in domestic newsprint production in this period. Concentration was low in the writing and book, and wrap and board markets, which dominated Lake paper production in this period. Few Lake mills produced draft and sanitary papers, so the concentration in these markets in the Lake region was relatively high. Although the sizes of the market-pulp mills in each category were approximately equal, concentration was lowest in the groundwood and sulphite markets due to larger total capacities of these grades. A total of only four mills produced soda pulp for market over the period (none in 1910 or 1920). Kraft concentration gradually declined as that market developed, as in each of the other regions.

The concentrations of the developing markets in the South and Pacific Coast regions were generally much higher than in the North and Lake regional markets. The southern concentration ratios are shown in Table C–3. Among the paper grades produced in the South, concentration was relatively low only in the wrap and board markets and the kraft wrapping paper market in 1940, where regional capacity was greatest. With little production of newsprint, book and writing, sanitary, and industrial papers, concentration was very high in these markets. Southern pulp production was dominated by kraft mills by the end of the period, so it is not surprising that concentration was lowest in this category (although still fairly high) and typically 100 percent in all other pulp grades.

In the Pacific region, market concentration was very high in all markets, which was consistent with the small number of mills operating in Washington, Oregon, and California in this period (see Table C–4). However, concentration in the sulphite pulp market steadily declined as this market flourished to become a major source of sulphite pulp for export to East Coast and foreign markets. The concentration of the wrap and board market also tended downward after 1920 with increased Pacific Coast capacity in these products.

Table C–1
Regional Concentration of Top Four Northern Mills, by Product
(Four-Mill Capacity as Share of Total Product Capacity in North)

NORTH	1900	1910	1920	1930	1940
PAPER CAPACITY					
Newsprint	40%	34%	30%	41%	62%
Book & Writing	15	20	19	20	22
Wrap & Board	9	12	14	16	15
Kraft	–	65	44	40	46
Sanitary	85	55	56	59	56
Industrial	33	24	22	23	22
PULP CAPACITY[1]					
Groundwood	28%	25%	25%	35%	53%
Soda	83	67	81	88	99
Sulphite	48	60	35	57	64
Sulphate (Kraft)	–	100	100	100	100
Semichemical	–	–	–	–	–

Source: Compiled by the author from Lockwood's Directory of the Paper and Allied Trades.

[1] Pulp produced for market; based on total pulp capacity of specialized pulp mills or pulp capacity in excess of paper capacity of integrated mills.

Table C–2
Regional Concentration of Top Four Lake Mills, by Product
(Four-Mill Capacity as Share of Total Product Capacity in Lake Region)

LAKE	1900	1910	1920	1930	1940
PAPER CAPACITY					
Newsprint	33%	47%	50%	43%	100%
Book & Writing	21	28	18	28	22
Wrap & Board	10	11	16	17	1
Kraft	–	100	61	40	40
Sanitary	100	100	78	95	50
Industrial	47	38	39	26	33
PULP CAPACITY[1]					
Groundwood	56%	43%	43%	57%	55%
Soda	100	–	–	100	100
Sulphite	61	53	47	65	69
Sulphate (Kraft)	–	100	100	69	87
Semichemical	–	–	–	100	–

Source: Compiled by the author from Lockwood's Directory of the Paper and Allied Trades.

[1] Pulp produced for market; based on total pulp capacity of specialized pulp mills or pulp capacity in excess of paper capacity of integrated mills.

Table C–3
Regional Concentration of Top Four Southern Mills, by Product
(Four-Mill Capacity as Share of Total Product Capacity in South)

SOUTH	1900	1910	1920	1930	1940
PAPER CAPACITY					
Newsprint	100%	100%	–	100%	100%
Book & Writing	94	100	100%	90	94
Wrap & Board	54	47	48	28	47
Kraft	–	100	76	51	39
Sanitary	–	–	100	100	100
Industrial	85	100	60	84	90
PULP CAPACITY[1]					
Groundwood	96%	94%	100%	100%	100%
Soda.	100	100	84	100	100
Sulphite	100	100	100	100	100
Sulphate (Kraft)	–	–	100	58	67
Semichemical	–	–	–	100	100

Source: Compiled by the author from Lockwood's Directory of the Paper and Allied Trades.

[1] Pulp produced for market; based on total pulp capacity of specialized pulp mills or pulp capacity in excess of paper capacity of integrated mills.

Table C–4
Regional Concentration of Top Four Pacific Mills, by Product
(Four-Mill Capacity as Share of Total Product Capacity in Pacific Region)

PACIFIC	1900	1910	1920	1930	1940
PAPER CAPACITY					
Newsprint	99%	99%	100%	90%	92%
Book & Writing	100	100	100	100	82
Wrap & Board	57	75	67	51	49
Kraft	–	–	100	97	96
Sanitary	–	–	100	95	100
Industrial	100	97	100	86	73
PULP CAPACITY[1]					
Groundwood	82%	100%	89%	70%	82%
Soda	100	–	–	–	–
Sulphite	100	98	89	60	51
Sulphate (Kraft)	–	–	–	99	100
Semichemical	–	–	–	–	–

Source: Compiled by the author from Lockwood's Directory of the Paper and Allied Trades.

[1] Pulp produced for market; based on total pulp capacity of specialized pulp mills or pulp capacity in excess of paper capacity of integrated mills.

Bibliography

Adelman, Morris A. "Concept of Statistical Measurement of Vertical Integration." In G. J. Stigler, ed., *Business Concentration and Price Policy*. Princeton: Princeton University Press, 1955.

American Paper Institute. *The Dictionary of Paper*. 4th ed. New York, 1980.

Blair, Roger D., and David L. Kaserman. *Antitrust Economics*. Homewood, Ill.: Richard D. Irwin, 1985.

"Border War Breaks Out Over Ticonderoga Paper Mill." *Democrat and Chronicle*, 15 December 1991, 5B.

"Building and Forest Products." *Standard & Poor's Industry Surveys* (December 14, 1989): B75–B80.

"Building and Forest Products." *Standard & Poor's Industry Surveys* (February 21, 1991): B75–B80.

Buzzell, Robert D. "Is Vertical Integration Profitable?" *Harvard Business Review* 61 (January–February 1983): 92–102.

"Capacity Survey." *Pulp & Paper* (February 1991): 27.

"Capital Spending Plans: 1990–92." *Pulp & Paper* (January 1991): 101–8.

Caves, Richard E., and David R. Barton. *Efficiency in U.S. Manufacturing Industries*. Cambridge, Mass.: MIT Press, 1990.

Caves, Richard E., and Ralph M. Bradburd. "The Empirical Determinants of Vertical Integration." *Journal of Economic Behavior and Organization* 9 (April 1988): 265–79.

Chandler, Alfred D., Jr. *The Visible Hand: The Managerial Revolution in American Business*. Cambridge, Mass.: Harvard University Press, 1977.

Churchill, Betty C. "Age and Life Expectancy of Business Firms." *Survey of Current Business* 25 (December 1955): 15–20.

Clark, Victor S. *History of Manufactures in the United States*. Volume III, 1893–1928. New York: McGraw-Hill, 1929.

Coase, R. H. "The Nature of the Firm." *Economica* 4 (November 1937): 386–405. Reprinted in G. Stigler and K. Boulding, eds., *Readings in Price Theory*. Homewood, Ill.: Richard D. Irwin, 1952.

Cohen, Avi J. "Technological Change as Historical Process. The Case of the U.S. Pulp and Paper Industry, 1915–1940." *Journal of Economic History* 44 (September 1984): 775–99.

——— . "Factor Substitution and Induced Innovation in North American Kraft Pulping. 1914–1940." *Explorations in Economic History* 24 (April 1987): 197–217.

Cohn, Edwin J., Jr. *Industry in the Pacific Northwest and the Location Theory*. New York: Kings's Crown Press, 1954 (c. 1952).

Cooke, David C. *How Paper Is Made*. New York: Dodd, Mead & Co., 1959.

Creamer, D., D. Dobrovolsky, and I. Borenstein. *Capital in Manufacturing and Mining, Its Formation and Financing*. Princeton: Princeton University Press, 1960.

Deutsch, Claudia. "A State-of-the-Art Plant Refines Newspaper Recycling." *The New York Times*, 18 March 1990, F9.

Duetsch, Larry L. "Structure, Performance, and the Net Rate of Entry into Manufacturing Industries." *Southern Journal of Economics* 41 (January 1975): 450–65.

Dunne, Timothy, Mark J. Roberts, and Larry Samuelson. "Patterns of Firm Entry and Exit in U.S. Manufacturing Industries." *Rand Journal of Economics* 19 (Winter 1988): 495–515.

——— . "The Growth and Failure of U .S. Manufacturing Plants." *Quarterly Journal of Economics* 104 (November 1989): 671–98.

Eberle, Irmengarde. *The New World of Paper*. New York: Dodd, Mead & Co., 1969.

"Economics of Paper." *Fortune* 16 (October 1937): 111.

Ellis, L. Ethan. *Print Paper Pendulum: Group Pressures and the Price of Newsprint*. New Brunswick, N.J.: Rutgers University Press, 1948.

"The Essentials of Recycling." *Dollar$ense*, Fall 1990, 10–12.

Evans, David S. "The Relationships Between Firm Growth, Size, and Age." *Journal of Industrial Economics* 35 (June 1987a): 567–87.

——— . "Tests of Alternative Theories of Firm Growth." *Journal of Political Economy* 95 (August 1987b): 657–74.

Evans, John C. W. "Use of Neutral Size, $CaCO_3$ Filler Gaining Wide Use in Papermaking." In John C. W. Evans, ed., *Trends and Developments in Papermaking*. San Francisco: Miller Freeman Publications, 1985.

Fabricant, Solomon. *The Output of Manufacturing Industries, 1899–1937*. New York: National Bureau of Economic Research, 1940.

Federal Reserve Bank of Minneapolis. "Proposed Paper/Pulp Mill Has Groups Drawing Battle Lines." *Fedgazette* 1, no. 3 (September 1989): 3, 7.

Feller, Irwin. "The Draper Loom in New England Textiles, 1894–1914. A Study of Diffusion of an Innovation." *Journal of Economic History* 26 (September 1966): 320–47.

"Fifteen Paper Companies." *Fortune* 16 (November 1937): 132.

The Financial World 3, no. 6 (March 1905): 10.

——— . 4, no. 4 (November 1905): 8.

Fraser, C. E., and G. F. Doriot. *Analyzing Our Industries*. New York: McGraw-Hill, 1932.

Fuchs, Victor R. *Changes in the Location of Manufacturing in the United States Since 1929*. New Haven, Conn.: Yale University Press, 1962.

Globerman, Steven, and Richard Schwindt. "The Organization of Vertical Related Transactions in the Canadian Forest Products Industry." *Journal of Economic Behavior and Organization* 7 (June 1986): 199–212.

Gort, Michael. *Diversification and Integration in American Industry*. Princeton, N.J.: Princeton University Press, 1962.

Guthrie, John A. *The Newsprint Paper Industry*. Cambridge, Mass.: Harvard University Press, 1941.

————. *The Economics of Pulp and Paper*. Pullman, Wash.: The State College of Washington Press, 1950.

————. *An Economic Analysis of the Pulp and Paper Industry*. Pullman, Wash.: Washington State University Press, 1972.

Hagenauer, John P. "Labor Cost of Production in the Paper and Pulp Industry." *Paper Trade Journal* 50 (April 25, 1935): 29–39.

Hennart, Jean-François. "Upstream Vertical Integration in the Aluminum and Tin Industries." *Journal of Economic Behavior and Organization* 9 (April 1988): 281–99.

Hessen, Robert. "Do Business and Economic Historians Understand Corporations?" Working Papers in Economics E–89–14, The Hoover Institution, Stanford University, May 1989.

Holusha, John. "The Tough Business of Recycling Newsprint." *The New York Times*, 6 January 1991, F9.

Hyman, David N. *Modern Microeconomics, Analysis and Applications*. Boston: Irwin, 1988.

"International Paper and Power." *Fortune* 16 (December 1937): 135.

International Paper Company. *International Paper Company After Fifty Years*. New York, 1948.

Jovanovic, Boyan. "Selection and the Evolution of Industry." *Econometrica* 50 (May 1982): 649–70.

Judkins, C. J. *Trade and Professional Associations of the United States*. U.S. Department of Commerce Industrial Series Number 3. Washington, D.C.: Government Printing Office, 1942.

Judkins, Jay. *National Associations of the United States*. U.S. Department of Commerce, Washington, D.C.: Government Printing Office, 1949.

Kane, Nancy Frances. *Textiles In Transition: Technology, Wages, and Industry Relocation in the U.S. Textile Industry, 1880–1930*. New York: Greenwood Press, 1988.

Keeler, Theodore E. "Deregulation and Scale Economies in the U.S. Trucking Industry: An Econometric Extension of the Survivor Principle." *Journal of Law and Economics* 32 (October 1989): 229–53.

Keeley, Michael C. "The Economics of Firm Size: Implications from Labor-Market Studies." *Economic Review* (Federal Reserve Bank of San Francisco) (Winter 1984): 5–21.

Kendrick, John W. *Interindustry Differences in Productivity Growth*. Washington, D.C.: American Enterprise Institute, 1982.

Kingsbury, Read. "Newspapers Pressing on with Recycling." *Democrat and Chronicle*, 15 February, 1990, 12A.

Klein, Benjamin, Robert G. Crawford, and Armen A. Alchian. "Vertical Integration, Appropriable Rents, and the Competitive Contracting Process." *Journal of Law and Economics* 21 (October 1978): 297–326.

Labarre, E. J. *Dictionary and Encyclopedia of Paper and Paper-Making.* 2nd ed. Amsterdam: Swets and Zeitlinger, 1952.

Lamoreaux, Naomi R. *The Great Merger Movement in American Business, 1895–1904.* Cambridge, Mass.: Cambridge University Press, 1985.

Levy, David T. "Testing Stigler's Interpretation of 'The Division of Labor Is Limited by the Extent of the Market'." *Journal of Industrial Economics* 32 (March 1984): 377–90.

———. "The Transactions Cost Approach to Vertical Integration: An Empirical Examination." *Review of Economics and Statistics* 67 (August 1985): 438–45.

Lindstrom, Diane. "Domestic Trade and Regional Specialization." In *Encyclopedia of American Economic History,* ed. Glenn Porter, vol. 1. New York: Charles Scribner's Sons, 1980, 264–80.

Livesay, Harold C., and Patrick G. Porter. "Vertical Integration in American Manufacturing, 1899–1948." *Journal of Economic History* 29 (September 1969): 494–500.

Lockwood Trade Journal Company. *Lockwood's Directory of the Paper and Allied Trades.* New York, 1887–1888, 1901–1902, 1931.

———. *Lockwood's Directory of the Paper and Stationery Trades.* New York, 1941.

———. *250 Years of Papermaking in America.* New York, 1940.

MacDonald, James M. "Market Exchange or Vertical Integration: An Empirical Analysis." *Review of Economics and Statistics* 67 (May 1985): 327–31.

McGaw, Judith A. *Most Wonderful Machine: Mechanization and Social Change in Berkshire Paper Making, 1801–1885.* Princeton, N.J.: Princeton University Press, 1987.

McGee, John S. *Industrial Organization.* Englewood Cliffs, N.J.: Prentice-Hall, 1988.

McLaughlin, Glen E., and Stefan Robock. *Why Industry Moves South.* Kingsport, Tenn.: Kingsport Press, Inc., 1949.

MacPhee, Craig R., and Rodney D. Peterson. "The Economies of Scale Revisited: Comparing Census Costs, Engineering Estimates, and the Survivor Technique." *Quarterly Journal of Business and Economics* 29 (Spring 1990): 43–67.

Maddala, G. S. *Limited-Dependent and Qualitative Variables in Econometrics.* Cambridge, England: Cambridge University Press, 1983.

Marcus, Matityahu. "Firms' Exit Rates and Their Determinants." *Journal of Industrial Economics* 16 (November 1967): 10–22.

"Markets for Recyclables Shrinking." *Democrat and Chronicle,* 18 February, 1990, 20A.

Markusen, Ann Roell. *Profit Cycles, Oligopoly, and Regional Development.* Cambridge, Mass.: M.I.T. Press, 1985.

Masten, Scott E., James W. Meehan, Jr., and Edward A. Snyder. "Vertical Integration in the U.S. Auto Industry: A Note on the Influence of Transaction Specific Assets." *Journal of Economic Behavior and Organization* 12 (October 1989): 265–73.

Miller Freeman Publications. *Lockwood-Post's Directory of the Pulp, Paper and Allied Trades.* San Francisco, 1989, 1991.

Moody's Manual of Investments: Industrial Securities. New York: Moody's Investor Services, 1931, 1941.

Mouzon, Olin Terrill. "The Social and Economic Implications of Recent Developments Within the Wood Pulp and Paper Industry in the South." Ph.D. dissertation, University of North Carolina, Chapel Hill, 1940.

Organization for Economic Cooperation and Development (OECD). *Integration in the Pulp and Paper Industry in OECD Countries.* Paris, 1982.

———. *Industrial Revival Through Technology.* Paris, 1988.

Organization for European Economic Cooperation (OEEC). *The Pulp and Paper Industry in the USA.* Paris, 1951.

Orr, Dale. "The Determinants of Entry: A Study of the Canadian Manufacturing Industries." *Review of Economics and Statistics* 56 (February 1974): 58–66.

Pakes, Ariel, and Richard Ericson. "Empirical Implications of Alternative Models of Firm Dynamics." Reproduced, Yale University, February 1990.

Paskoff, Paul F. *Industrial Evolution: Organization, Structure, and Growth of the Pennsylvania Iron Industry, 1750–1860.* Baltimore, Md.: Johns Hopkins University Press, 1983.

Perloff, Harvey S. *How A Region Grows.* New York: Committee for Economic Development, 1963.

Perry, M. K. "Vertical Integration: Determinants and Effects." In R. Schmalensee and R. Willig, eds., *Handbook of Industrial Organization.* Amsterdam, The Netherlands: North-Holland, 1989.

Porter, P. G., and H. C. Livesay. "Oligopoly in American Manufacturing and Their Products, 1909–1963." *Business History Review* 43 (Autumn 1969): 282–98.

Reese, Richard A. "Fourdrinier Rebuilds: Keys Are Common Sense, Proven Methods." In John C. W. Evans, ed., *Trends and Developments in Papermaking.* San Francisco: Miller Freeman Publications, 1985.

Riche, Richard W. "Impact of Automation in the Pulp and Paper Industry, 1947–60." *Monthly Labor Review* 85 (October 1962): 1114–19.

Schary, Martha A. "The Probability of Exit." Reproduced, Boston University, March 1988.

Scherer, F. M., and David Ross. *Industrial Market Structure and Economic Performance.* 3rd ed. Boston: Houghton Mifflin Co., 1990.

Shepherd, William G. "What Does the Survivor Technique Show About Economies of Scale?" *Southern Economic Journal* 34 (July 1967): 113–22.

Shughart, William F., II. *The Organization of Industry.* Homewood, Ill.: Richard D. Irwin, 1990.

Smith, David C. *History of Papermaking in the United States (1691–1969).* New York: Lockwood Trade Journal Co. 1971.

Stevenson, Louis Tillotson. *The Background and Economics of American Papermaking.* New York: Harper & Brothers Publishers, 1940.

Stigler, George J. *Capital and Rates of Return in Manufacturing Industries.* Princeton, N.J.: Princeton University Press, 1963.

———. "The Division of Labor is Limited by the Extent of the Market." *Journal of Political Economy* 59 (June 1951): 185–93. Reprinted in *The Organization of Industry.* Chicago: The University of Chicago Press, 1968a.

———. "The Economies of Scale." *Journal of Law and Economics* 1 (October 1958): 54–71. Reprinted in *The Organization of Industry.* Chicago: The University of Chicago Press, 1968b.

———. "Barriers to Entry, Economies of Scale, and Firm Size." In *The Organization of Industry.* Chicago: The University of Chicago Press, 1968c.

Sutermeister, Edwin. *The Story of Papermaking.* Boston: S. D. Warren Co., 1954.

Temin, Peter. *Iron and Steel in Nineteenth-Century America: An Economic Inquiry.* Cambridge, Mass.: The M.I.T. Press, 1964.

———. "Product Quality and Vertical Integration in the Early Cotton Textile Industry." *Journal of Economic History* 68 (December 1988): 891–907.

Tucker, Irvin B., and Ronald P. Wilder. "Trends in Vertical Integration in the U.S. Manufacturing Sector." *Journal of Industrial Economics* 26 (September 1977): 81–94.

Ullmann, John E. *The Anatomy of Industrial Decline.* New York: Quorum Books, 1988.

United Nations. *The Growth of World Industry, 1967.* New York, 1968.

———. *Yearbook of Industrial Statistics, 1977.* New York, 1979.

———. *Industrial Statistics Yearbook, 1988.* New York, 1990.

United States Bureau of the Census. *Manufactures, 1905.* Washington, D.C.: Government Printing Office, 1908.

———. *Census of Manufactures, 1914.* Washington, D.C.: Government Printing Office, 1919.

———. *Abstract of the Census of Manufactures, 1919.* Washington, D.C.: Government Printing Office, 1923.

———. *Biennial Census of Manufactures, 1921.* Washington, D.C.: Government Printing Office, 1924.

———. *Biennial Census of Manufactures, 1923.* Washington, D.C.: Government Printing Office, 1926.

———. *Biennial Census of Manufactures, 1925.* Washington, D.C.: Government Printing Office, 1928.

———. *The Growth of Manufactures 1899 to 1923.* Washington, D.C.: Government Printing Office, 1928.

———. *Biennial Census of Manufactures, 1927.* Washington, D.C.: Government Printing Office, 1930.

———. *Biennial Census of Manufactures, 1931.* Washington, D.C.: Government Printing Office, 1935.

———. *Biennial Census of Manufactures, 1933.* Washington, D.C.: Government Printing Office, 1936.

———. *Biennial Census of Manufactures, 1935.* Washington, D.C.: Government Printing Office, 1938.

———. *Biennial Census of Manufactures, 1937.* Washington, D.C.: Government Printing Office, 1939.

———. *Census of Manufactures, 1947.* Washington, D.C.: Government Printing Office, 1949.

United States Congress House. Pulp and Paper Investigation Report. 60th Cong., 1st Sess., 1908. H. Rept. 1786.

———. Pulp and Paper Investigation Hearings. 60th Cong., 2nd Sess., 1909. H. Doc. 1502, 5 volumes.

United States Department of Commerce. "Trade Association Activities." Domestic Series Number 20. Washington, D.C.: Government Printing Office, 1927.

United States Department of Commerce. "Paper and Allied Products." *1990 U.S. Industrial Outlook* (January 1990): sec. 10, 1–24.

———. "Paper and Allied Products." *1991 U.S. Industrial Outlook* (January 1991): sec. 10, 1–21.

United States Industrial Commission. Report on Trusts and Industrial Combinations. 57th Cong., 1st Sess., 1901. H. Doc. 182.

"U.S. Paper Industry Will Manage Economic Slowdown This Year." *Pulp & Paper* (January 1991): 57–65.

United States Pulp Producers Association. *Wood Pulp, A Basic American Industry.* New York, 1944.

————. *Wood Pulp: A Basic Fiber.* New York, 1955.

United States Tariff Commission. *Report to the United States Senate on Wood Pulp and Pulpwood.* Number 126, Washington, D.C.: Government Printing Office, 1938.

Veverka, Arthur C. "Economics Favor Increased Use of Recycled Fiber in Most Furnishes." *Pulp & Paper* (September 1990): 97–103.

Vogel, John H. "The Paper and Pulp Industry." In John G. Glover and Rudolph L. Lagai, eds., *The Development of American Industries: Their Economic Significance.* 4th ed. New York: Simmons-Boardman Publishing Corp, 1959.

Weeks, Lyman Horace. *History of Paper Manufacturing in the United States, 1690–1916.* New York: Lockwood Trade Journal, 1916.

Weidenmuller, Ralf. *Papermaking.* San Diego, California: Thorfinn International Marketing Consultants, Inc., 1984.

Weiss, Leonard. "The Geographic Size of Markets in Manufacturing." *Review of Economics and Statistics* 54 (August 1972): 245–57.

Westmoreland, Jerry, and Ashok Majmudar. "Dyeing Pulp in an Alkaline System Requires Special Considerations." In John C. W. Evans, ed., *Trends and Developments in Papermaking.* San Francisco: Miller Freeman Publications, 1985.

Whitney, Roy P. *The Story of Paper.* Atlanta, Georgia: Technical Association of the Pulp and Paper Industry, Inc., 1984.

Whitney, Simon N. *Antitrust Policies: American Experience in Twenty Industries.* New York: The Twentieth Century Fund, 1958.

Wilder, Ronald P., and Irvin B. Tucker. "Trends in Vertical Integration: Reply." *Journal of Industrial Economics* 32 (March 1984): 391–92.

Williamson, Oliver E. *The Economic Institutions of Capitalism: Firms, Markets, Relational Contracting.* New York: The Free Press, 1985.

York, John W. "Paper Machine Rebuilds Gain in Popularity as Industry Recovers." In John C. W. Evans, ed., *Trends and Developments in Papermaking.* San Francisco: Miller Freeman Publications, 1985.

Index

About the Author

NANCY KANE OHANIAN is a consulting economist and the author of *Textiles in Transition* (Greenwood, 1988).